¡Pistoleros!
The Chronicles of Farquhar McHarg
I: 1918

¡Pistoleros! The Chronicles of Farquhar McHarg – 1: 1918
Farquhar McHarg

ISBN: 978-1-60486-401-4
Library of Congress Control Number: 2010916483

Cover and interior design by briandesign

10 9 8 7 6 5 4 3 2 1

PM Press
PO Box 23912
Oakland, CA 94623
www.pmpress.org

Printed in the USA on recycled paper, by the Employee Owners of Thomson-Shore in Dexter, Michigan.
www.thomsonshore.com

Contents

Introduction

Pistoleros! 1: 1918 is the first volume of the memoirs and notebooks of Farquhar McHarg, a seventy-six-year-old anarchist from the Govan district of Glasgow, its writing prompted by the murder, in October 1976, of his lifelong friend, Laureano Cerrada Santos. McHarg's *Chronicles* record his evolving beliefs and sense of mission, and the remarkable adventures he experienced from the day he sailed into the neutral port of Barcelona in the spring of 1918, a naïve but idealistic eighteen-year-old, and 1976. Farquhar's *Chronicles* are folk history, bringing the changes that shook the political and social landscape of Spain (and the world) between 1918 and 1976 into the framework of adult lifetime. They make a vexatious but fascinating story that provides a deep insight into the spirit that moved the selfless, generous, occasionally naïve, and recklessly idealistic people who were involved in the bitter social struggles that marked the hectic insurrectionary and utopian aftermath of the great imperialist war of 1914-1918.

Contemptuous of traditional political parties and professional politicians, and inspired by the example—and the myth—of the Russian Revolution, these men and women aimed to rid the world of a cruel, corrupt, arbitrary, and oppressive political and economic system that abused authority and exploited, degraded, tortured, and murdered in the name of profit and power.

The transformation of the unworldly young Farquhar, in the climactic and rebellious years between 1918 and 1924, is fascinating to observe as he acquires consciousness and identity through his experiences in a world for which he is little prepared. The journey he embarks upon in these pages is not simply a personal memoir or an exploration of his own psyche; the many hitherto untold stories that unfold along his way provide profound understanding of the circumstances, thoughts, and deeds of people who tried to rescue the Europe of the twentieth century from the cycle of disaster, war, and death.

Stuart Christie
Hastings, 2011

Paris, Belleville, 18 October 1976

It was 11:15 p.m. on a wet October night in the heart of working-class Belleville. The tall, heavily built man with a weathered face and a shock of silver-grey hair that curled under a broad-brimmed black fedora stood alone at the zinc of the Café de l'Europe. For a man in his mid-seventies he was remarkably handsome. Deep in thought, his brow was furrowed and shoulders hunched as though expecting the heavens to fall, he was waiting for his friend Laureano to return from an urgent meeting with his lawyer.

The Café de l'Europe, a café bistro in the Rue des Couronnes, was a friendly place, albeit in a slightly squalid, mind-your-own-business sort of way. It was late but the bar was still busy—and noisy. The clinking and rattling of coffee cups, saucers, and spoons came accompanied by occasional explosions of pressurised steam escaping from the valves of the large brass- and eagle-mounted Gaggia espresso machine parked on the zinc counter like some extraterrestrial steam driven flying machine preparing for takeoff. In the background outbursts of laughter and raucous banter punctuated the murmured conversations. A professeur des parfums might have described the room's blend of 'fragrances' as that of freshly brewed coffee, cognac, beer, pungent tabac noir, and damp wool, with top notes of patchouli and 4711 Eau de Cologne, and a base note of stale sweat. It was Edward Prince's local, a rendezvous for the dispossessed and hardboiled desperadoes alike. Its clients were mainly immigrants from France's old colonies of the Maghreb and Indochina, émigré lowlifes, intriguers, hustlers, and incorrigible chancers who mingled indistinguishably with idealists, 'Les Justes', and plain ordinary folk—complicated and uncomplicated: the good, the bad, and the banal.

During Belleville's guinguette days of shady bars and dance halls, the Café de l'Europe acquired a certain reputation as a hangout for the neighbourhood gangsters known as 'Apaches'. Not a lot had changed in the interval between then and now.

This man, known to everyone as Edward Prince, was the only Scot in the bar, a Govan man, a fact no one would have guessed so totally did he merge into his cosmopolitan surroundings. He was at home there with the rest of the human flotsam who drifted around the sociometric Sargasso Sea that was Paris's nineteenth arrondissement.

Edward was irritated—and worried. Laureano was very late. His appointment with Maître Dumas had been scheduled for eight o'clock; it had been a last-minute meeting that was unlikely to have gone on for more than an hour.

A wave of melancholy, the unique, poignant melancholy of love known in Spain as duende, *unexpectedly engulfed him as another face emerged from the past—his Lara. 'I'm becoming maudlin in my old age,' he thought ruefully and with a barely audible sigh he drained the gritty dregs of his* carajillo. *Giving Laureano the benefit of the doubt, he pushed the cup across to the bartender for a last refill before heading home to the single end apartment in the nearby Rue des Cascades, his refuge for the past ten years.*

As the bartender splashed the brandy into his cup, two gunshots, fired in rapid succession, rang out in the street outside. The babble of voices in the bar stopped as though someone had lifted the stylus from a gramophone record. Despite his age, Edward's reflexes kicked in and made him dive for cover. The sudden movement knocked his right knee cartilage out of place; the pain was excruciating. At first he thought he'd been shot, but the pain slowly eased as he lay on the floor massaging the affected joint. The bar was a disaster zone. Chairs and tables were overturned as customers and bar staff sought cover, falling over each other in their panic to escape. The floor was awash with a broth of vin rouge, pastis, beer, coffee, and shards of broken glass.

Rolling over onto his good knee and putting all his weight against the floor with the palms of his hand, Edward succeeded in levering himself up and, keeping low, he made his way to the window. Across the road, he saw a shadowy group of half a dozen men silhouetted under the sulphurous yellow light of the street lamp. They were looking at a figure slumped on the pavement at their feet. A man in a dark topcoat was bent over the body, his features obscured by a broad-brimmed fedora. He had a gun in his hand. As he leaned closer, the figure on the ground lashed upwards with his fist, punching his would-be executioner in the face with a blow that was sufficiently forceful to knock off the man's spectacles. Unperturbed, the gunman retrieved them from the pavement, stood up and pulled a handkerchief from his coat pocket, studiously cleaning the lenses before adjusting them on his face. He dabbed gingerly at the blood trickling from his nose. Bending over his victim again, he spoke to the wounded man then raised his gun and fired another four shots at point-blank range. It was the coup de la colère. *The killer straightened himself, slipped the gun into his pocket and turned up the collar of his coat. Speaking briefly to the others he stepped over his victim and walked off calmly into the dark night. Street theatre, Belleville style.*

The remaining men exchanged a few words, then they too disappeared into the wings of the night. Down the street a car door slammed, an engine revved, and tyres screeched as the vehicle carrying the killer drove off into the inky blackness beyond the street lights.

Back in the Café de l'Europe, the gunmen gone and their courage partially restored, customers and staff milled around the doorway, cautiously peering out to see what was happening without exposing themselves to any further dangers that might still be lurking outside. Pushing his way through the crowd, Edward limped across the road to the figure sprawled on the pavement. Drawing closer to the body his heart beat faster; he recognised the victim. The body lying in a congealing pool of its own blood was that of his oldest friend and comrade, Laureano Cerrada Santos, his thinning grey hair now matted with blood from a bullet hole on his left temple. Dark stains spread across what had been an immaculate white shirt, like spilt ink over a blotter. Edward tried to swallow, but his saliva had turned to ash. His heart pounded in his chest, as if ready to burst. Then he retched. Glinting in the yellow light was Laureano's lapel pin, a red and black enamelled oblong, bearing the letters CNT-AIT, the acronym of the Anarchist International and the Spanish anarcho-syndicalist National Confederation of Labour, his beloved labour union from which his sworn enemies in the national leadership had engineered his expulsion more than twenty years earlier.

Laureano's briar pipe lay next to his body. Smouldering embers still glowed faintly through the grey ash in the heavily reamed bowl with its worn-down rim. Wailing sirens and flashing blue and red lights signalled the approach of an ambulance. Numb and in shock, Edward levered himself to his feet as an ambulance technician and her partner pushed through the onlookers. Easing backwards into the crowd he watched as she and her colleagues examined the body, then manoeuvred it onto a stretcher, covering Laureano's staring, lifeless eyes with a coarse red woollen blanket. As the ambulance drove off, silently now, Edward Prince hobbled away shivering uncontrollably, his mouth still unable to produce spit. He had no desire to be there when the police came asking for witness statements. They might have uncovered his true identity—Farquhar McHarg.

Over the years McHarg had successfully camouflaged his colourful past with many different identities, but in his current role as journalist and writer he had readopted his first nom de guerre. Like all his other identities, it was Laureano who had provided the necessary documentation. He had worked as an occasional columnist and freelance sub-editor for Libération under the name Edward Prince, ever since that newspaper's launch, three years ago, by his old friends Jean-Paul Sartre and Serge July. Laureano had provided most of the capital.

Farquhar McHarg's apartment was small, though not by Parisian stand-

ards. *Every square metre was precious in that crowded City of Light. He had a bright, airy room on the third floor, a former atelier, with tall windows and a couch that served as his bed at night, a tiny galley kitchen in one corner, a door that led into a simple bathroom the size of a large cupboard. Against a wall stood the large mahogany American roll-top desk which held his sky-blue 1956 Smith Corona portable typewriter, squeezed between stacks of papers, files, and brown, varnished card index boxes, all containing research in progress.*

Taking comfort in the familiar surroundings, he pulled back the chair from the desk, switched on the green-shaded desk lamp and drew the typewriter towards him. When not freelancing at Libération, *he was writing a history of the Spanish anarchist action groups, a subject ignored by academia, but one that was dear to his heart. It was also his story. He was of that generation consigned to history, condemned by it in fact, and he—as had Laureano—wanted their voices to be heard and their motives understood. For Farquhar McHarg writing wasn't self-expression; it was action—action continued by other means. It was the only way left to him to cast light on the dark psychological and ethical undercurrents in the never-ending struggle against injustice and indifference.*

That night Laureano had come to meet him to help him write that very story, by arranging to turn over his journals and the newly acquired police files held on him since 1944. His lawyer had purchased these on his behalf earlier that day. It could not have been coincidence that Laureano's enemies had found him only a few steps, a few minutes away.

Feeding a crisp new sheet of paper into the roller, Farquhar carefully aligned it with the type guide, adjusted the carriage return and lightly ran his fingers over the typewriter keys.

Without warning, he felt the shock of adrenaline in the pit of his stomach as the awful memory flashed back. His heart rate soared while his stomach squirmed and twisted into a tight knot. The portal of Hell—over which each and every one of us is suspended by the slenderest of threads—opened beneath him. It had been a long time since he had experienced that sense of imminent dread— the feeling that a vexatious God was about to cut that slender thread. Pouring a large Glenmorangie, his one concession to the place of his birth, he adjusted the platen knob on his typewriter and tried to rewind his mind into the past.

'Tonight,' he typed, 'my old friend and comrade Laureano Cerrada Santos was murdered. I may be next. I must write my story while I still have time.' He paused. He thought back to the fortuitous, pivotal event that brought about that cosmic shift from engineering apprentice in Scotland to international revolutionary. He searched for the letter 't' and pressed the key shift: 'Time is a precious commodity, especially when it's running out. Only the other day I was just eighteen . . .'

GLASGOW, MARCH 1918

It was in the spring of 1918 that I first met Laureano Cerrada Santos. I was as old as the century; he was two years younger. I was an apprentice engineer and had just joined the crew of the freighter *Covenant*, an old tub that Lloyds, the Board of Trade and the Ministry of Shipping had all passed as seaworthy; it floated, had a steel hull, newly overhauled engines, and could carry freight. Such are the compromises of war.

It was my first time at sea, my first time out of Scotland, in fact. Howdens of Scotland Street, Govan, the marine engineering firm where I was serving my time as a fitter, offered me the opportunity to go to Spain with the *Covenant* as a Junior Engineer to oversee its new 'forced draught' fan system. This was a revolutionary new system developed by old man Howden himself to recycle waste heat by driving hot air into the boilers, drastically increasing the engine's efficiency and profitability—by reducing the amount of coal needed. Howden died the year before I joined the firm, but still I had helped build and install his system in the *Covenant*.

For a young lad like myself it was a wonderful opportunity. With the Kaiser's war at its height, the likely alternative was that I would end up as canon fodder in the sodden trenches of Northern France. As the time drew nearer I grew more and more excited at the prospect of going to Spain. I suspected that the real reason I had been offered the trip was because the managers wanted me out of the way. As an indentured apprentice I wasn't allowed to join a union or involve myself in union affairs, but even so I had acquired a reputation as a radical. Nesbitt, the foreman, was forever warning me about my vocal support for the anticonscription movement, the Clyde Workers' Committee, and the critical comments I had been making on the shop floor about the dangerous practice of throwing red-hot rivets from the braziers up to the riveters and 'hodders on' bonding the boiler plates.

'Yer a bbbloody troublemaker, McHarg. And a bbbloody unpatriotic tttroublemaker at that! Mark my words, lad, yer heading for tttrouble with all this bbloody political nonsense. It's time ye grew up and bbbloody well started to live in the bbbloody rreal world.'

Nesbitt savoured the word 'bloody', and when he wasn't around the lads all called him 'Bbbloody Nesbitt'. He spat a lot. Every time he told me, or anyone else, off he'd punctuate the admonition by spitting on the ground, as if he was trying to get the taste of me out of his mouth. It didn't help that I had enough of that arrogance of youth to wind him up whenever I could.

'If ye dinnae wipe that smirk aff yer face ye'll be hanged as a murderer wan day. And I'll tell you this fur nothin', son, if I hud ma way ye'd be oot on yer bbloody ear.'

But he couldn't sack me. And neither could Howdens. As an articled apprentice it was practically impossible for them to get rid of me. The next best thing, therefore, was to ship me off somewhere out of the way. No doubt they would have preferred to send me east of Suez, or even to the battle-fields in Northern France, but the best they could manage was Barcelona with a cargo of Welsh anthracite from Cardiff. At least I'd be out of their hair for a month instead of stirring things up on the plate shop floor.

The crew of the *Covenant* was entirely Protestant and Scottish, with the exception of Paddy Mullins, an old sea hand who, despite his name, was English. George Foulser, a later acquaintance who was active in the National Union of Seamen, told me that his uncle had sailed with him pre-1914 and that he was named Patrick after his Irish grandfather on his mother's side. Apparently Paddy had been a highly promising footballer and had played a whole season for Millwall juniors, with hopes of even an England or Ireland cap, but disappointment in love had driven him to sea at an early age.

In those days in Glasgow a person's religion mattered much more than it does now, and that's saying something. It was anti-Catholic prejudice that had helped me get my apprenticeship. From the day he launched the company in 1854, old man Howden only employed Protestants. Catholics knew better than to apply. It helped that my father was the deputy grand master of the Govan and Renfrew Apprentice Boys of Derry Lodge.

Although I didn't share my father's austere Protestantism, I certainly benefited from it. He and my mother believed in education for its own sake and, despite my youth, I was fairly well read. I was reared in an atmos-phere that stressed the importance of liberty and freedom of conscience, and encouraged the idea of personal achievement by facing up to life's difficulties, learning through a critical and scientific examination of the world—all that Roman Catholicism was not. My Presbyterian upbringing also imbued in me not only a deep sense of justice, but a faith in the idea of punishment for wrongdoing and reward for good, the final triumph of truth and liberty—and a stubborn belief in the perfectibility of man, or at least our ability to progress towards perfection. It provided the spirit that roused and animated me, and the star I was destined to follow.

My father delighted in telling me tales of the Covenanters, men and women of jaw-dropping integrity and bravery who took up arms against the state and the forces of reaction, placing liberty of conscience above respect for the arbitrary laws imposed by ruling elites. It's funny how—for good or bad—our young minds are kindled and flame up with ardour through the telling of old stories of how people through the ages have dealt with cruel wrongs, persecution, and the quandaries life has thrown at them. It is undoubtedly the means by which we acquire our sense of ethics, morality, and understanding of the world and people around us. James Grahame, the Scottish poet and divine, expressed this sentiment most eloquently in his poem, Sabbath, about the 'Killing Times' in seventeenth-century Scotland:

> Their constancy in torture and in death—
> These on Tradition's tongue still live, these shall
> On History's honest page be pictured bright
> To latest times.

Mother was quieter in her convictions, but in some ways she influenced me more than my father. She taught me how to feel morality, really feel it deep in my gut. My father furnished me with the intellectual arguments, but it was my mother who imbued in me the emotional commitment. Our brand of Presbyterianism was free of hierarchy, pomp, ritual, and idolatry, all of which made a big impression on me when I was young.

Although my father's religious sense was darker—or perhaps because of it—he was never afraid to stand up for what he believed to be right, no matter what the cost, a trait that left its indelible mark on me. He never tired of quoting from his well-thumbed copy of *Ringan Gilhaize*, and it was largely through that extraordinarily powerful and enduring book by John Galt that I came to feel, know, and understand what he called 'the divine right to resistance'.

Father and I disagreed on most things, especially my involvement in radical politics, and I strongly suspect he had a hand, through the Lodge, in getting me posted to the *Covenant* in a well-meaning attempt to remove me from what he felt were 'bad' influences. Paradoxically, despite his constantly extolling the moral virtues of those who—in the past—placed conscience above the law, my scepticism of his authority and lack of deference irritated my father enormously. The Kaiser's war was the most serious bone of contention between us; we argued about it relentlessly, but at no time did he badger me or try to burden me with guilt. It was to his great credit, too, that he remained consistent with his belief that, in life, room had to be found for 'tender consciences'; I had a right to hold my own views even if he believed I was seriously mistaken and was heading straight for the Seventh Circle of Hell. Like most people, he was a mass of contradictions.

It was the idea of evil that first led me to question and then drive me away from the Christianity I had grown up with. I found it impossible to equate the iniquitous suffering of the war with a belief in an all-powerful God who could create us and then leave us to fend for ourselves in a world full of pain and wickedness without attempting to alleviate mankind's dreadful suffering. Prayers didn't work, and as far as I could see there had been no divine intervention in human affairs since God turned his back on Christ in the Garden of Gethsemane. No, if the world was to be redeemed it was something we had to do ourselves.

By the time I was fourteen I was a regular at Guy Aldred's street corner anarchist meetings. One woman I met there, Annie Gordon, told me how, when she had been a little girl, Kropotkin had cradled her on his knee. Her dad, Willie Nairn, a stonebreaker, had brought the Russian revolutionary up to Glasgow to speak at a series of anarchist meetings on the ideas developed in his book, *Mutual Aid: A Factor of Evolution*—a book that was to have a profound influence on me. Aldred also introduced me to the life and work of Francisco Ferrer i Guardia, a well-known Spanish secular freethinker, a teacher whose tragic fate facing a firing squad had moved me deeply. My father and I often argued about Ferrer and his ideas on education.

'Farquhar,' my father would say in exasperation, 'you'd try the patience of Solomon himself.' Then, turning to my mother, he would add 'Dinna fash yersel', hen. It's a' jist boy's nonsense. He'll grow oot o' it.'

My mother would nod her head and go about her business. I never really found out what she thought about my father's homilies, but occasionally she would flash me one of her smiles, which seemed to say, 'Don't you worry about him, son.'

Yes, I owe my parents a great deal, even if I did go off on a tangent they didn't approve of; they certainly provided me with the ethical foundations and moral context from which I emerged into adolescence and young manhood.

SS COVENANT, MARCH 1918

The engine room of the *Covenant* had a full complement of First, Second, Third, and Fourth Engineers to look after the pair of twelve-year-old engines and auxiliaries, but no Junior Engineers. The crew, both deckhands and engineers, were mostly 'hielanders' or 'teuchters' from the Western Isles.

Our captain, Alexander Roy Macrob, was a 'Wee Free' martinet, a member of a branch of the Presbyterian Church of Scotland that adhered to a particularly sulphurous interpretation of fundamentalist Calvinism

whose model of the City of God was late sixteenth-century Geneva. He ran
his ship as though it were a beleaguered and insular parish congregation
on the Isle of Lewis and Harris under constant threat of subversion from
Romish 'ferryloupers' from Lochmaddy or Uig across the Hebridean Sea, or
from Episcopalian mainlanders from Ullapool, Oban, and Mallaig. He was
the reincarnation of William Barret Travis, leader at the Alamo.

Macrob—a cross between William Bligh and Captain Ahab, and as
strict a Sabbatarian as you could find on the high seas, he officiated at
two Church services every Sunday, one in the morning and another in the
evening; he would have tried to impose three services if he thought for a
minute it wouldn't lead to him being cast adrift in a lifeboat. He was forever quoting Scripture. At my interview I faced him across the desk in his
cabin, while he grilled me closely on my upbringing like a latter-day Jim
Hawkins in the presence of a fundamentalist Captain Smollett.

'I hope you're a decent Christian, lad, an' no wan o' they infidels that
carries the red-edged hymn books an' sits at prayer?'

I hesitated, uncertain as to which way the conversation was leading.
I was slightly disconcerted by the way he alternately caressed and then
drummed his fingers on the black leather binding of the large family bible
on his desk.

'A man canny be too cautious. There urr too many that ca' themselves
Protestant that behave like Papists. You're no' wan o' them, are ye?'

Despite my father's own radical interpretation of Presbyterianism I
had never before been confronted by this kind of zealous venom. I was at a
loss, wary of this little man who burned inside with something quite unnat-
ural. I have since come across one or two fundamentalist Presbyterian ministers on my travels, but none seemed quite as intense as Captain Macrob,
whose bituminous black eyes sapped all my youthful arrogance.

'They'll be sayin' there's no hell next! But there's still some o' us in the
merchant tred that are true to the faith; we'll show them, I'll assure ye o'
that! We are few, but firm—firm!'

His observations were rhetorical and, like Jesting Pilate, he didn't wait
for an answer. At the end of his 'welcoming address', which I took to be
an induction into the planet Macrob, he dismissed me with a peremptory
flick of his hand. I left with relief. But the man puzzled me. As I learned
more about him, it was clear that Macrob was a man obsessed by seagoing
superstitions and 'the wan true faith'. I often wondered if he'd read *Moby
Dick* and saw anything of himself in Captain Ahab. Conversations with
him—if they could be described as such, being so one-sided—inevitably

included the information that he 'couldnae abide neither Catholics nor "Piskies"'—Episcopalians, he meant. I thought it politic to keep quiet about my own views, not that he would have been interested. It was unlikely to have occurred to him that anyone on his boat could be a Godless anarchist!

Dan Macphail, the chief engineer, was my immediate boss, and a welcome relief after Macrob; he immediately put me at my ease, chatting pleasantly as he showed me around the ship and introduced me to the crew. His previous job had been with the Glenlight Shipping Company on their fleet of West of Scotland puffers, the small cargo boats that carried household removals ('flittings'), coal, gravel, and other everyday necessities up, down, and between the out-of-the-way ports of Scotland's West Coast.

Forty-three years old, a small, kindly man with a beer belly and salt and pepper eyebrows, the only hair on his shiny, bald head. The crew used to make fun of him, saying that when he washed his face, he never knew where to stop. He laughed at that and never seemed to mind. But he was fearsome if he thought someone was putting the ship or crew in danger. He'd been in the Merchant Navy all his life, but when war broke out he applied to join the Royal Navy, wanting to serve on the Dreadnoughts. He was far too old, of course, and was rejected, so it was back to the Mercantile Marine where he'd started out.

Macphail was an avid reader, consuming everything he could lay his hands on, from Comic Cuts to penny novelettes and the great philosophers. During the voyage, when we had the odd bit of free time, we would discuss books, ideas, people, and places. He was a lovely man and a great raconteur who kept everyone amused with his reminiscences and anecdotes. An adopted Glaswegian from Campbelltown, most of his stories were at the expense of the Gaelic-speaking Highlanders who crewed many of the ships that sailed from the Broomielaw. English was their second language, and inferior to their Gaelic, so often they didn't fully understand what was being said to them.

The rest of the crew were pleasant enough. Some were a bit aloof at first, and I found that hard. When I was first introduced to Mullins, the only Englishman on board, he burst out laughing.

'Fucker? What kind of a name is that? What kind of parents would give a kid a name like Fucker?'

I bridled at this; my face flushed with anger. But all I could do was bluster self-consciously:

'I'll have you know that Farquhar is an old and respected Scottish name ...'

'What, Fucker is?'

He laughed harder still. The other crewmembers smiled too, including Macphail, and then laughed uproariously as I grew angrier and more flustered and inarticulate. I hadn't expected this kind of reception. But then one of them spoke up:

'Leave the boy alane, ya ignorant sassenach bastard!'

Mullins laughed again, as did the other crewmen. Macphail turned to Mullins: 'Okay, that's enough, Paddy, let the boy alane.' Turning to me, he said: 'Dinnae tak it tae heart, son. He's only pullin' yer leg. The time tae worry is when they stop daein' it.'

I was too angry to reply. Even with all my bravado I was still really a boy, a callow youth far too easily offended by nonsense. If I hadn't been so full of my own importance, so protective of my mawkish sense of dignity, I might have realised that Mullins was actually welcoming me into the fold. I had similar things happen to me when I started my apprenticeship, but I hadn't made the connection. I remember being sent down to the fitters' stores at the yard for a long stand, and being left there for nearly three hours, before being asked if the stand was long enough for me. On another occasion I was sent down for a rubber hammer and half a dozen glass nails. It was all part of the apprentice's induction into the world of easily amused adult men, but I still hadn't learned not to take myself too seriously then. As it turned out Mullins and I developed a warm friendship during the voyage. He, too, was a socialist, but of Marxian persuasion, and was a great admirer of Lenin and the Bolsheviks—as were most socialists and even quite a few anarchists at the time. We spent much of our time off watch discussing the latest developments in Russia. I never did find out why he was called Paddy, though. I suspect it might have had something to do with his thinly disguised sympathies for the Irish Republican cause.

The voyage to Barcelona was uneventful, apart from a few tense hours navigating our way out of the Firth of Clyde and through the Irish Sea, which was notorious for German U-boat activity. Other than that the ten days passed relatively peacefully. But the lifejackets piled on deck and the lifeboats permanently swung out on davits were a constant reminder of the perils lurking below the surface. The Marconi ship-to-shore radio kept us up to date with the news. I remember hearing a story about a U-boat commander who had been taken prisoner in the Irish Sea; he was reported to have had in his pocket the counterfoils of two tickets for a concert given just a few days before by Sir Thomas Beecham in Glasgow's St Andrew's Halls.

Immediately, as we hit the Bay of Biscay, it became clear we were in for a rough passage; enormous waves regularly broke over the boat, making it roll and pitch for what seemed like forever. Great squalls blew up suddenly with driving torrential rain. I'd been queasy before, but that storm made me horribly sick and I had to take to my bed for the best part of two days.

I didn't see much of the sea. Most of my time was spent deep in the bowels of the ship in the searing heat and deafening noise of the engine room where it was easy to let your imagination run amok. One popular German trick involved using false-flag Spanish fishing boats to drop mines in the path of Allied ships. Not that the British navy didn't do the same. I was on tenterhooks with uncertainty most of the time, wondering when a torpedo or a mine might explode through the hull and blow us all to Davy Jones's Locker. The others felt the same, but despite the constant underlying tension, the cheery banter made it bearable, and I made some good friends among the crew, especially Dan Macphail.

Soon we passed the Cabo de Sao Vicente and made good speed through the Straits of Gibraltar, past Cadiz and Algeciras with its beautiful purple heather hills, then the great historic Rock of Gibraltar itself. Heading north we hugged the green, gold, and brown Spanish coastline dotted with little whitewashed sugar-lump houses, steaming at speed past the brilliant-white Arab town of Malaga with its castle-crowned hill of lavender. Then came Valencia with its wonderful polychrome tiles and serried ranks of orange trees as far as they eye could see.

Macphail was impressed with the difference the overhauled engines made to our speed.

'Holy smoke, Farquhar!' he declared one day. 'Ye've done a grand job, man. She's chust sublime; a better boat than ever she was.' He patted the bulkhead affectionately. 'She might be an auld wifie, but she's behavin' like a young girrul, like a Lever watch she is. I canny see mony U-boats catchin' us nappin.'

'Man! It's no coals we should be cairryin' but tourist passengers. If we chust had the accommodation!'

The other crew members laughed. 'Careful, there!' cried Mullins. 'I think Macphail is falling in love again! Don't you think you're past it, man?'

'I've still got plenty of lead in ma pencil, Mullins. An' when we get ashore I'll show you.'

'That a challenge, Macphail?'

'Chust wait till we get ashore, that's all I'm goin' to say.'

He winked at me and smiled. He liked it when the lads were in this mood.

'Well, you'd better get a good wash before leaving the ship,' continued Mullins. 'Or is that greasy blot on your face a birthmark?'

We all laughed. Looking around none of us were a particularly pretty sight. Mullins wiped a dirty rag across his forehead, smearing a dark smudge across his brow. The proud mark of an engineer aboard a steamer. The camaraderies of those ten days are among my fondest memories. The lads were great company and despite the difficulties of the work and the bout of seasickness it was a memorable time.

Reflecting on it I see now that the contrast between Nesbitt, Macrob, and Macphail made a lasting impression on me. They all exercised power, each in different ways: Nesbitt, the workshop bully, despised by the men he thought he controlled; Macrob, the messianic fanatic who scared everyone, but Macphail was special. His authority was unquestioned, but somehow he held it lightly; no one ever thought to challenge him directly, although they did argue with him, openly—and made fun of him, even in his presence—but always good-naturedly. They respected him. I didn't know it at the time, but Mr Macphail taught me a great deal about working and living with my fellow man.

BARCELONA, APRIL 1918

The morning we arrived in Barcelona harbour I was in the engine room tending to the engines, with their exposed cylinder heads and their shiny valves moving rhythmically like a beating heart, when Macphail tapped me on the shoulder, shouting over the din: 'Come up top with me, son.'

I followed, a bit nonplussed. I thought perhaps I'd done something wrong and was about to be hauled over the coals, or perhaps he had bad news for me. I chewed nervously at my bottom lip. The idea of upsetting Macphail bothered me. We had been getting on really well, and I didn't want to fall from his good opinion. On deck he turned to me and I braced myself to hear the worst, but Macphail was beaming widely at me.

'Tak a guid look, son,' he said, putting his hand on my shoulder. 'Is it no' magnificent?'

The view was like a vividly coloured picture postcard.

'This is yer first foreign port as a seafarin' man. Enjoy it, lad, because there'll never be another first time.' I began to stammer: 'But, wwhat about Captain Macrob? Shouldn't we be in the engine room for docking?'

'Relax, lad,' he replied. 'The lads know whit they're daein', an' they can manage withoot the two of us for a while. I'll sort it oot wi' the captain if he says anything. Old Macrob might be a scary old so an' so, but he's no' completely lackin' in a' humanity. He kens fine that the first port of call for a young seaman is somethin' special. When he gets into port he's a different man entirely, much nicer—for a wee while onyway.'

I gulped, not quite believing him, but I soon relaxed and began looking around me. It truly was magnificent. Accustomed more to the leaden skies of the West of Scotland, the fierce glare of the Catalan sun in springtime made me squint as I took in my first, vivid images of Spain against the backdrop of a cornflower-blue sky. It was still early spring, but to me it felt like the height of summer. To feel the sun gently warming my face so early in the year was a new experience.

Macphail pointed out a tall bronze column close to the front: 'Wan o' Genoa's hardy sons,' he said approvingly. 'Columbus,' I replied, as much to let Macphail know that I knew a thing or two as to answer him. 'Aye, Columbus. An' a seafarin' man chust like yersel',' and he patted my shoulder gently.

From his vantage point two hundred feet above us, Christopher Columbus, ignoring the *Covenant*, was pointing across the shimmering horizon towards new worlds real and metaphorical. Behind him in the distance, sloping up to the dark purple heights of Tibidabo, stretched a slate grey and terracotta mosaic of tenement rooftops, factory chimneys, elliptical domes, bell towers, and spires. And there, dominating the skyline to my left, six hundred feet up, was the great hill of Montjuïc, crowned with the brooding silhouette of its seventeenth-century fortress citadel. It cast a long shadow.

'You stay here, son,' said Macphail, 'while I go back doon tae see whit the lads are up tae. Dinnae worry, the captain'll no bother ye, I promise.'

And so it was that I watched like a tourist as the ship docked and the mooring ropes were heaved to the quay for tying up. The sound of a bell rang out from the bridge as Captain Macrob relayed his orders down to the engine room, and I felt the harsh judder of the engines beneath my feet and heard the frantic thrashing of the propeller as the ship came to rest at the dockside. The thump of the ship colliding with the fenders reminded me of the excitement and anticipation I felt on board the *Glen Sannox* or the *Duchess of Argyll* paddle steamers as we tied up at Brodick pier in Arran for the annual Glasgow Fair holidays.

Macphail rejoined me on deck. It was very hot. 'By chove,' said Macphail, wiping the sweat from his brow with an oily rag. 'It's the first time for years I've bin in sich heat withoot a sight o' a mudgie.'

'Is that right?' I replied half-heartedly, too absorbed in taking in the sights before me.

'Ay, man,' said he. 'Tak' Tighnabruaich, fur example. The mudgies in Tighnabruaich, they're that bad they bite their way through corrugated iron tae get tae ye. They're that ferocious ye'd think they hud spurs on their feet!'

THE RAMBLA SANTA MONICA

Spain had been neutral throughout the Great War, a neutrality its government and capitalists were quick to exploit. The disruption to international commerce provided the ideal opportunity for Spain's entrepreneurs to trade goods and raw materials to both sides in the murderous conflict. So, despite the country's supposed neutrality or, rather, because of it, everyone was working for the war in one way or another, whether it was making clothes, hides, shoes, canned goods, armaments, machine parts, or by picking and packing Valencia oranges. But not today! Today was a fiesta in Barcelona and there were no dockers or stevedores available to unload our coal or load our return cargo of oil from Tortosa, wood from Galicia, and ore from Asturias.

Captain Macrob, anxious to prevent the devil corrupting the minds of his idle deckhands, set the crew to painting, scrubbing, and polishing his beloved *Covenant* from the funnel to the Plimsoll line. Fortunately for me, however, replacement parts were needed for one of the bilge pumps, so it was agreed that Macphail and I should go to the manufacturer's agents in town to purchase them. I wasn't really needed, but Macphail had taken a shine to me, probably because I laughed at his jokes and his baurs, but he had become my moral as well as my mechanical mentor, and he wanted to give me the chance to explore Barcelona. I jumped at the opportunity, especially as it meant not sweating buckets in a hellishly hot engine room, dismantling and cleaning pumps, filters, and ventilation systems in a temperature of 120 degrees or more.

Macphail, too, was pleased to be out of his own engine room. 'Man it's hot, most desperate hot, Farquhar!' he continued, apropos of nothing in particular other than the fact that we were free of the ship and the furnace door: "An' Caesar's spirit rangin' fur revenge, Wi' Ate by his side, come hot frae hell, Shall in these confines, wi' a monarch's voice Cry, Havoc! an' let slip the dugs o' war." Shakespeare, you know,' he explained.

Walking along the quay, past the sinister-looking Customs House building and across the busy boulevard towards the Columbus monument—a man who had also sought new worlds—I looked up towards the dark silhouette on Montjuïc and impotently shook my fist. Macphail turned and scrutinised me closely, raising a quizzical, hairy caterpillar eyebrow: 'Whit on earth did ye dae that fur, son?'

'Because, Mr Macphail,' I replied, 'that charnel house up yonder is Spain's Bastille, the place where they murdered Francisco Ferrer—an' God knows how mony others.'

Although it was my first time in Barcelona, the image and history of Montjuïc—the 'hill of the Jews'—was well known to me. For over a hundred years, this monument to injustice overlooking the city from the south had represented Castilian military and political power over the working people of Catalonia. Just nine years earlier, it was where my hero, the Catalan teacher and educationalist Francisco Ferrer i Guardia had been marched to a wall by the trench of Santa Eulalia and murdered by a firing squad of infantrymen.

Macphail raised the other eyebrow: 'Ye'd better watch oot that ye dinnae end up in a Montjuïc cell as weel, son. Captain Macrob'll definitely no staun bail an' the *Covenant*'ll sail withoot ye. Then whaur'll ye be?'

The question was rhetorical. Macphail and I had spent hours in the engine room or on deck discussing life, politics, ideas, and current affairs. I had read and reread the translation of Ferrer's book, *The Origins and Ideals of the Modern School*, by the former Franciscan professor of theology, Joseph McCabe. It accompanied me everywhere and was in my cabin at that very moment.

Macphail and I parted company by the Columbus monument at the foot of the Rambla de Santa Monica. We arranged to meet again at five o'clock that afternoon.

I strolled aimlessly but captivated, up the crowded, tree-shaded Ramblas in the direction of the Plaça de Catalunya. The street seemed to be carpeted with yellow roses. It was the fiesta of San Jordi, the day of books and roses, when men presented their girlfriends with a rose and the women presented their men with a book. It all felt very civilised. The entire population of Barcelona seemed to be on the streets, strolling, chatting, or just whiling away the time watching the world go by from the bustling café terrace tables that filled the pavements and central promenade of the long, green-arched avenue of plane trees. I stared in fascination as the waiters weaved their way expertly between the obstacle course of tables and chairs, delivering glasses of beer and wine, cups of coffee, and pastries on trays with all the theatrical agility and bravura of the plate-jugglers' act I had seen in the Trongate's Britannia Panopticon just before leaving Glasgow.

I was in a state of exhilaration, bombarded on all sides with exciting new sights, sounds, smells—and emotions. The myriad colours of the flower stalls blazed in the afternoon sun. The breeze was warm, the perfume of the flowers and señoritas heady. The effect was narcotic. Despite their sorry plight, the caged birds chirped and whistled, providing a musical counterpoint to the cacophony of backfiring taxis and the cries of street traders, and the general constant commotion. I couldn't make out from animated gestures whether or not the passers-by were conversing or quarrelling, but all these things added to the acute sense I felt of being alive and free—and eighteen.

Something was in the air, but exactly what it was I couldn't tell. Ingénue that I was, I failed to pick up on the underlying tension and resentment. I had noticed, absentmindedly, pairs of swarthy-faced, moustachioed, and bearded men patrolling the avenue in olive-green uniforms crisscrossed with canary-yellow belts and shiny black leather three-cornered hats fitted tightly to their heads. With rifles slung over their shoulders, some were on foot, others seated menacingly on horseback, the iron hooves clattering on the cobbles, their maleficent essence captured by the poet, dramatist, and theatre director Federico García Lorca:

> Black the horse
> Black the horses.
> Black the horses' shoes.
> Ink and wax spots
> glinting on the capes.
> Heads made of lead,
> which explains why they do not weep.
> Coming along the road with their patent leather.
> Hunchbacked denizens of the night.

I didn't know then that these picturesque but sinister creatures, the Guardia Civil, were the visible tip of the vast repressive iceberg that policed Borbón society: below the surface crept or slithered the informers, gimlet-eyed Hawkshaws, secret policemen, provocateurs, double agents, and mercenary gunmen. It was a society whose prisons were filled with political and social prisoners locked away in dungeons where torture and physical abuse were routine.

Like the Glasgow 'polis', recruited from the Scottish Highlands and Islands, the Guardia Civil in Catalonia tended to be poor Castilians enlisted from the rural hinterlands, serving far away from their native communities. They were the shock troops of the Borbón-Hapsburg regime—a paramilitary rural police force with the status of an army unit and a fearsome reputation for 'preventive brutality' and for applying 'exemplary violence' against anyone daring to challenge the social order. They played a crucial role in maintaining public order in Barcelona's inner city and in the industrial suburbs. Well-fed and well-housed in posts and barracks, they were directly subsidised by the employers and big landowners whose class interests they defended—and when the state executioner slowly tightened the iron collar of the garrotte around the neck of the condemned man who gasped for breath as the infernal machine crushed his vertebrae, it was the Guardia Civil who surrounded the scaffold.

Another discordant memory of that first stroll up the Ramblas was the sight of black-soutained priests with their tall birettas and broad brimmed parsons' hats, the 'gentry of the long skirts,' moving in clusters through the crowds like carrion crows scavenging a cornfield.

Turning off the noisy Rambla Santa Monica, I wandered into the Plaça Reial and found an empty bench beneath one of the tall palm trees that dominated the quiet, colonnaded square. After a time, when the sun's glare and the stifling humidity grew too much for me, I looked around for somewhere cooler. To my right, at the far corner of the square, I noticed an alleyway that seemed worth exploring. It led me into a labyrinthine network of fortress-like tenements, deep and narrow stone canyons where the sun shone only briefly at the top of the day. I was in the Carrer dels Escudellers. I didn't know it at the time, but I was now in the heart of the Old City, the Ciutat Vella, one of the most disreputable parts of Barcelona. I had crossed my own personal 'event horizon' into another world.

THE BAR IN THE CARRER DELS ESCUDELLERS

At the point where this medieval street narrows and curves deeper into the Old City, I passed a bar from whose dark open doors wafted the delicious and unfamiliar aromas of a Catalan kitchen, the pungent smell of garlic, onions, potatoes, and bacon sautéing in hot olive oil. Hunger and the hypnotic melodies of a flute and a classical guitar lured me through the entrance into its cool, shadowy interior. My eyes were still adjusting to the gloom when I suddenly remembered I had no pesetas with me. All I had in my pocket was two shillings and sixpence, and my seaman's card. As I turned to leave, the young waitress, a self-assured dark-haired girl in a diaphanous turquoise cotton dress, approached me with a beguiling smile and merry twinkles dancing in her eyes. Clutching my arm, she asked me, in English, if she could be of help.

'No, but thanks anyway, hen. I'm just lookin' around—I've no money on me,' I replied, flustered by her attentions—and unexpectedly firm touch. I stood there, rooted to the floor, with an embarrassed rictal grin on my adolescent face, my heart raced as my whole body registered the first thrill of romantic excitement. She was petite with a flawless complexion, long and wavy dark auburn hair, chestnut brown pupils set in the whitest and clearest of eyes, a slightly upturned nose, and, as my eyes slipped instinctively downwards, two perfect little apple breasts.

'*Me llamo Lara*,' she said. 'What's your name, stranger? Where are you from?'

Lara? I thought, my mind working twenty to the dozen. Was she some sort of Catalan Lorelei, luring a young sailor into who knows what perfidy—hopefully her bed?

'I'm a sailor,' I said, exaggerating slightly. 'A Scottish sailor who's far from home.' Why I added that last bit I've no idea, probably for sympathy, or the subliminal thought that 'all the nice girls love a sailor.'

I wasn't sure if she had the foggiest idea what I was talking about—I spoke with a broad Glaswegian accent at the time—but she pulled me towards a table.

'Sit down, sir, and I'll bring you something to eat,' she said.

'But I haven't any money,' I replied, backing away.

'Don't worry,' she insisted, still steering me towards the table. 'You can pay us when you have money.'

I didn't argue. I was ravenous by this time and could have eaten a scabbyheided dug.

Forty minutes or so later I was on the outside of a saucerful of olives, a potato and bacon omelette, figs, a prickly pear, and the best part of a carafe of vino tinto. The food was a pleasant surprise. I'd never tasted olives, figs, or prickly pear before, and the music was hypnotic and calming. As the dog said when he ate the bagpipes, 'There's baith meat and music here.'

Full of continental sophistication and contentment I basked in the convivial atmosphere, a glass of wine in one hand and listening to a young guitarist play classical guitar. He was playing Bach, an unusual choice of music for a guitarist in Spain in those days. Then Lara reappeared behind me, placed her hands on my shoulders and announced, at the top of her voice: 'Listen, everyone. Here's a poor young Scottish sailor who has no pesetas. Who will help him out?' She proclaimed this loudly for everyone's benefit, in Catalan of course. Her voice was soft, but there was an immediate hush, such was the force of her presence. Then she leant down and

whispered in my ear in English what she had just told everyone. Her close-
ness and the scent of her body excited me, making the hairs on the back of
my neck stand up, especially when her lustrous hair brushed against my
cheek and her warm breath eddied around my ear. She smelled of roses. My
heart beat faster. I felt a pulse of excitement, the promise of illicit thrills,
throbbing in my stomach. I wondered where this chance meeting might
lead, hoping it just might take me to her room, and my becoming a man
sooner than I expected.

Everyone in the bar turned to look at me; my cheeks blazed with
embarrassment as I stared hard at the floor, not knowing where else to
look. A drinker at the bar broke the silence by raising his glass in my direction, saying '*Salud! Escocés.*' The rest of the bar followed suit, which paradoxically heightened my embarrassment and put me at my ease.

Lara, my lovely guardian angel, then went round the room with a plate,
like a church beadle after the sermon, collecting money from every cus-
tomer. When she returned and presented it to me I counted out twenty
pesetas. I could now pay for my food and drink, and still have a bit left over.

A group of men seated around an adjoining table waved me over. They
seemed an affable bunch so I took my drink and joined them. The youngest, a lad with thick, dark hair that flopped over his face and a big friendly
grin, spoke to me in English.

'*Hola, Señor Escocés!* Please allow me to introduce my friends and myself.
My name is Laureano Cerrada Santos and these are my friends Ramón,
Eusebio, Andrés, Gregorio, José and, Juan,' pointing to each man as he
named them. Their ages, I guessed, varied from late teens to late thirties.

'Today is a fiesta, and we would be very happy if you would join us. We
don't often meet Scotsmen. I have read many stories by your great writer,
Robert Louis Stevenson, and I am always anxious to improve my English.
I study in the evenings, at the *ateneu* in my *barri*.'

'What's an ateneu?' I asked. 'Is it a sort of a night school?'

'Hmm, similar, I think' he replied. 'They are workers' social centres with
schools, lending libraries, shops, cafés, and meeting rooms.' He paused to
take a drink of his wine, then resumed.

'They provide a lot of services for the barris'—he paused—
'neighbourhoods?' I nodded and he smiled.

'They are a bit like your Cooperative movement in Britain, but mainly
providing day schools for . . .' he hesitated again 'analphabets?'

I must have looked puzzled because he began searching for another
word, finally settling on 'illiterates.'

'Yes, lessons for illiterate working-class children. And evening classes for adult workers.'

He took another drink from his glass of wine and lit up a cigarette before continuing.

'Most ordinary working people cannot read or write, but they thirst for knowledge, especially *los obreros conscientes*, those who are politically conscious. Knowledge is the best path to freedom, and without it we can never be free.'

That phrase tripped a switch in me, and I could feel a deep excitement uncurling inside. My parents' voices echoed in Laureano's as I remembered my father's stern lectures on the benefits of education and my mother's kindlier but no less committed encouragement to learning. This stranger, a man, boy, had just touched a deep point in my soul, and I was captivated.

'We have about seventy-five ateneus in Barcelona. They are mostly funded by our union, the CNT—the National Confederation of Labour—and the rationalist and Modern School movements . . .'

'Ferrer,' I muttered.

'Yes!' He was delighted. 'Francisco Ferrer i Guardia! You have heard of him?' It was actually more of a statement than a question.

I nodded and smiled. I was still feeling a little shy, but now I was on firmer ground.

'He's one of my heroes. I have a copy of *The Modern School* in my cabin.'

Laureano translated the news to his friends who took it as a signal for toasts, cheers, and laughter. When I added hesitantly that I too was an anarchist their faces cracked into the widest smiles imaginable and everyone jumped up to shake my hand with great enthusiasm. Lara was called over to order a bottle of Cava, a white sparkling wine, with which to toast new comrades.

Laureano and his friends were railway workers, employed by RENFE, the national railway company; they were all *cenetistas*, members of the anarchist led labour union, the CNT. They also, I learned later, belonged to an anarchist friendship or 'affinity' group calling themselves 'Los Indomables'—'The Indomitables'—all close-knit friends, bonded by mutual loyalty and a shared vision of a society without injustice, poverty, ignorance, or exploitation.

Although only sixteen and the youngest of the group, Laureano was clearly accepted by the others as an equal. He told me he was from an anarchist family in the village of Miedes de Atienza in Guadalajara and had been taught in a rationalist school there by the famous anarchist teacher José Alberola. He was continuing his education in L'Ateneu Enciclopedic

Popular in the Carrer de la Carne in the Raval district, where he was also learning English.

Through Laureano I explained a little about my background and upbringing: that I was an apprentice engineer and had been brought up not by anarchists but by churchgoing parents to believe that wrongdoing was something to be resented and confronted, that we had a duty to diminish suffering and pursue justice and liberty—in short, to rectify in creation everything that was rectifiable. I had been politically aware since at least the age of fourteen, but the war had deepened my radicalism, especially after coming into contact with anarchists in the Clyde Workers' Committee and the Clydeside anticonscription movement at the workers' forums and popular street corner meetings of the Independent Labour Party, the ILP.

I had started out as a zealous pacifist but now felt ambivalent about the war, a shift in belief that may have had something to do with the relentless moral pressure brought to bear on the British people to support the war, and the vicious public belittling and denigration of those daring to protest against it. Antiwar activists were consistently portrayed in the newspapers as cowards, traitors, or agents of the 'German hidden hand'— usually all three.

The idea that a German hidden hand was behind political opposition to the government, even industrial accidents, was profoundly pernicious, a conditioning catchphrase designed to prey on people's deepest and darkest fears. Anything not fitting the state's self-serving definition of patriotism was either seditious or the work of saboteurs, a view bolstered daily by the hysterical, jingoist propaganda of the national press. If you weren't 'with us' you were 'agin' us'. Even Glasgow's socialist paper *Forward* succumbed to the populist hysteria. It was painful to see the extent to which even the most intelligent minds were manipulated by the newspapers and the church—the other big opinion-former—to respond to the political interests of their masters and respective nation states.

My new acquaintances seemed intrigued by what Laureano was telling them about me as they talked among themselves. One of them said something to Laureano, who translated:

'Señor Farquhar, my friend would like to invite you to his apartment this evening for a meal—and to introduce you to some compañeros from the CNT. They would be most interested to meet you. Will you come?'

'I'd love tae,' I replied, 'but I'm not sure if I'll be able to get away from the ship.'

'Don't worry,' said Laureano. 'I'll meet you by the gangway at seven o'clock. You'll be safely back on board by eleven o'clock at the latest. *Por favor*, say you'll come?'

I hesitated for a moment, glancing at the watch my parents had given me for my eighteenth birthday. It was quarter to five: 'Okaydokay,' I said. 'Agreed!'

It was time for me to be heading back to meet Mr Macphail. I stood up and shook hands with everyone, then I went to the bar to thank Lara and say goodbye, shaking hands with her, formally, as I'd been brought up to do.

'Perhaps I'll see you again sometime?' I said, hopefully.

'That would be nice,' she replied with her endearing smile. Did I realise at that point how important she would become to me? Did we recognise each other? I like to think we both knew.

Laureano and Lara accompanied me to the doorway. As I stepped out into the late afternoon shadows of Escudellers, it seemed that an eon had passed. 'Until later, then,' said Laureano.

Waving goodbye to my new friends I hurried down the narrow street towards the Ramblas filled with elation and foreboding. Escudellers wasn't the most salubrious of streets, in fact I'd never seen anything like it; very unlike anything in Govan or the Gorbals. I stopped by the corner charcoal rotisserie of the Los Caracoles restaurant and lingered for a few moments, like one of the Bisto Kids in the newspaper advertisements, savouring the mouth-watering aromas of the roasting chickens and suckling pigs that were sizzling and flaring on the revolving spits. A bit further down the road, I halted outside the Quixote Bar, drawn to it by the exotic posters and photographs of partially dressed women in provocative poses. Two elderly men, laughing heartily, walked past me and went inside. One day, I thought, I must go into one of these places and see for myself. Here, at least, I wouldn't be seen by anyone who knew me, but it would have been shameful to be seen coming out of a place like that in Glasgow, if they had them, which I didn't think they had. It would have been bad enough if I'd been caught looking at the pictures.

I moved swiftly on, past bars with knots of swarthy-looking men standing around the entrances, thin, handrolled cigarettes drooping from their bottom lips, flat caps pulled low over their foreheads with white silk aviator scarves knotted as cravats and tucked under their waistcoats. It seemed to be the fashion because many men sported these scarves at the time. Carefully avoiding eye contact I kept my head down and, prudently, crossed the street, walking briskly to discourage the prostitutes, young and old, who tried to accost me. One of them, with her bloated postbox-red lipstick, rouged cheeks, dyed ginger hair and ugly Hapsburg jaw, looked remarkably like 'Big Gertie' from Helen Street in Govan—same mean street, different town.

To my relief I reached the end of Escudellers and emerged into the still sunny Ramblas. A pair of craggy-faced Guardia Civil looked me over suspiciously as I waited for a break in the traffic to cross to the Columbus monument where Macphail sat waiting for me.

'So whit dae ye think o' Barcelona then, son?'

'Great!' said I. 'Thanks for getting me the afternoon off work, I really appreciate it, Mr Macphail.'

'Me and some of the lads were thinkin' o' goin' oot on the toon fur' a wee dram or two tonight, son. Wid ye like to jine us?' asked Macphail.

'No, but thanks very much anyway, Mr Macphail. I'm fair wabbit from trailing around the town all day. I think I'll read for a bit and have an early night if you don't mind.'

'Suit yirsel' son. It's probably fur the best. Ah widnae like fur ye tae get intae ony trouble. Yir paw and maw wid never forgive me!'

THE DEFENCE COMMISSION

As I stood at the foot of the gangplank at seven that evening, Laureano and a slightly older, walnut-skinned man, Patricio Navarro, a member of the CNT's Transport Workers' Union, emerged from the shadows of the warehouses. Both men were obviously known to the night watchman as we walked straight past him through the dock gates with a nod and without question.

We carried on along the waterfront towards Montjuïc, past the strange Customs House building, which looked to me remarkably like a scaled-up version of the building housing the entrance to St Enoch Square Underground Station in the centre of Glasgow. I wondered if they had the same architect. In the Carrer Conde de Asalto we stopped outside a café bar called La Tranquilidad, one of the many French style cabaret venues along the Paral·lel. Laureano explained it had been a popular meeting place for anarchists since it opened in 1901. We slipped inside for a quick look round the cavernous smoke-filled room. It was a human beehive, buzzing with vitality, swarming with people from the four corners of Spain and beyond, some playing cards and dominoes or engrossed in newspapers, magazines, and books, others chatting, arguing, and debating all things mortal and divine against the noisy backdrop of an accordion orchestra and the clatter of countless domino pieces on marble table tops.

We didn't stay long. From La Tranquilidad we headed towards the Plaça d'Espanya where Laureano pointed out El Español, another café popular with anarchists.

Turning left off the Paral·lel into the Carrer de Bobilla, Laureano led us into a pitch-black close with a steep, unlit wooden staircase as dark as a Glasgow tenement dunny at midnight. Groping my way to the stairwell, clutching Laureano's shoulder, I found the first step by tripping over it. Cautiously we climbed the steps, up four flights of stairs, without once letting go of the handrail, until we reached the top landing. In my mind's eye I was conjuring up images of Robert Louis Stevenson's hero David Balfour on the brink of tumbling into the empty void at the top of the crumbling Gothic tower of the House of Shaws, but the landing proved solid.

Laureano lit a match to read the apartment numbers tacked to the three doors. He rapped with his knuckles on the door of the furthest apartment, which was opened by the shadowy figure of Andrés, one of the men I had met that afternoon. Ushering us inside, he directed us along the short lobby with its worn linoleum and fading yellow wallpaper into a dimly lit room. It was pure chiaroscuro. Had Dan Macphail been there he would have told you himself, the scene was straight out of one of his penny novelettes, or a Caravaggio painting. A long table covered with a waxed floral tablecloth occupied the centre of the room on which burned two paraffin lamps, their delicate golden light casting flickering shadows, alternately burnishing and shading the faces of the five men seated around it.

Each man rose from his chair to shake my hand and give me his name and trade union affiliation, which Laureano translated for me. The men before me were members of the Defence Commission of the Catalan Regional Committee of the CNT. Ramón Archs Serra was the one I immediately warmed to. A metalworker in his early thirties, from Igualada, he was bony and fit looking, with disconcertingly flinty blue twinkly eyes set deep in a rugged, weather-beaten face. I recognised in him a kindred spirit, a charismatic man with a sense of humour—one who didn't take himself too seriously. Behind his calm, cheery exterior, however, Archs was a complex character whose formal education consisted of night classes at Ferrer's Modern School, lectures and debates in the ateneus, complemented by his experiences and understanding of men that he acquired in the army. His role in the Defence Commission—together with another battle-hardened comrade, Pedro Vandellós, whom the Special Services Brigade had been attempting to frame for the previous January's murder of an important Catalan manufacturer—was to coordinate the union's defence groups.

Among other things, they provided prominent union activists with body-guards and armed security for the collectors of union dues in the work-places or in the streets outside the factories, a hazardous job at the best of times. The defence groups were to become the core of the urban guerrilla action groups that were preparing to take the social war to the capitalist bourgeoisie. There weren't many people around capable of adapting to the semiclandestine lifestyle required to pursue the CNT's revolutionary objec-tives. Some comrades worked within the parameters of the system; others did not. Archs and Vandellós were among those who 'did not'.

Next to Archs sat Salvador 'Sugar Boy' Segui, a lugubrious-looking, jowly, ba' faced *'caballero de la triste figura'*—a 'knight of the sad counte-nance'—with heavy bags under his hooded eyes, one of which was discon-certingly 'lazy'. I say disconcertingly because in Glasgow a 'skeely eye' was a defect closely associated with the 'evil eye'. Everyone in the room appeared to defer to Segui, who struck me at first as slovenly, but being young and judgmental I couldn't tell the difference between bohemian and shabby. He was in his work clothes: a well-worn flat cap, paint-splattered blue overalls, white rope-and-canvas slip-on shoes—*alpargatas*—with a red-and-black silk neckerchief tied around his neck. I learned later, however, that if he was going anywhere special, such as to a restaurant or a public meeting, he paid considerably more attention to his appearance, or rather his part-ner, Teresina, did, ensuring he wore 'proper clothes'—leather shoes, a fedora hat, a jacket, and a clean white shirt with a high butterfly collar and a tie.

Whenever he was in a position to indulge himself, which wasn't often in those hard times, Segui was partial to a brandy, a cigar, and good food. This sybaritic aspect of his character was frowned upon by some of the more puritanical and judgmental anarchists whose lifestyle preferences tended towards the monastic and self-denying, which meant Segui was often the subject of sanctimonious and hypocritical gossip.

Opposite Segui was Ángel Pestaña, another prominent anarcho-syndi-calist. He motioned for Laureano and me to sit beside him. Like Segui and Archs, Pestaña was dynamic, strong-willed, quick-witted, and resourceful, but whereas the former two were extroverted and flamboyant, Pestaña was markedly more reserved, with a pronounced tendency towards mor-bidity. When I first met him he still retained a certain peasant simplicity, preferring to remain in the background, and although a highly competent public speaker, he lacked Segui's charisma, that special ability to enthuse and carry an audience with him.

Austere and priestlike with a concave chest that made him look tubercular, Pestaña's features—his gaunt face, full lips, and prominent hooked nose—were markedly Levantine, and no matter how often he shaved his bony jaw, three times a day sometimes, he always seemed to have a heavy blue growth of beard.

This thirty-two-year-old union leader was from Santo Tomás de las Ollas, a small village near Ponferrada in León Province. Abandoned by his mother at the age of three, Pestaña had been brought up by his violent father, a railway worker. But, like most kids of the time, his childhood was ephemeral and he had to support and care for his sick father, who eventually died when Pestaña was fourteen. After that Pestaña had to fend for himself, acquiring, along the way, an unusual mix of trades and skills, including acting, journalism, and watchmaking. Like Segui and Archs, he too was only fifteen when he had his first run-in with the police, spending three months in jail in Sestao in the Basque Country for 'disorderly conduct' during a public meeting. The onetime artisan watchmaker and autodidact was now a seasoned journalist on *Solidaridad Obrera*, the newspaper of the Catalan CNT.

After the introductions, we settled around the table. Andrés and his wife emerged from the kitchen bearing two large pots of steaming fabada Asturiana, a bean stew with spicy pork sausage and black pudding. These were placed in the centre of the table for everyone to help themselves. There was no wine, only a clay *botijo* of ice-cold water, a saltcellar, and a couple of straw baskets with bread and fruit.

The meal was accompanied by a passionate and heated discussion punctuated with occasional alarmingly raised voices and arm waving—all of which I was told was friendly banter; very different from the heated and considerably more uncivilised arguments in Glasgow pubs and street corners. Laureano explained a little of what the debate was about—none of it particularly important as far as I could make out—and translated my occasional observations for the others when I was asked a direct question about life in Glasgow. Miguel, Patricio, and Pablo left after the meal, leaving only Archs, Pestaña, Segui, Laureano, and myself at the table, Andrés and his wife having withdrawn earlier, either to bed or into the kitchen.

Segui disappeared into the kitchen and emerged soon after with another jug of coffee. He filled our cups, lit a chunky Partagás cigar, then settled back into a comfortable leather armchair in the corner, quietly contemplating the blue-grey column of aromatic smoke as it drifted upwards. It smelled of moist raisins and cherries. Pestaña struck the flint of his *mechero* lighter and blew hard on the wick until it glowed furnace red. Lighting his cigarette from it, he inhaled deeply, and then released a stream of smoke towards the ceiling. Taking a sip of his black coffee, he put down his cup and addressed me in surprisingly good English.

What he told me was extraordinary—his proposal even more so.

THERE'S BEEN A MURDER!

'Señor Farquhar, you may be wondering why we have asked you to come along this evening. We'd like to ask you a favour. But I must explain.

'Let me begin. In January,' he said, 'two men were killed by *pistoleros*, gunmen, outside the Industrial School here in Barcelona. They had been going to give a talk on new developments in mechanical engineering. More than fifty shots were fired. It was a massacre.

'The victims were Señor Pastor, a lecturer in mechanical engineering at the Industrial School, and his friend, Josep Albert Moner Barret, a munitions manufacturer and one of Barcelona's biggest employers. Barret was the *pistoleros*' real target; he was one of the most intransigent and hard-line members of the Federación Siderúrgica y Metalúrgica—the metal manufacturers' organisation—president of the Society of Industrial Mechanics, and the managing director of Industrias Nuevas, one of the main manufacturers of strategic war matériel. He produced grenades and howitzer shell fuses for the French army, among other things.

'It is four months since these murders and Chief Superintendent Manuel Bravo Portillo, head of the secret police, has been trying to pin these murders on our members. He has done everything in his power to frame innocent cenetistas for the crime, including planting explosives and weapons in the homes of militants and in union halls. He has the support of the local newspapers and the employers, La Federación Patronal. Since January, they have barraged the CNT with these accusations.

'The CNT was not responsible for the murders. The whole thing is untrue.' His fingers tapped rhythmically on the table, emphasising the words. 'It is another excuse for the authorities and employers to blacken the name of the *sindicato único*, to attack the workers.' Weariness passed briefly across his face, and for a moment he was no longer with us but lost among his own painful memories. With a snap he returned to the room, took a mouthful of coffee, and resumed.

'We were not responsible,' he repeated. 'We are not terrorists. Anarchosyndicalism is not about murdering employers, not even bad ones.' He looked around the room for approval.

'What we want is to organise the workers until we are strong enough to paralyse capitalism. Then we can take over the means of production and distribution for the benefit of everyone. Killing employers like Barret is a distraction. It only benefits the State, and the enemies of the working class. We have a lot of enemies, a lot ... but I'm not telling you something you don't know,' he looked directly into my eyes.

I cleared my throat, which had tightened. I was flattered, and anxious. What did this hard-bitten class warrior want from me? I could feel my face burning with flattery and apprehension. To cover my disconcertion I reached for my coffee. The others were watching me intently.

'I, er, I ...' I stammered. This was all a bit overwhelming.

Pestaña patted my hand gently and smiled, reassuringly, but without mirth.

'I apologise, Señor Farquhar, a bit much I imagine for a young man whom we've only just met. But please understand. We are fighting a war, and our enemies want to destroy us, destroy the hopes and aspirations of the working people.'

The others nodded, barely perceptibly, and for a moment the room became as silent as a tomb as each became lost in their own thoughts.

'More coffee?' said Archs, breaking the silence.

The jug was passed around, and each of us concentrated on the dark liquid as if it were a crystal ball.

Pestaña touched my hand to attract my attention. I met his eyes and I could see the urgency there.

'Señor Farquhar,' he said in a whisper, 'we need your help.'

'H—how can I ...?'

'I will explain later. Please forgive me but I must tell you the rest of the story. We do not know exactly who is behind these killers, although we do have our suspicions, but we do know they are mercenaries killing for money, not principle. But someone is directing them and it is not us. We believe in this case it is the German special services working with the employers and the police.

'It is true that some of our people do get frustrated sometimes, how could they not? And sometimes some of them get violent, but never as union policy. Violence does not and cannot help our cause, and vengeance, even if satisfying, seldom resolves the problems we face. No matter how impatient some of our compañeros are,' he threw a sideways glance at Archs, 'and no matter how good it feels to see bad people getting their just desserts, most of our people reject violence. *Words* are our weapons, education, persuasion, propaganda—and *solidarity*. We are proselytists, not terrorists.

We can die for our ideas, but we can never kill for them.' He paused again, waiting for his words to sink in.

'Not so our enemies. The Catalan bourgeoisie is degenerate, and the European war has made them more so. They place no value on lives other than their own, and certainly none on those of their employees. They are more than happy to burn two candles, one for God, the other for the Devil.'

Pestaña paused, lighting another cigarette from the burning tip of his previous fag end, blowing out another stream of smoke. Between the fumes from the paraffin lamps, Segui's cigar, and everyone else chain-smoking, the room had filled with a fug as acrid and dense as a pea-souper fog. When I started coughing and spluttering in the smoky atmosphere, Archs, considerately, opened a window.

Pestaña resumed: 'To return to the Barret murders; the main suspect is Eduardo Ferrer. Until 6 January this year he was chairman of the local Metalworkers' union, but he resigned suddenly and unexpectedly the day after Barret's murder. It was the timing of his resignation that made us suspicious; branch elections weren't due for some time, that and the fact that the examining magistrate ignored Ferrer and investigated, instead, his successor as the prime suspect—a man who clearly had no involvement with the affair.

'We now know that Ferrer is a *confidente*, an informer and provocateur on Chief Superintendent Manuel Bravo Portillo's payroll.'

'Bravo Portillo's Brigada de Servicios Especiales are called the "untouchables", interjected Segui, 'so when Pestaña here first exposed his links to the German special services in *Solidaridad Obrera*, describing him as the "captain of murderers", the authorities became extremely 'touchy'. The story caused Madrid enormous diplomatic and political embarrassment because it exposed the fiction of Spain's neutrality. Bravo's bosses knew he worked for the German secret services and they were probably complicit in his activities. A few years ago, in 1916, he was caught red-handed photographing secret documents for the Germans in his own office, but nothing ever came of it, nor was he prosecuted for espionage.

'Worse still,' added Pestaña, 'the German secret service has also suborned and corrupted our comrades, and to add insult to injury the German embassy in Madrid has actually been funding *Solidaridad Obrera*, our newspaper, handing out large sums of money to comrades who should know better.

'I have the evidence of their payments to the *Soli* administration, which I am about to present to the Catalan CNT's Regional Committee,' said Pestaña, 'along with a demand that they sack the editor, José Borobio, and *Soli*'s publisher, José Negré. The problem is that both men are highly respected compañeros from the Serrallonga Workers' Centre in the Carrer Mercador, and were directly elected to run *Soli* and its supplements. So you see, it's not at all clear-cut how to resolve this messy situation—unless they agree to resign of their own accord. And there is absolutely no suggestion that they have used this money for their own personal benefit; everything has been ploughed back into the paper.

'I hasten to add,' continued Pestaña, 'that *Soli* isn't the only leftist paper funded by the Germans. Niceto Alcalá Zamora's liberal daily, *El Dia*, is another—and they have also bought off most of the Cortes, our parliament. From the union's point of view the effect of the German actions has been to compromise our integrity and credibility, and seriously undermine rank-and-file morale—which will be to the detriment of our nationwide recruitment drive later this summer, after our Congress in Sants, when we intend to restructure and relaunch the CNT to incorporate as many different labour organisations as possible in each industry.

Segui picked up the narrative: 'If we can convince enough of the country's smaller and regional labour unions to affiliate en bloc to the CNT the consequences for the ruling classes could be devastating. Look at what's happening in Russia; a semifeudal agrarian society that mirrors Spain in so many ways—politically, socially, and economically. These people know only too well that they've got trouble right here in Merchant City, and that what is happening now in Russia could so easily happen here in Spain. For the ruling class that is a prospect that doesn't bear thinking about. For them the CNT has to be stopped in its tracks, and they will do everything in their power to ensure that happens.'

THE CAIRO GANG

I shifted uneasily in my seat, bemused and overwhelmed by this torrent of information. Why was Pestaña telling me all this? I had only just turned eighteen, I was a foreigner who couldn't speak a word of Spanish or Catalan, and my boat was due to sail within forty-eight hours. How could I possibly be of help? I felt the wheels turning inside my head.

Pestaña saw the look of panicky incredulity on my face. 'Por favor, señor Farquhar, the reason I am telling you this,' he said, 'is because we need your help—and we don't have much time. Laureano tells me you are a compañero of the 'Idea'. I trust his judgment, and I think, I hope, that is—that you can be trusted. Let me explain. A compañera who works for the British Consul General here as a confidential secretary has learned that twenty or so British secret service agents will be arriving shortly from Alexandria in Egypt. In fact, they are probably here already. These men are soldiers, loyal servants of His Majesty, the King of England, professional killers of the backstreet variety, as opposed to the battlefield kind. Until last week they were based in Cairo, assassinating German, Austro-Hungarian, and Ottoman agents who were spreading pan-Islamic propaganda, and subverting and sabotaging British interests in Egypt, Persia, and Central Asia.

'Now, with Germany escalating its submarine campaign, the British are focusing their attention on the Central Powers' proxy agents operating here in Barcelona. And although Bravo Portillo recruits and pays these killers, the money itself comes from the Baron de Rolland, the head of Section III (b) of Germany's secret service in Barcelona, the man responsible for all their operations in Catalonia and the Levante, operations that he runs from his mansion in the Carrer de Balmes. His orders, in turn, come from the Madrid embassy, which oversees all Central Power secret service activities in the peninsula; the top men in Madrid are von Kalle, the military attaché, and the naval attaché, Korvettenkapitän von Kroch, a dilettante and a playboy but dangerous all the same.

'The mission of the British agents is to "neutralise" the Baron de Rolland's network of spies and saboteurs. So, for the moment at least, we share a common cause and common enemies with the British and the French—by which I mean the German special services and their plutocratic collaborators in the Employers' Federation, the Patronal—along with their gangster lackeys and vigilante auxiliaries among the police, the Carlists, and Sometent (a reactionary, officially sanctioned vigilante militia).

'Our problem is an ethical one: whether or not to form a strategic alliance with these people. They say you need a long spoon to sup with the devil, and they don't come more diabolical than the British Secret Service Bureau. However, needs must when the devil is driving, and at the moment he's driving fast and loose with our compañeros' lives and the good name of the sindicato único! They are certainly not fighting for the things we fight for, but right now their enemies are our enemies. If we can work together on this—purely short-term of course—we should both benefit from the relationship. The war in Spain is a covert one, with the German Consulate in Barcelona smuggling in explosives, ammunition, and guns to sabotage Britain and France's strategic supply chain, arming and funding employers' vigilante groups, and assisting the employers to compromise and destroy the CNT.

'The oligarchs, their acolytes, wire pullers, intriguers, and men of property and power are terrified by what is happening around the world, and even now they are preparing for Armageddon as the established order of capitalism and feudalism glides towards collapse and chaos. When the war ends, social revolution will spread as quickly and devastatingly as the influenza pandemic; empires are unravelling and thrones across Europe will soon be falling like skittles. This senseless imperialist war they have imposed on humanity has the potential to trigger a global confrontation between the classes the like of which has never been seen since 1789. If the Russians can do it, so can we. This time, however, we need to be better prepared; we can't afford a repeat of last August's disastrous general strike. We lost over seventy compañeros then, and hundreds more wounded, and we still have over two thousand comrades rotting in prisons and hulks across the country.' He stopped abruptly, took a deep breath and pinned me with his eyes with mingled urgency and anticipation.

'To get directly to the point, Farquhar, we would like you to act as an intermediary, an *enlace*, with the British Secret Service Bureau here in Barcelona. Bravo Portillo's men have the British Consulate under twenty-four-hour surveillance, and they know most of our activists. Apart from that, all Catalans or Spaniards entering the Consulate are stopped and questioned and therefore filed, compromised, and exposed, possibly even arrested. You, on the other hand, are "clean"—a British subject with a legitimate reason for visiting the Consulate.'

So now we had it. My goodness, what a proposition! My mind dashed off in every conceivable direction, like the poor affrighted elephant in Stephen Leacock's *Literary Lapses*. I don't know if it was a panic attack, adrenaline, excitement, anxiety, or . . . what. I just needed to move. I needed to stand. Pacing backwards and forwards in the cramped, smoky room I tried to work out my turmoil. This was not at all what I expected from a supper with comrades whom I had met barely a few hours ago. I needed air, and moved towards the open window.

The cool breeze from the street steadied me a bit, and the old Presbyterian pragmatism began to assert itself. But . . . spies! International espionage, secret agents, intrigue, murders? I turned back to the room. The others were all standing, looking at me anxiously. They obviously thought I had been going to jump. I smiled to myself. It was a bit of a leap of the imagination from shop-floor and street-corner radical to life-endangering deeds of derring-do like John Buchan's ubiquitous hero Richard Hannay.

My voice trembled as I spoke. Still reeling from trying to absorb what I'd been told and what had been asked of me, I stammered: 'My ship will probably be leaving tomorrow, or the day after . . . I, er, can't,' I cleared my throat, 'I can't see how I can do anything in that time.'

'We know. That is why,' Pestaña said, glancing to the others 'we would like you to stay.'

Another bombshell! Now I had to sit down. I was hardly listening as he continued.

'We know this is a big thing we are asking of you, but would you consider staying in Barcelona for a couple of months to help us? We are appealing to your comradeship and solidarity.'

By now his earnest appeal was palpable, and my head swam once more as I tried to focus on him in the dim light through the smoke haze.

'What do you say?'

I was dumbstruck, perhaps even suffering from mild hysteria, but I managed to regain some presence of mind, such as it was. Fresh off the boat from Glasgow, I had somehow drifted into a parallel world of intrigue, espionage, and who-knows-what else. I desperately tried to sort out and catalogue everything I had just heard, contemplating all the possibilities, but my hesitation began to evaporate. There was no question as to what my decision would be; here was something I could do that would actually make a difference. I'd felt jaded and a bit complacent about life recently; now I was being presented with an opportunity to be part of something— and definitely exciting. Excitement—the irresistible narcotic for all youth. My heart pumped purple adrenaline at the prospect of living so close to the edge of danger. My mundane life had unexpectedly veered off course straight into a plot from *Nick Carter Weekly* or a William Le Queux novel. For a brief moment I thought about my parents, how worried they would be. Then the image of Lara flashed into my mind. Those eyes! That smile! Those breasts!

'All right,' I said, feeling half reckless, half convinced, but wholly excited. 'I'm game. It's not a time for hummin' an' hawin'! So, tell me, how you propose we go about this?'

'Good man!' said Pestaña. Pointing to Archs, he said: 'Ramón here coordinates the Defence Commission's clandestine planning group. He'll be responsible for everything from now on. He will explain the plan to you.'

ARCHS—THE MAN WITH THE PLAN . . .
But there were practical questions to think through first. My apprenticeship, for example. How was I to explain not returning home with the *Covenant*, and how would I support myself while in Barcelona?

'Don't worry,' said Archs, when I explained the reasons for my hesitation. 'You may have gathered we have a flu pandemic sweeping the country at the moment. What we propose is to have one of our compañeros, a doctor, register you into a clinic with the appropriate symptoms. For those lucky enough to recover, this particular strain takes at least two or three weeks to run its course—far too long a time for your ship to wait for you. Also, your captain won't risk spreading the influenza among the rest of the crew so he'll probably make arrangements with the British Consul for you to return to Britain on another ship when you are fully recovered. As for your apprenticeship, I'm sure your employers will understand; a couple of months won't make much difference. You'll also learn some Catalan and Spanish—and maybe a few other things besides. As for supporting yourself, that won't be a problem. We'll look after you.

'Laureano will take you to the clinic of Dr Felípe Alaíz where you will be admitted to the Hospital de la Santa Creu I Sant Pau. It's in the city centre, close to the Ramblas, not far away. We have many compañeros there—porters, auxiliaries, nurses, and doctors, including a young intern by the name of Dr Isaac Puente who will look after you and liaise with Laureano and Archs until we can get you into more appropriate accommodation with compañeros.

'Once you are admitted to hospital, Laureano will let your captain know what's happened and where you are. He'll say he found you collapsed in the street and took you to the clinic. Your ship should be gone soon, so you won't have long to wait. Meanwhile, I suggest you start learning Spanish. I'm sure Laureano will be happy to teach you in return for improving his English—or Glaswegian.'

Belleville, 18 October 1976

Farquhar stopped typing and sat back. Rummaging through the effluvia on his desk he uncovered a rumpled pack of Partagás cigarettes, shook one out, tapped it on the back of his wrist, struck a match with one hand, lit the cigarette, and blew out the match. The smoke rushed from his mouth and nostrils, twisting its way upwards, like ivy up a telephone pole. He poured himself another Glenmorangie and savoured the mellow, caramel flavour of the whisky as it trickled down his throat, warming him as it went. Writing this familiar story was helping to steel his nerves. He hadn't fully appreciated it at the time, but his decision all those years ago to join the defence groups had been the moment he had set off down the road 'less travelled by, And that has made all the difference.'

Somewhere, Dostoevsky has written about the second part of a man's life being made up of nothing but the habits and values he acquired during the first half—Abeunt studia in mores. Farquhar's young self was about to acquire a lot of unusual values, if not habits. Spain had taught him about good and evil, hate and love, greed, hardship, injustice, and corruption. It had also widened his experience of men, and it was there, through adversity, he had learned the value of comradeship and dignity. Spain had enhanced and reinforced his belief in goodness—and redemption. Stubbing out the cigarette in the saucer of his coffee cup, he leaned over the typewriter to pick up his narrative again. Time was pressing.

BARCELONA—NEW BEGINNINGS

By the end of that evening I was tucked up in bed in a small isolation ward in the Hospital de la Santa Creu, which was where Macphail visited me early the following afternoon. I felt uneasy deceiving a man who had become such a good friend to me over the last month or so, but I had no choice.

'Man, yer no lookin' weel. Whit happened tae ye?' said Macphail when he entered the room, carefully keeping a safe distance from the bed and covering his nose and mouth with a large khaki handkerchief. Dr Puente had given me the pharmaceutical equivalent of snake oil that had raised my temperature and made me look suitably feverish. I explained that I had gone out to explore the city at night and had taken a bad turn and collapsed in the Ramblas. Next thing I knew I'd woken up in this hospital bed with a pounding headache. A porter had kindly volunteered to go to the docks to let him and Captain Macrob know what had happened.

But as we talked and I lied to my old friend I could feel the guilt seep into the pit of my stomach, drop by drop.

Dr Puente came in with a nurse to take my temperature and check my pulse. After making a show of examining me, Puente explained to Macphail that they would need to keep me in for at least a week to monitor my progress. They suspected influenza but couldn't be certain. I didn't have the telltale blue-black marks of cyanosis, the worse outcome effect of the virus as fluids flooded the lungs, but if I did have the disease and it didn't attack my chest, I would survive.

Macphail was visibly taken aback at this news; the *Covenant* was due to sail at first light the following day and he didn't want to leave me behind, but I reassured the chief engineer that I was in good hands and would be all right. Dr Puente promised him he would keep the British Consul informed as to my situation and that I would be well looked after until I could be repatriated.

Macphail returned that evening with my canvas kitbag, my books, and a large, crisp, white five-pound note the size of a hanky with the best wishes of Captain Macrob.

'The money will see you all right for a couple of weeks, Farquhar my lad, and the Consul,' he said, 'will handle all the hospital bills and repatriation costs. They have all your details.'

Macphail, ever the optimist and having had a dram or two, was in reflective mood. Throwing all caution and his protective hanky to the winds, he talked wistfully about how he missed his time on the steam puffers, especially the *Vital Spark* with its eccentric skipper Peter Macfarlane, better known around all the harbours between Bowling and Stornoway by his byname of Para Handy.

'I've made up my mind, son. This'll be my last trip on the *Covenant*. I've seen enough o' foreign pairts and I hae a strong inclination to go back on the puffers. Nothing in the wide world can beat sailing into Lamlash Bay on a bright June morning to collect a cargo o' gravel, or tie up at Tarbert quay wi' a cargo o' coals. There isn't a rock, no, nor a chuckie stane this side o' the Cumbrae Heid that I do not have a name for. I ken them a' fine, in the dark, by the smell—and that's no easy, I can tell you.

'An auld verse my grampa was fond of quoting keeps drumming in my head. In fact he liked it so much he had it carved on his gravestone. No name, he didn't want his name or any dates on it, only the verse:

> I live and know not how long,
> I die and know not when,
> I travel and know not whither,
> Strange that I am so cheerful.

'That's me, my boy. So, I've decided I'll be haunin' in my notice when we get back to Glesca. I had a dram wi' Para Handy before we left, and the *Vital Spark* is being refitted wi' a new boiler. Ay, man, wi' a new boiler there'll be nae stoppin' her. It may no be as good as the wan you put intae the *Covenant*, but she'll still go like the duvvle—six knots at least. I hope ye'll look us up when ye get back.

'Wi' a new coat o' paint an' a touch o' gold bead, she'll be the smertest boat in the tred. My, you should see her, Farquhar. She is all hold, wi' the boiler behind, four men an' a derrick, an' a watter butt an' a pan loaf in the foc'sle. Oh, man! She's the beauty. Chust sublime! It's gentry for passengers, or nice genteel luggage for the shootin' lodges she should be cairryin'. My bonnie wee *Vital Spark*!'

Tears appeared in his eyes so I hurriedly said how tired I was; it was time to say goodbye. In an emotional farewell—at least as emotional as male Glaswegians could be without embarrassingly over-the-top displays of unmanly affection—Macphail got up to leave, shook my hand, and wished me good luck, promising to let my parents know I was in good hands and would soon be back home. I never saw him again.

GOODBYE TO ALL THAT

Dan Macphail never did deliver my message. Three days later I received a visit from a Consular official with the tragic news that a German U-boat had sunk the *Covenant* the previous day, just a few hours out of Barcelona. There were no survivors. I felt sick, as though I had been sucker punched in the solar plexus. I couldn't sleep that night; my mind raced twenty to the dozen thinking of Dame Fortune's arbitrary turn of the wheel that had saved my life and taken the lives of Macphail and the other crew members.

That power which erring men call Chance.

I have never been able to shake the lurid images in my head of their last moments. How did they die? Was it in the explosion when the torpedoes hit? Were they scalded or burnt to death in the engine room—or did they drown? What was Macphail thinking as the sea closed around him? Probably of his wife and five kids. That he'd never see Greenock, Upper Loch Fyne, or the Kyles of Bute again?

I was neither religious nor superstitious, but I now felt certain that my decision to remain in Barcelona, fortuitous as it was, had to be life-changing as well as lifesaving. It's never easy to jettison prejudices, but that was when I finally stopped being a pacifist, and the war against Germany, for me, became a 'just' cause.

I spent a little over a week in hospital, during which time Laureano, whom I'd started to recognise as a true friend, visited me mornings, afternoons and evenings. That first day he turned up with a jotter, a pencil, a book of Spanish verbs and a dictionary that he'd borrowed from the ateneu, and every day thereafter he tested me relentlessly on the meaning and conjugations of the three common verbs he had given me the previous day. It helped keep my mind off the fate of my shipmates.

Some people had problems understanding my accent, and I worked hard to modify my speech patterns, if only to avoid the irritation of having to repeat myself, so it was a learning process for the both of us. Whenever someone from the Consulate visited, Laureano made his excuses and left.

When I was signed off from the hospital, Laureano took me to the home of a compañero called Josep Maria Foix. When the consular official next called to check on my progress, Dr Puente told him that I had been discharged into the care of one of the nursing staff, with whom I was now staying. With the influenza epidemic worsening, the hospital needed all the beds it could get. I left a note with Puente confirming this, promising to check in with the Consulate within the week.

Josep Maria Foix and his partner, Maria Antonia Foix, lived in a spartan two-room apartment on the third floor of a crowded slum tenement building in the Carrer San Pablo, deep in the proletarian barri of Poble Sec between Montjuïc and the Paral·lel. The Foixes were lucky; they didn't have to share, as did many at that time. Apartments built for one family sometimes accommodated six or more families who shared a single stairhead toilet for two floors. The entrance to Foix's close was framed by two shops, one of which was a hatters, the other a butchers whose window was festooned with strings of garlic and dark red sausages of horse, mule, and pig meat.

I slept on a camp bed in a half-tiled, windowless room lit by a shimmering green-hued gas mantle. A low, stone butler sink stood against one wall and beside it a double gas-ring with a coffee pot, which was always on the go. Above the cooker hung a large frying-pan and an enormous smoke-blackened cooking pot; against the facing wall stood a dark mahogany chest of drawers with a Willow Pattern china vase containing four or five pink paper carnations. Next to the chest of drawers was a worm-eaten pine trunk. The centrepiece of the room was a large scrubbed pine table, which at mealtimes was covered with a frayed floral oilcloth. It was the centre of the family's universe; around this table everyone ate and socialised. It was also where I spent most of my time learning verbs and practising my Spanish. It reminded me of home.

Josep Maria and Maria Antonia couldn't do enough for me. Square jawed with a pleasant smile and kind eyes, Josep was short and sinewy, and walked with a mariner's roll. His head of fuzzy thick hair gave him the look of an Abyssinian, with two moons on his broad forehead. Maria Antonia was cadaverously thin and her skin ashen, almost translucent, and although her cheeks had begun to sag with dark circles and crows' feet about her deep-sunk eyes, she was still a handsome—and passionate woman. She wore her auburn hair gathered up in a tight bun—a topknot they called it—which, when she undid it in the evening before going to bed, hung over her shoulders. Black clothes accentuated the aura of melancholy that surrounded her.

Photographs on the dresser of her as a young woman showed how beautiful she had once been. She had the straight carriage, grace and compassion of a lady of breeding who welcomed every visitor to her apartment as a valued friend. When Laureano was around to translate she would talk endlessly about her past and the terrible conditions in the factories, and the dirty tricks and the abuse the workers received from the employers and the foremen—the *encargados*. Aggressive sexual advances from foremen and managers were a common problem facing most women factory workers. If the men didn't get their way they could make the women's lives even more difficult and miserable.

Women didn't work on Saturday afternoons, but they still laboured one day more than the men. Sunday was for housework: cleaning, washing, and mending clothes. It was a woman's lot to work from the time she had a bit of strength until she was old and done with no stopping for rest. If she was unlucky enough to survive her partner, she was usually left destitute at the end of her days, forced to beg in the streets—or enter an asylum or a convent-run poorhouse.

In Spain, as in the West of Scotland, although there were few female union leaders, even in the textiles industries, it was the women who gave the movement spirit and backbone, especially in the domestic sphere, supporting their partners. They fought for more than just workers' rights or the eight-hour day. In the early days they kept themselves separate from the men in the barri committee meetings—much as in Scotland—but gradually that mentality, weaned in religious indoctrination, broke down as companionship and solidarity took over. Once those initial barriers were broken down, everyone mixed as one united group.

Maria Antonia was a passionate woman with an extraordinary fighting spirit. When crossed or angered she would seethe quietly until finally exploding in terrifying bursts of articulate fury. Nor did she think twice about landing a punch on any man. She was heavily involved in the almost daily protest demonstrations against escalating rents and the soaring cost of food, fuel, and everyday necessities. These protests had been going on since hyperinflation gripped the economy the previous December; they usually ended with the women organising mass raids on grocery stores, bakeries, lorries and carts carrying foodstuffs, and coal yards. They were dangerous too; anyone caught 'liberating' shops stood a good chance of being shot dead by either the Sometent or the Guardia Civil—women and children included.

Maria was usually first on the picket lines, and in times of hardship she was always to the fore helping organise a mutual aid welfare system. Instead of simply doling out money to needy families, the barri committees—which were akin in many ways to small self-managed, self-contained neighbourhood republics—bought chickpeas, lentils, rice, beans, and sacks of flour that sympathetic bakers would knead and bake for free. Most of what the strikers' families needed could be obtained from the union hall, which was always filled with the aroma of freshly baked bread. In the Poble Sec centre, for example, there were around fifty women volunteers who took it upon themselves to distribute food to the most needy families.

Stories like these closely paralleled what was going on in Glasgow at the same time. Before I left home it wasn't uncommon for organised groups of women to attack shopkeepers and the offices of the factors, the landlords' agents. I vividly remember one occasion when a horse-drawn coal cart turned into our street and was immediately ambushed by a crowd of desperate men, women, and children who emerged almost as though choreographed from the tenement closes and stripped it in minutes, like coal-eating locusts.

In Barcelona, large crowds of angry women would surge en masse into the bakeries and empty them. The shouting and screaming during these attacks was ear-splitting. One image in particular, of a Catalan woman, Lola, sticks in my mind. She was a wonderful public speaker and although I had no idea what she was talking about, the emotion she conveyed was spellbinding! Inevitably, after one of her impromptu street corner speeches, crowds would march to the nearest bakeries and coal yards and strip them bare.

Lola reminded me of the socialist women who had been involved in the Singers strike in Clydebank in 1911 and were now on the Clyde Workers' Committee.

RAMÓN ARCHS

After I'd been living at the Foixes's rooms for a week or so, Laureano came to tell me that Archs had convened a meeting of defence group delegates that evening and that he wanted me to come along as well. The venue was a ground-floor apartment in a tenement in the Carrer Alcano, in Pueblo Seco, near the Paral·lel. Laureano and I arrived late so we squeezed into the crowded room, hugging the wall, close to the door. The smoky room held almost two dozen men, including Pestaña, Segui, and Archs, who sat behind a table at the far end. Everyone, apart from myself, represented a defence group linked to a particular sindicato único or to a neighbourhood anarchist group.

Archs was briefing the meeting when we arrived. Laureano whispered a translation for me: '...The Germans, Austro-Hungarians, and their proxy gangsters of the Barcelonan milieu are,' he said, 'dangerous people running a terror campaign intended to make the CNT appear responsible for their outrages. They are also murdering our compañeros on the streets of Barcelona and Valencia with impunity—to say nothing of the waterfront bombings and the torpedo attacks at sea killing our fellow workers. As long as Superintendent Bravo Portillo's proxy gangs remain unchallenged and unpunished they pose a serious threat not only to the sindicato único, but to our lives and livelihoods as well. There is no alternative. We have to take them on; because if we don't stand up to them now they'll become even more arrogant and efficient—murdering, maiming, and terrorising anyone and everyone who opposes them.

'The question is—do we collaborate with the British special services against a mutual enemy? Some of you have problems with this, understandably. I, too, have problems with it and am conscious of the moral and ethical questions these raise for us as libertarians, but the fact remains we have to defend ourselves.

'Everyone has their own opinion on the subject. For the British, theirs is a war of empire; for us it is the class war. For the moment, however, we share a common enemy whom we both need to destroy—or at least neutralise.

'The British no longer have any reliable intelligence sources in Barcelona—or anywhere else in Spain come to that. They can't trust their former police, army, and naval contacts who are mostly in the pockets of the Central Powers; the others are petty crooks and institutional criminals like Juan March, who can be bought and sold by the highest bidder. That is why the British have brought in their own team of agents to eliminate Germany's espionage and sabotage rings.

'These café society gangsters are British army officers who were trained and brought together last year on the orders of Sir Henry Hughes Wilson, chief of the British Imperial General Staff. They have been shipped in from Egypt where, under a man by the name of Erskine Childers, they have been assassinating Ottoman saboteurs, spies, and agents of influence. Now they have come here to do the same thing under the orders of their controller, John Chartres, Wilson's chief of Intelligence.

'Their boat docked yesterday and a Greek compañero who works for a shipping agency in Alexandria has sent us a list of their names along with a photograph of the group taken in the docks. We have been able to identify eighteen in the group so far—three colonels, two majors, eight captains, and five lieutenants. Interestingly, there are no enlisted men or NCOs in the group.

'Also, for the past couple of months other British Secret Service Bureau types have been coming and going between Barcelona, Madrid, Malaga, Valencia, Morocco, and Gibraltar—a Captain George Marshall and a Colonel Osbert Brice Ferguson Smyth—but we have no more information on these two—yet.'

When Archs finished speaking a short and heated discussion followed on the 'ifs' and 'buts' of collaborating with the British Secret Service Bureau. In the end everyone agreed to the proposal, but many had misgivings all the same.

Archs asked Laureano and me to stay behind after the meeting. His English, acquired from British and American volunteers in the Legion, was good.

'What I would like you to do, Farquhar,' said Archs, when the others had gone, 'is to go to the British Consulate tomorrow morning and tell them you are now fully recovered from your illness and that you are ready to be repatriated. Once inside ask to speak to Captain George Bruce, the

new temporary military attaché. He is in fact attached to the Secret Service
Bureau of the British Imperial General Staff operating out of 41 Rue Saint
Roche in Paris.

'I know Bruce from Algiers, and I get on well with him, in spite of his
job. It was he who told us about the machinations of another secret branch
of the British government, the Department of Intelligence and Statistics
section of the British Ministry of Munitions, the MMDIS, who had infiltrated an agent into the CNT here in Barcelona. Bruce detested these people,
whom he describes as "incompetent amateurs". They were trespassers on
his territory.'

Archs knew only too well that the reason Bruce told him about the
MMDIS infiltrator had more to do with interdepartmental and territorial
infighting than having any particular sympathy for the CNT, but he appreciated the gesture. The MMDIS/PMS2 agent in Barcelona had been sending back reports to his boss, Lynden Macassey, claiming that the CNT's
strikes were not linked to genuine wage demands or to do with negotiating improved working conditions; they were, he claimed, instigated and
funded by Germany's special services for their own geopolitical ends.

'Your job, Farquhar,' explained Archs, 'is to pass on a letter to Bruce
proposing joint actions targeting the German espionage and sabotage networks operating here in Spain.

'If they agree, I would like you to liaise with the British. You and
Laureano here will, with our help, identify for them the main Central
Powers' agents and their gangster proxies operating between Port Bou
and Valencia—and beyond.'

I nodded. Arch's confidence, briskness and lucid sense of purpose
impressed me. I had gone one more fateful step down that road 'less taken':

> ...And it's time to turn on the old trail, our own trail, the out trail,
> Pull out, pull out, on the Long Trail—the trail that is always
> new!

THE BRITISH SECRET SERVICE BUREAU

That was how I came to stand and knock at the door of His Britannic
Majesty's Consul General in Barcelona at ten o'clock the following morning.
'Having explained to the haughty uniformed doorman that I had come to
arrange my repatriation, I was ushered into a walnut-panelled parlour with
a thick-piled red and brown carpet. On three of its walls hung life-size gilt-
framed portraits of stern-eyed military and diplomatic heroes of Empire

sporting enormous moustaches and sideburns. Against the far wall stood a wide glass-fronted bookcase, its shelves tightly packed with gold-tooled, leather-bound tomes that looked as though they had never been opened.

After what seemed an age listening to the relentless tick-tocking of a rosewood grandfather clock, the door opened and a small, middle-aged man slouched in. He stared at me, briefly, with rheumy, washed-out pale-blue eyes framed by rimless pebble eyeglasses. Introducing himself as the Third Secretary he indicated that I should sit opposite him at an intricately carved partner's mahogany desk topped with red leather. We eyed each other up across the desk; I wondered what he saw—an uncouth, ignorant, pale faced, scruffy, Glaswegian working-class youth to be patronised? His breathing was laboured and wheezy and he stopped every so often to catch his breath. He seemed to be either consumptive or asthmatic or both, and didn't look long for this world, especially if he caught the influenza. I gave him my particulars, explaining about my influenza scare, the sinking of the *Covenant* and that I was now ready to be repatriated. He laboriously wrote down everything in an enormous leather-bound ledger—a book of reckoning, obviously—with a scratchy dipping pen without once looking up. When I finished my story, he stopped writing and blotted the wet ink. He fiddled with his pen for a time as he skimmed over his notes, repeating everything I'd just told him, stopping regularly to gulp in more air. Only when he finished did he look up and, adjusting his glasses in a headmasterish sort of way, proceeded into a rote lecture about my rights and obligations as a British citizen abroad, along with considerable humming and hawing about British Consular responsibilities in the great scheme of foreign affairs.

After his spiel he told me that His Majesty's Government would 'graciously' arrange for my repatriation to Britain—with the proviso that I forfeited my passport or my seaman's card until such time as His Majesty's Foreign and Colonial Office had been repaid in full. I was to return to the Consulate the following Monday, by which time the necessary paperwork would be ready and the appropriate arrangements made. I thanked him politely. As he rose from his chair, indicating that the meeting was over, I said:

'Can I speak to Captain Bruce, please? It's a private matter.'

This request from a young Glaswegian ingénue clearly just off the Govan ferry as it were, took the man aback. His jaw dropped.

'Can I ask what possible business you could have with our military attaché?' he asked, with all the hauteur he could muster.

'I'm afraid that's somethin' I can only discuss wi' Captain Bruce himsel',
but I assure you it is a matter of national importance.'

The man stared at me, flummoxed.

'I'll see if he is available,' he said, leaving me to the trance-inducing
ticking of the grandfather clock. After no more than five minutes or so I
heard the muffled sound of footsteps and voices in the lobby outside. The
door opened and two smartly dressed men entered with the official.

'Mr McHarg, these are Captains Bruce and Marshall. Gentlemen, this is
Mr McHarg who wished to speak with you on what he claims is "a matter
of national importance".'

Muttering some sarcastic comment under his breath, which I didn't
catch but whose tone I understood perfectly, he left the room. The two men
came over, shook hands and we sat down around the desk.

'So, Mr McHarg, can I ask what this is all about?' said Bruce. 'I'm
intrigued as to why you asked for me by name . . . ?'

I explained as succinctly as I could the circumstances of how I came to
be in Barcelona, without mentioning either my politics or my new friends.

'. . . And so, I was sitting in the café across the street waiting for the
Consulate to open when I was approached by a man, whom I didn't know,
who asked me if I was British, and if I would be kind enough to hand deliver
a letter to yourself, personally, and wait for a reply. I was to be sure to tell
you it was from Ramón and that it was a matter of great importance.'

A flicker of recognition crossed Bruce's face when I mentioned the
name Ramón. The two men looked at each other quizzically, then at me.
They obviously didn't buy my story; I wouldn't have bought it either, but
they didn't make any comment.

Dressed in brash Harris tweed suits with pointless leather elbows,
Bruce and Marshall looked like Eechie and Ochie, thirty-something Scottish
Tweedledum and Tweedledee, minus caps and bulging midriffs. Bruce's suit
was green, Marshall's was hodden grey check—which struck me as being a
bit affected for secret service men, but then again I wasn't of their class or
au fait with the dress code of the British Secret Service Bureau. Both wore
highly polished brogue shoes—Bruce's brown and Marshall's black—and
freshly laundered brilliant white cotton shirts. Apart from their suits, what
distinguished them were their ties, but not being one of them, I couldn't
tell whether they were regimental, club, or old school.

Both men spoke with refined, barely noticeable but identifiable East
Coast Scottish accents. I guessed they were probably Royal High School
or Fettes College boys from the more salubrious suburbs of Edinburgh,

whose educations had been polished at one of the more exclusive Oxford or Cambridge finishing colleges. They oozed confidence and intelligence, but didn't strike me as arrogant. They were like a pair of well-heeled and urbane commercial travellers, frequenters of fine restaurants and railway hotels. I wondered which one was the comedian and which was the straight man—or if they were both straight?

George Bruce—slightly built with alert cornflower-blue eyes, mousy hair greying at the temples, and a military moustache—put on his spectacles and read the letter, remarkably impassively I thought, given its contents. Marshall, meanwhile, scrutinised me with curiosity. When he finished reading, Bruce passed the letter to Marshall and he too examined me closely with penetrating eyes.

I tried to keep my expression blank, but I felt my face redden and found it difficult to maintain eye contact with the men on the other side of the desk. I knew they knew I was lying—or at least that I hadn't been entirely truthful. I shifted uneasily in my seat. Despite what I had hoped was an outward show of self-assurance, I found the situation and the men facing me across the desk quite intimidating.

Deftly pulling out a crisp white handkerchief jammed into the cuff of his jacket, Bruce took off his spectacles and breathed on both sides of each lens, again, in turn before polishing each lens in turn. He looked at me intently.

'So, Mr McHarg, tell me,' he said, pleasantly, 'how old are you?'

'Eighteen,' I replied, trying to appear nonchalant.

'And why do you think this man asked you to deliver the letter?' asked Bruce.

'No idea,' said I. 'Perhaps it was my "honest, sonsie face", or it could have been the five pesetas he gave me,' I replied cheekily. I didn't want to mention my political sympathies. Least said, soonest mended, as my old granny never tired of reminding me.

'Mmm,' purred Bruce, 'Strange. Bit of an odd choice, don't you think?' Marshall's hypnotic green eyes bored into mine from under puckered brows. Clearly they weren't taken in by my story.

'I've been asked to wait for a reply,' I said. 'Will there be one?'

Bruce thought for a moment, tapping the blotting pad with his index finger as though he was wrestling with an idea. Then, opening the desk drawer, he took out a sheet of cream-coloured paper, carefully tearing off the red embossed Consular Office address and the Foreign Office coat of arms. Taking a dipping pen from an inkwell embedded in a white porcelain base as big as a dinner plate, he scratched out a short note in neat copperplate writing in green ink which he carefully blotted on the large desk pad then folded, meticulously, in three and slipped into an envelope. Lighting a small candle he melted the end of a stick of blood red sealing wax, which he carefully dripped onto the flap and sealed it with his signet ring.

In the lobby, on my way out, I caught sight of myself in the full-length mirror in the vestibule. Gazing back at me were the eyes of a tall, enigmatic-looking young man with dark Celtic looks, someone barely recognisable as the unworldly adolescent who left Glasgow only a few weeks previously. The sensation was almost that of an out-of-body experience. I felt I was viewing someone else remotely. Which was the real me, myself or the mirror image? The uniformed and plainclothes policemen standing by the steps of the British Consulate looked me over with only passing interest as I left to find Laureano and Archs in a bar in the Travesera de Gracia where I handed Bruce's reply to Archs.

'Excellent,' he said, after reading the note. 'They want to meet as soon as possible. We'll convene a meeting of the Defence Commission tonight to discuss our options. First we need to compile an up-to-date list of all the German agents known to us, along with their gangsters and police contacts. Farquhar, I'd like you to deliver a reply to Bruce tomorrow morning, proposing a meeting for the evening.'

Next morning at ten o'clock sharp, I stood again outside the great mahogany door of the Consulate and knocked, and was promptly ushered straight into the waiting room by the liveried doorman. Bruce and Marshall arrived within minutes and, while Marshall read Archs's letter, Bruce poured me a cup of coffee from a vacuum flask on the sideboard. Marshall passed the letter to Bruce, who read it in turn. I, meanwhile, sipped my coffee and gazed blankly at the Establishment heroes gazing down at me from the walls. 'Good,' said Bruce, folding the letter and putting it in his pocket, 'We'll find the bar.'

WILL YOU STAY A LITTLE LONGER?

As I rose to leave, Bruce asked me to wait a moment; he had something to ask me.

'Mr McHarg—Farquhar, if you don't mind me calling you that—I know you are hoping to return home next week, but I wonder if you would consider staying on a little longer? If you agree, I'll have a word with the Consul General and arrange for your repatriation to be deferred for as long as is necessary. For some reason you are obviously trusted by these people, and it would be useful to His Majesty's Government if you could stay on and help us. It would be an important contribution to the war effort, you know. We would also be happy to help with a small contribution towards your living expenses.'

I was about to make a smart-arsed comment about what His Majesty's Government could do with the war effort, but I thought better of it and held my tongue. As for staying on, I wouldn't have missed it for the world. Not only had I suddenly been transformed from a naïve but earnest, callow youth into a confidential agent, an international man of mystery—now I had a new role as double agent. What next?

'Sure! No bother! Thanks!' I said, with the air of doing him a favour. 'I don't mind hangin' around a bit longer. How much will I get paid?' Always the pragmatist, me!

He grunted: 'We'll see what we can manage. By the way, when it's convenient I'd like to arrange a time with you to explain a little about how we will be communicating.'

I grinned. 'What about tomorrow mornin'?'

'Fine, ten o'clock sharp, here, at the Consulate. It'll only take a few hours. It's nothing too complicated.'

The war had made the secret services gluttonous for agent fodder, irrespective of age or experience.

The following morning Bruce gave me a crash course in invisible inks, opening letters discreetly, and encoding, or rather transposition, substitution and Caesar ciphers. Because time was so limited he taught me a simple book code based on an English translation of two novels from *La Comédie Humaine* by Honoré de Balzac: *Cousin Bette* and *Cousin Pons*. When I got round to reading them that weekend, for lack of anything else to read, I wondered if he was being ironic in his choice of titles, with their theme of poor people dependent on wealthy relatives. They struck me as the sort of books that would appeal to a man of his class and profession— with their vile, greedy, and cold characters—and humanity depicted as unredeemed and irredeemable. I seriously misjudged him, however. He proved to be a cheery cove who was a Balzac aficionado; I later thanked him for introducing me to the author, whom I wouldn't otherwise have considered reading.

Only once, many years later, did I use a cipher in my dealings with Bruce, when I was arranging to meet him in occupied France, prior to his departure for Bordeaux where a submarine was waiting to take him to

Portsmouth. In the meantime everything else that passed between us was as received—mainly documents.

'Suppose I want to send you the word "betrayal"?' said Bruce.

'Interestin' thought,' I said.

'Well,' says he, '"betrayal" appears on page 248 of *Cousin Bette*, on line 8, and is the seventh word in the line. So I would send "CB 248 8 7". Do you get it? Simple enough, isn't it?

'Sounds like a good way to get to read a book,' said I, 'but I'm a wee bit concerned about your choice of word.'

Our first meeting with Bruce and Marshall took place that evening in El Tastevins, a bar bodega in the Carrer Ramón i Cajal, halfway down a narrow backstreet off the Travesera de Gracia, near the Plaça de la Revolución. Its location made it easy to see if we were being followed. Another advantage was that it was leased by a compañero, and had a private dining room with a rear door to the kitchen and another that led out into a rear alley. It was the ideal location for clandestine meetings and quick getaways.

Archs, Laureano, and I arrived first; we settled ourselves in the backroom as the *patrón* uncorked a bottle of Somontano from his family vineyard, filled our glasses and set out saucers of salted almonds, olives, *chorizo* (a spicy pork sausage), anchovies, and sardines. Bruce and Marshall arrived a quarter of an hour later. Bruce, who as I've already said, knew Archs from Algeria, greeted him as an old friend. Glasses were filled and we toasted to good fortune and health.

Archs argued the CNT's case for working with the British. It was, he said, in both sides' interests to work together to neutralise the Central Powers' agents—and the gangster and police proxies who carried out their dirty work for them.

'We need to counter the antiunion activities of these gangsters,' said Archs, 'and end the police frame-ups and murders of our members. All of them can be laid at the feet of the military governor's office, the *Capitania*, the employers' organisation, the Patronal, and the pro-German elements in Bravo Portillo's Special Services Brigade. We have an important union congress coming up in July and we need, in the meantime, to take as much pressure off the sindicato único as possible.'

Archs gave no indication that he knew of the Cairo Gang's presence in Barcelona, but the British officers must have guessed that the unspoken preferred outcome for the Defence Commission was the physical elimination of the Patronal's puppeteers and footsoldiers.

The British officers knew they were dealing with revolutionaries, committed men and women with a clearly stated agenda to topple capitalism, displace the state, and replace it with a classless, federalist, cooperative society. They were, however, also realists. Anarchism was certainly not their 'cup of tea', but it wasn't their problem either—at least not yet. Over the years, especially during the Nazi occupation of France, the British Secret Intelligence Service and the Special Operations Executive relied heavily on Spanish, French, and Italian anarchists for intelligence and collaboration in mutually advantageous actions, especially when it came to organising Resistance networks and the escape and evasion lines in South-Western France and across the Pyrenees.

Archs was an accomplished poker-player and widely read: more than just Bakunin and Kropotkin. His face gave nothing away. The books he carried with him everywhere were well-thumbed and annotated translations of Carl von Clausewitz's *On War*, and Niccolò Machiavelli's *The Discourses*. Archs studied power politics and was well aware that the British officers were motivated by practical considerations of power, not altruism, ideals, or friendship. For them it was just another exercise in national self-interest. Trust didn't enter into the equation. What Archs and the Defence Commission were offering the British was a readymade, peninsula-wide network of well-placed informants and experienced agents from Port Bou to Alicante, La Linea, Cadiz, Huelva, to Lisbon and Bilbao, and from Ceuta to Melilla in Spanish Morocco. The icing on the cake was that the Defence Commission had already compiled extensive dossiers on most of the known and suspected pro-German agents in Spain. They also had an unsurpassed local knowledge of the chic bars, cafés, restaurants, and brothels they frequented. The British secret service officers wanted leads and quick results, and were anxious to tap into the network of confederal activists that covered almost every industry, profession, and neighbourhood in Spain. For Bruce and Marshall it was risk-free—all quid and no quo. Almost!

Bruce stressed to Archs that they would only work with him, Pestaña, and Segui; no one else was to know about their relationship, apart from any immediate compañeros in the Defence Commission who needed to know. Their concern—and ours too—was that some union members had been seriously compromised by their connections, real and imaginary, with the Germans. According to Bruce, only the previous month, Sir Arthur Hardinge, Britain's ambassador in Madrid, had sent a memorandum to Prime Minister Balfour briefing him on the extent to which they believed the CNT had been infiltrated by German agents who were allegedly 'handing out money left, right, and centre to Spanish anarchists'—exactly as they had been doing with Lenin and the Bolsheviks. The British Secret Service Bureau couldn't afford to be seen to be meddling in the internal affairs of a sovereign state, especially one that was allegedly neutral.

Bruce and Marshall left the dining room to discuss the matter between themselves, returning ten minutes or so later to confirm that they did want to work with us. We had a drink to celebrate, then settled down to working out procedures for making contact, which was to be through me. I was only to visit the Consulate if absolutely necessary. When the British needed to communicate with Archs it was to be by means of a letter addressed to the 'patrón' and left with the head barman—a compañero—at the Café Español on the Paral·lel. Letters for Bruce, marked 'Jorge', would also be collected from the Café Español. Bruce, meanwhile, was to arrange with the Consul General for me to remain in Spain indefinitely, so there would be no need for me to worry about my repatriation. They also agreed to provide me with a small stipend to help defray my living expenses, which was timely as by that time I was nearly down to my last peseta.

Archs promised that a dossier with the names of known German agents would be delivered to the two British officers the following Monday afternoon. I was to deliver it to them at the Café Tranquilidad in the Paral·lel, next to the Victoria Theatre. Almost as an afterthought Archs added: 'Laureano and Farquhar will accompany you or your people to act as watchers, and help identify the targets and their associates.'

'Gee, thanks, amigo!' I thought to myself, sardonically.

The secret service officers left through the front door. We waited a few minutes then left through the kitchen exit—just in case.

THE MILIEU

Laureano collected me at the Foixes the following afternoon. He was taking me on a tour of the Barcelonan milieu, one of whose centres was the Paral·lel, the two-mile-long 'boulevard of broken dreams' that runs from the port to the Plaça d'Espanya in the shadow of Montjuïc. On the Montjuïc side, hidden behind the brightly lit theatres, bars, nightclubs, and dance halls, the parlours of the poor, was another, darker, world—the *barraqas*, a crowded, verminous, shantytown of corrugated iron and cardboard shelters, occupied mainly by Murcianos and economic refugees from poverty-stricken Andalusia. Here, too, was the so-called barri of degradation, a neighbourhood of crumbling tenements swagged with drying laundry, a haunt of cutthroats, pimps, and lowlifes for whom anyone who didn't speak Catalan, eat *churros* (doughnuts) or drink anis was a potential victim. The smell of fish grilling on smoky charcoal braziers made me nauseous.

Our first stop was the crowded and poorly lit Café Español. As we entered, Laureano pointed out the segregated areas, indicating a section of the terrace and a double row of tables inside the entrance.

'Those tables are usually reserved for anarchists; the adjoining ones are normally taken by agents of foreign powers, secret policemen, and inform-ers—*confidentes*—while aspiring *toreros* (bullfighters), longhaired bohemi-ans, would-be writers and artists acting out their fantasies, reciting poetry to each other and arguing about the finer points of Futurism all use the other part of the terrace. You can easily identify them by their theatrical posturing and affected dress sense: broad-brimmed hats, long capes and cloaks, silver-topped canes, and the trademark flouncy black artists' cra-vats or knotted red and black bandanas tied around their necks.'

I stuck close to Laureano as we edged through the noisy smoke-filled room towards the bar, squeezing past tables of workingmen chapping domino pieces and arguing, *tertúlias* (debating circles) of pundits, teach-ers, intellectuals, and students nursing ten-centimo coffees over loud, book-ish, and ideological debates among friends and acquaintances, or single men lost to the world around them, deep in newspapers, books, or pam-phlets. Everything seemed to be done with the maximum of noise and a dramatic waving of arms.

The Café Español was a *milonga*, a venue where they danced and sang the Argentine tango. At the back of the room, on a small stage, a man played a *bandoneón*—a small accordion with buttons instead of keys. Beside him was a woman *cantante* in front of whom, in a tiny floor area, a couple danced, bonded in close embrace, chest-to-chest, hip-to-hip. I watched, transfixed by the driving, pulsating rhythm, the intricate choreography and brazen sexuality of this syncopated 'walking about' spectacle. It was a surreal visual and melodic counterpoint to the discordant hubbub that resonated around us. The image I have etched on my memory of the scene is that of a Hogarthian 'Rake's Progress' painting. A long, wide, cavernous room with cast-iron columns and heavy gilt-framed mirrors hanging from the walls, their manifold reflections making the room appear even larger, extending into infinity even—with no hiding place. Around me, in the all-seeing mir-rors, I saw images of Laureano and me, repeated a hundredfold. Although he—dark, short, and stocky—only came up to my shoulder, we could have been brothers, and in a sense, of course, we were: brothers in the 'Idea'.

Laureano ordered two *fino* sherries and spicy potato and *piquante* (savoury) *chorizo tapas*. He emptied his glass in a single gulp; I sipped mine, slowly. I wasn't keen on sherry. It reminded me of Sunday afternoons at my aunty's in genteel Bearsden. We stood at the bar, engrossed, tapping out the hypnotic 2/4 tempo on the counter. When the cantante finished her song and the audience was applauding her performance, Laureano discreetly pointed out some of the known police informers, the confidentes around the room. A few he knew, but he insisted he could tell an informer by their body language: their darting eyes, nervous hands, and straining ears; to me, however, they all looked fairly nondescript types.

Like Rick's bar in the film *Casablanca*, the Café Español was a popular haunt for secret agents of all nationalities, but without Rick. Laureano advised me to be especially careful if approached by Germans, Czechs, or Hungarians claiming to be comrades—be they deserters, pacifists, socialists, revolutionaries, or personal emissaries of Karl Liebknecht and Rosa Luxembourg. There were lots of these characters in town, apparently, the majority of them informers, provocateurs, and spies.

The rear of the bar was reserved for the Paral·lel's underclass, the so-called 'young barbarians'—Left Republican followers of the overpowering Alexander Lerroux, the shit-stirring demagogue and venal leader of the populist Partido Republicano Radical. He was a 'bought' man, an out-and-out scoundrel who cynically mixed and poured the most volatile passions. His role in the political scheme of things was thwarting the *Catalanista* (Catalan separatist) and anticentralist movements by convincing Catalan workers to vote Republican. He stopped at nothing to achieve his ends—power, influence, and money. The Paral·lel was his power base, his constituency, and it was to the anti-Catalanista prejudices of these low-browed 'barbarians' that he brazenly pandered.

In his younger days Lerroux had been a serious political influence in Spain, but by 1918 he was a spent force—or so we thought—unable to match his poisonous rhetoric with action. Even so, he was still capable of dredging up powerful emotions in his audiences. Decent Republicans, by which I mean those who retained some degree of integrity, supported the more genuinely idealistic Vicente Blasco Ibañez, whose pro-French novel *The Four Horsemen of the Apocalypse* had become the bible of Spain's pro-Entente-Cordiale party. Republicans, in general, supported 'compulsory' trade unionism, which, they believed, would force up wages, antagonise the pro-German Catalan employers and rally the liberal army officers to overthrow Madrid's pro-Central Powers clique of King Alfonso XIII—and establish a pro-Entente republic. Very simple ...

A GRAND DAY OUT

Laureano and I continued our grand tour the following morning, moving on from the bars and cafés of the Paral·lel to the preserved medieval quarter of the Old City, to explore the symbols of tyranny—the cathedral, the palaces and the museum that was once the arsenal of the kings of Aragón. The fortress-like slums of Barcelona's Old City are difficult to describe. The Old City's labyrinthine and dark, intimidating streets and byways conjured up the mental images of François Villon's fifteenth-century Paris described by Robert Louis Stevenson in his *Familiar Studies of Men and Books*, a collection of essays I had read only a few months earlier.

Barcelona's La Seu Cathedral is among the most oppressive buildings in Spain; its wide, carved doors gaped open like the portals of hell. Standing on the concourse, at the top of a wide flight of steps, we peered into the cool semidarkness at the shadowy figures drifting around inside this Gothic monstrosity, their occasionally dense silhouettes fleetingly outlined against the soft ochre glimmer of diffused candlelight. Laureano claimed that the reason all the churches in Spain were so dark was because the priests had the monopoly on the candle trade.

Returning to the Ramblas, we dodged the traffic and jumped on board a whining juggernaut of a tramcar that shoogled and thrummed its way up the long tree-lined boulevard, past the flower stalls and the market, along straight avenues past dozens of parallel streets and blocks of modern offices and apartments, until, slowly, it began to grind its way uphill past the grand, imposing, rococo homes of the very rich towards the northern outskirts of the city. It made me think of Bearsden, similarly located in the leafier northern suburbs of Glasgow.

'Where are we going?' I asked.

'To Tibidabo. I want to show you the finest view of the city,' he replied.

At the terminus we transferred to the funicular railway, but even that didn't take us to the very top, and for the last stage of the journey we had to trudge along a steep path through a pine wood until—puffing, panting, and sweating—we reached the summit.

He was right about the view. The panorama was magnificent. From 1,600 feet up we looked down on a mosaic of the city's rooftops with its spider's web of streets and alleyways spun out below us in stone and brick. Tibidabo, according to Laureano, was reputed to have acquired its name from the words used by Satan to tempt Christ: 'All these things will I give thee' (*tibi dabo*).

It was still early; the air was crystal clear, the sun was shining in the cloudless, china-blue sky. Laureano pointed out the city's landmarks. Over the rooftops, beyond the three famous factory chimneys of the Paral·lel, the cathedral tower of Santa María del Mar, the building site and unfinished bell towers of Gaudí's Sagrada Familia, the port cranes and the fortress of Montjuïc, was the silvery Mediterranean, an immense carpet of blue diamonds, its hundred thousand facets stretching out as far as the eye could see. And there, far out on the shimmering, hazy horizon, forty miles or so distant, I could make out mirage-like smudges through the heat haze that Laureano assured me were the Balearics. For a brief moment I was that 'watcher of the skies' . . . 'silent upon a peak in Darien'.

BRAVO PORTILLO EXPOSED

Ángel Pestaña, the anarchist journalist, meanwhile, had been busy. On 9 June, *Solidaridad Obrera* broke its biggest story ever, exposing Chief Superintendent Manuel Bravo Portillo as Germany's top agent in Catalonia. For at least two years, Bravo Portillo had been passing information on port traffic—from Port Bou in the north to Cartagena in the south—to German Naval Intelligence, providing them with shipping destinations and cargoes, information that was immediately transmitted to German submarines standing by in the Mediterranean and the Atlantic.

Pestaña's seemingly incontrovertible evidence consisted of signed, handwritten letters from Bravo Portillo directly linking him to the notorious incident of the sinking of the *SS Joaquín Mumbrá*, a Spanish cargo ship that had sailed from Barcelona for Britain the previous December and had been torpedoed off Madeira in January. The German U-boat captain who picked up the *Mumbrá*'s crew boasted that he had been waiting for them, and that his information had come from Barcelona. That week *Soli*'s circulation jumped from 3,500 to over 18,000 copies.

The first lead came in January, shortly after the sinking of the *Mumbrá*, from dockers of the CNT's Maritime Workers' Union in the small Catalan port of Palamos. For months they had been sending in reports to the Defence Commission about German U-boats anchoring regularly in a nearby cove and uniformed German naval officers being entertained in the office of the local harbourmaster, a virulently anti-labour and pro-German Carlist and Sometent—who made regular mysterious visits to Barcelona on 'official business', without any explanation to his second in command, a CNT sympathiser.

Suspicious as to what their boss might be up to, a couple of local compañeros followed the harbourmaster to Barcelona where they were astonished to see that his first call was to the headquarters of the Special Services Brigade in the Paseo de Isabel II. They were even more surprised when he emerged shortly afterwards, arm-in-arm with none other than Chief Superintendent Bravo Portillo.

The two men walked to a nearby bar where they sat at an outside table and took an aperitif; they talked for about half an hour. At the end of the conversation Bravo Portillo opened his document case and produced a notepad on which he wrote something, tore out the sheet of paper, folded it and handed to the harbourmaster. The men stood up, shook hands, and went their separate ways, Bravo Portillo returned to police headquarters while the harbourmaster walked up the Rambla de Estudios to the Café Royale where he sat at a terrace table and ordered from the waiter.

Ten minutes later he was joined by a seedy-looking man in his mid-forties whom we later identified as Royo de San Martín, a well-known low-life of the Barcelona milieu, a morphine addict, a gambler with a penchant for the gaming tables—and a close confidente of Bravo Portillo. The men exchanged a few pleasantries then the harbourmaster handed Royo de San Martín what appeared to be the piece of paper given to him earlier by Bravo Portillo. A close head-to-head discussion followed, which lasted for about twenty minutes, after which the men stood up, shook hands, and went their separate ways.

The two compañeros who had followed the harbourmaster all the way from Palamos split up; one followed their quarry to the railway station where he caught the train home. The other shadowed Royo de San Martín to his apartment in the Carrer Sant Pau. This information was passed to Archs by the CNT's Carrer Toledo defence group who already had a file on Royo because of his connections with Bravo Portillo and other officers of the Special Services Brigade. Royo's name was also on the list of German agents that Archs passed to Captains Bruce and Marshall.

A few days later, Laureano and I accompanied Bruce, Marshall, and another man by the name of Alfred Mason, an Englishman in his mid-fifties, recently arrived from Gibraltar on his steam yacht. They wanted us to identify Royo for them and show them where he lived. Mason also wanted to talk to the Palamos compañeros as to the whereabouts of the cove used by the U-boats. A bar opposite Royo's apartment building provided good cover to keep watch on him. We sat at a terrace table, drinking and chatting until, finally, Laureano saw our man emerge from his tenement close.

My first thoughts on seeing Royo looking up and down the street were of Dan Macphail and my former shipmates in their final moments—and of their families. Oddly, I could hear Mullins teasing 'Fucker' and something caught in my throat. Suddenly I was overwhelmed with seething anger and a desire for revenge. Only a few yards away from me stood the man who was probably responsible for supplying the information that led to the sinking of the *Covenant* and the deaths of my friends—and who knows how many others. My heart raced twenty to the dozen; I wanted to run over and tear him apart with my bare hands. If I'd had a gun I think I would have shot him there and then. Something deep in my Cameronian psyche stirred, calling to mind a hymn by Henry Van Dyke:

> ...And yet there is a hatred that purifies the heart:
> The anger of the better against the baser part,
> Against the false and wicked, against the tyrant's sword,
> Against the enemies of love, and all that hate the Lord.

Fortunately, the others picked up on my zealous mood of righteous revenge and calmed me down before I did something stupid and compromised the operation.

'Bide your time, son,' said Mason. 'Just pause and consider. If you react with anger foremost in your mind, you'll only expose yourself, making it all the easier for your enemy to kill you. Rushing straight in when you're in a temper will probably end with you being arrested or killed because you are not thinking clearly and lack caution. You need a clear mind to fight well, and you have to be able to think while you are fighting. Just wait, son. Your time will come—but only when your forces are equal to the contest.'

Mason's advice was another important life-lesson, that survival in this new world, in which I found myself, demanded discipline and single-mindedness.

MY SECRET LIFE

For the next two weeks Laureano and I accompanied a succession of British army officers every day to the same bar to monitor Royo's movements. These men were all from the so-called 'Cairo Gang'—the café society military cut-throats shipped in from Cairo. Some were cultured, a few were charming and friendly, most, however, were arrogant, hubristic, cold, and distant. One man I took an immediate dislike to was a chap called Chartres, an English 'gentle-man' type with an irritating, clipped, and affected drawl, a monocle permanently clamped in his right eye, slicked back, heavily oiled hair tucked under a trilby hat and a thin black line of hair running horizontally a quarter of an inch or so above a taut, lipless mouth. He also affected a black silver-knobbed swagger cane that presumably doubled as a swordstick. A real William Le Queux type who might as well have hung a sign around his neck saying 'Spy'.

Some of the younger officers were chatty and forthcoming. Two of them, Lieutenants Henry Angliss and William Peel, had recently returned from Russia where—with their boss Captain Francis Cromie, RN, the British naval attaché in Petrograd, Secret Intelligence Service officer Bruce Lockhart and his sidekick Sidney Reilly—they had been involved in clandestine jiggery-pokery to assassinate Lenin. They had been sending back highly partisan reports to the Foreign Office about how the Bolsheviks were fomenting revolution on 'Red Clydeside' through 'agents' such as John MacLean, the Glasgow teacher, whom they asked if I knew. Diabolical nonsense, I told them, angrily, but they ignored my comments with a disdainful look that said, 'What would you know about such matters?' Another gang member I took an instant dislike to was an arrogant piece of work by the name of Captain G.T. Bagally, a cold, emotionless and solitary type—a sociopath if ever there was one, and I have seen a few in my time.

Whenever Royo appeared, Laureano, two British officers, and I took turnabout at following him until he reached his destination, at which point we'd split up and one or other of us would follow Royo, or whomever he was meeting. It didn't take long for us to put together a comprehensive audit of names and addresses of every identifiable person in Royo de San Martín's friendship network, and those of his associates. In the process we acquired as lot of anecdotal information on these individuals and their connections from local barri and union branch committees, all of which was collated and analysed by Archs, Vandellós, and Pestaña.

Meanwhile, Marshall—with whom I had now established an unlikely but affectionate rapport—told me that his seafaring colleague, Alf Mason, who worked for a Colonel Thoroton of the British Secret Service Bureau in Gibraltar, had been busy. Mason's somewhat extraordinary job was to identify and destroy Central Power U-boat provisioning and refuelling sites around the Spanish, Balearic, Moroccan, and Canary Isles coastlines, which he did from his steam yacht, the *Privet*. This was actually a disguised warship, 'Q boat' of No. 3 Special Service based in Glasgow, and was fitted out with one of the new ASDIC sonar systems, depth-charges, and heavy machine guns disguised as capstans.

Mason and his skipper, 'Hurricane' Jack Maclachlan of the Royal Naval Reserve, together with a Royal Marine crewman by the name of Jenkins, had come to Barcelona in pursuit of the *SS Ganeko*, a ship chartered by the German intelligence 'front' company, Ceuta Impex, which had loaded a suspiciously large cargo of barrels listed as 'bicarbonate of soda' in Alicante. Archs heard about this unusual cargo from the local branch of the Maritime

Workers' Union, and had passed on the information to Bruce and Marshall as part of our quid pro quo arrangement. Mason's *Privet* had trailed the boat to a cove near Palamos and he and his colleagues watched from a vantage point on the cliffs while the crew transferred the barrels and boxes to rafts and floated them ashore, hiding them in a cave under the watchful eyes of men he later identified as the Palamos harbour master and the local Guardia Civil captain.

With everyone gone and the beach deserted, Mason climbed down to explore the cave where he discovered the barrels contained submarine diesel. He also found boxes of detonators, metal tubes containing hydrofluoric acid time fuses of the type that had been used in industrial sabotage operations in France and Britain, as well as in Spain. The *modus operandi* was for German agents working in the munitions factories to slip a couple of these tubes into their mouths before clocking in for work, then shortly before the mid-morning, lunch, or mid-afternoon break they would set the timer and leave them close to explosives, shells, bullets, or other strategic matériel—then move as far away as possible to await the big bang. One of the boxes contained small wooden cases with carefully packed glass phials filled with a yellowish liquid; another contained sugar cubes that were later shown, on analysis, to contain anthrax and glanders microbes. Inside was a note, in German, which read:

> Enclosed find 100 small bottles for horses and a similar amount for horned animals, 50 of which are for onward shipment to Buenos Aires. Use as previously discussed. Each tube is sufficient for 200 head. If possible, administer directly into the animals' mouths, otherwise into their fodder. We ask for a brief report of any success that you have there, and if detailed results are obtained, we request the presence for one day of Dr Wuppermann.

Archs told Mason about another regular U-boat refuelling point at an isolated cove near Cartagena. Compañeros from the local CNT defence group took him to a small bay where two U-boats of the German Mediterranean submarine flotilla had surfaced and were at anchor, bold as brass. One of these was the infamous U35, commanded by submarine 'ace of aces' Kapitänleutnant Arnauld de la Perière, which was being refuelled and provisioned in full daylight. Mason photographed the whole operation, and later had postcards printed of the scene that the British government made sure were circulated throughout Spain—and the world. This caused great embarrassment to Maura y Montaner's government, coinciding as it did with Ludendorff's tightening of the U-boat blockade of Spain, which meant more Spanish ships were being torpedoed.

With the failure of the spring Central Powers' offensive and fresh American troops arriving daily in Europe, the balance of the war was fast slipping away from the Central Powers' High Command. Increasingly desperate, they issued orders that all vessels approaching Spanish waters—including Spanish vessels—were now 'legitimate' targets for the German navy, a development that brought Spain's economy even closer to collapse. The final straw occurred early in June when Arnauld de la Perière's U35 sank a French merchant ship, the *Provence*, off the Costa Brava, a day out of Barcelona. Eight men died in that disaster.

That was when the Cairo Gang made their move. The operation began at 4:30 a.m. on the morning of 4 June with the British murder squad—and, presumably, French army and navy Deuxième Bureaux agents—closing in on Bravo Portillo's spies and saboteurs in a series of coordinated dawn raids on their offices and apartments across Catalonia and the Levante. The only one who escaped was Bravo Portillo. In Palamos they broke into the harbourmaster's home, dragged him from his bed and shot him dead in front of his wife. Luciano González and three of his men were blown to smithereens when powerful bombs destroyed two of Ceuta Impex's main offices and a fire gutted the company's massive dockside warehouse. Next day the press reported fourteen murders, all of which were blamed on interunion score settling—by the CNT, of course!

The Cairo Gang didn't kill Royo de San Martín. They needed him to tell them what he knew about Bravo's network and to testify as to 'where the bodies were buried'. And he did talk: 'He sang like a lintie,' as my grampa used to say, telling Bruce and Marshall everything they wanted to know. He even gave them a signed letter in Bravo Portillo's handwriting proving his complicity in the sinking of the *SS Joaquín Mumbrá*, which had sailed from Barcelona on 20 December 1917:

Police Department, Atarazanas District
First Section, Barcelona

My dear Royo: The bearer is the friend I told you about; he has my complete trust, and will provide you with information about the *Mumbrú*, which will depart the 20th at 9 a.m.; please refer him to the person you know. A thousand thanks from the friend who embraces you.

Bravo

This was one of the letters Bruce gave me for Pestaña, who published them shortly after in *Solidaridad Obrera*. With them was a dossier containing Royo San Martín's signed statement naming his confederates and their compromising connections with local and national personalities. When they'd finished with Royo, the British agents handed him over to one of the few Barcelonan police contacts they trusted to press for a conviction—Inspector Francisco Carbonell, a Grand Orient freemason and a liberal who detested Bravo Portillo. They should have put a bullet between Bravo Portillo's eyes when they had the chance, but they felt there was more political and diplomatic mileage to be had in exposing him rather than killing him. That was the background to Pestaña's scoop, which was the splash headline in *Solidaridad Obrera* on 9 June, five days after the raids.

CUB REPORTER—I JOIN *SOLI*

Towards the end of June 1918, after the initial publicity surrounding Bravo Portillo's arrest had died down, Pestaña asked me to join his new editorial team at *Soli*. The job, unpaid, involved compiling a weekly news roundup of developments in the English-speaking labour movements. It meant monitoring the international English-language anarchist and syndicalist press and précising and rewriting important international stories for translation into Spanish. I accepted his offer enthusiastically; it was the ideal way to keep my finger on the pulse of world affairs and improve my Spanish grammar and vocabulary.

Every evening I carefully scoured the pages of the latest English-language newspapers, magazines, or leaflets that had arrived by mail, selecting what I thought to be the most interesting pieces and writing up a rough first draft, which Laureano then helped me translate, rewrite, and edit. Lots of foreigners, many of them stateless refugees—Swedes, Germans, Frenchmen, Belgians, Italians, Mexicans, Argentineans, Greeks, and so on—also came to the *Soli* office to read and translate the latest international papers we had on file, but the English papers were much more regular, and covered a wider range of topics.

Once we'd cobbled our pieces together, Pestaña subedited the copy and gave our prose a final polish before passing it on to be typeset and fitted onto the page. My first news piece for *Soli* was a report on the mass trial of 250 Wobblies in Chicago—lumberjacks, harvest hands, and miners—who had been charged with sedition, sabotage, and 'conspiring to obstruct the war'. Like the Spanish government with the CNT, the US government's aim was to destroy the Wobblies and all other manifestations of militant, organised labour.

FORGING AHEAD

As well as translating and crafting my articles into polished Castilian prose, Laureano found himself increasingly fascinated by the technical aspects of printing. He spent more and more of his free time working evenings and weekends in Tomás Herrero's print shop, running off books, pamphlets, leaflets, and posters, learning to be a printer and, more importantly, acquiring what we called 'shoemaking' or forgery skills. He went to extreme lengths to befriend, cultivate, or bribe any functionary, civil servant, or embassy or consular employees he could identify who might be able to supply him with genuine passports, naturalisation and birth certificates, or any other legal documents, papers, or stamps they might be able to lay their hands on.

The design of official rubber stamps and the collecting of inks became an obsession for Laureano, and for a time it was his sole topic of conversation—the different colour tones, sizes, shapes, and designs, and how they might look—clear, legible, or smudged. His greatest coup at the time was 'acquiring' a package of a thousand blank Spanish passports direct from a securities printer in Luxembourg. Apart from English lessons with me, Laureano's free time was now spent deep in conversation with printers and paper salesmen, absorbing everything he could about the latest printing techniques and technology, and about paper and inks.

I was Laureano's first guinea pig. That autumn he created for me a tailor-made Spanish identity, complete with birth certificate, identity card, and passport—all in the name of Eduardo Principe, the name I use today. Somehow he obtained a batch of blank birth certificates through a contact in the Ministerio de Gobernación, the equivalent of the British Home Office, and had began experimenting with authorisation stamps and inks. We spent the whole of one weekend working on that first birth certificate project. Before that we'd never even looked at one properly, let alone examined the stamps on it.

'Most people don't bother,' said Laureano's printing mentor, Miguel Castro de Castro, the master printer in Tomás Herrero's printshop. 'If it looks official it'll be accepted, mostly.' But to a perfectionist like Laureano it became a challenge to make as near perfect a copy as possible, even though he knew that it was unlikely to be checked closely, or compared with the original. For the first time I began to realise just how meticulous and thorough Laureano was in all his endeavours. I, on the other hand, was more a 'will that do?' sort of person. Laureano wasn't only trying to find a way to make one single stamp impression; he wanted a method that would enable him to make lots of them in quick succession. Together we worked out a technique. The stamp had to be an imprint rather than a one-off drawing, so for our first attempt, using fine tracing paper and a soft pencil, he traced an outline of the original stamp, which he then transferred to a small square of linoleum. We thought that would be the ideal medium, as it was easy to get hold of and could be washed and used repeatedly. In the end, however, lino proved too hard and thick to make a satisfactory impression, and without using pure-white wax pencil it was impossible to see the tracing.

Next we tried tracing the image using a fine cartographer's pen and rubberstamp ink—and a compass to ensure the circle was perfect—inking in the tracing as accurately as possible. He then gently pressed the drawing itself—a reverse mirror image—onto the document while the ink was still wet. After a bit of experimentation we found we could make perhaps three reasonably good impressions from one pressing on an inkpad, and another two that were lighter and fuzzier. Our next attempt involved thicker tracing paper, the sort used by draughtsmen and architects—soft and light in colour—but it wasn't sufficiently absorbent for our purposes, and after the first good impression it left an oval instead of what was supposed to be a round stamp. Also, the straight lines curved and became more pronouncedly distorted with each subsequent impression. We tried everything from the thinnest paper to the heaviest cardboard. Magazine covers seemed a good possibility, but because the paper quality varied so much it was impossible to tell how it would turn out without actually testing each cover, which was very time-consuming.

It was one of those Einsteinian 'Aha!' moments that led us to trying the back of an old photograph—bromide paper—that was sufficiently firm without being too thick. Carefully transferring the tracing, Laureano inked in the drawing, leaving the ink sitting smoothly on the surface, and then pressed the drawing against a sheet of paper. When it worked we understood how Archimedes must have felt after stepping into his bath, swamping the floor and discovering the solution to the problem that had eluded him for so long. The impression was close to perfect. The only drawback was the paper's low absorbency, which meant we had to wait a long time before the ink dried sufficiently for it to make a good first imprint, but we overcame this by gently blotting the impression with newsprint, which absorbed just the right amount of ink and allowed us to use the stamp immediately. With the stamp laid on the document in the required position, a gentle stroke on the back with a comb was all that was needed to make a perfect impression and ensure that every part of the stamp was legible. After that, all we had to do was to wait until the stamps were completely dry before rubbing out all evidence of the pencil tracings.

With more practice we were able to complete a stamp in less than ten minutes. The next project was replicating blind embossed stamps, the sort used on passports and identity cards, a much easier nut to crack once we discovered the properties of dental compound. Heated in water it becomes highly malleable and—with talcum powder to prevent it sticking—is perfect for taking impressions of all manner of things, from keys to embossed stamps. Castro de Castro also told us the secret recipe for weaving watermarks into the grain of paper using Canada balsam from the Canadian Balsam fir, which has the unique property of remaining transparent even when heated or dissolved. The watermark fades after a few years, but false documents aren't normally meant to last forever. In the meantime, however, it was undetectable.

Belleville, 18 October 1976

Hearing noises from the street outside, Farquhar McHarg rose from his desk and walked to the window. He was still in shock from the night's events. His stomach felt like a bag of six-inch nails. The little he could see of the monochrome street below was illuminated by moonlight. Beams from the street lamps cast long geometric bars of light into the inky black shadows. He could see nothing untoward other than a couple of working women walking, loitering, then retracing their steps, waiting for business. His thoughts returned to his dead friend, probably the most talented forger in Europe, certainly of his generation.

The skills Laureano began to acquire that summer in 1918 had not only helped Farquhar himself, and countless other compañeros, out of tight corners in later years. They had also played a crucial role in providing identity documents for many of the anti-Nazi Resistance groups and escape and evasion networks in occupied France during the Second World War, as well as the anti-Francoist Resistance movement from the 1940s through to the late 1960s. But it was this same reputation as the main document facilitator to the French, Corsican, Italian, Levantine, and Jewish criminal milieu of Paris, Marseilles, and Perpignan that also led him—unintentionally—into venality. It was through his wartime connections with the Jewish Resistance groups in occupied France that, after the war, he began supplying weapons and matériel from Republican Army and anarchist arms dumps for, among others, the Zionist Irgun Zvai Leumi. Was it perhaps these or Laureano's other equally sinister intelligence and criminal connections in the European and Latin American demimondes that caused his murder in Belleville fifty-eight years on? He had, after all, since the war, created new identities for countless major criminals and double agents, many of whom were ruthless killers with much to hide—and answer for. Men such as these did not want simply to remain invisible. Like the Devil in Baudelaire's story Le Joueur généreux, *he needed to persuade people that he did not exist.*

Or could it have been the work of the sinister Hiéron du Val d'Or who continued to operate under many different names? A closer examination of the fifty-odd years of diaries and fifteen-hundred-page dossier Laureano had been arranging for him to have access to might throw some light on that night's events.

Laureano was meeting his lawyer to arrange the release of this archive to Farquhar, his lifetime friend and confidant, who was writing the history of the defence groups. Farquhar was the only man Laureano ever really trusted. Somehow, someone had learned of the existence of these long buried and potentially explosive records and that they might be made public. Whoever they were, they were clearly determined to prevent that happening, no matter what the cost.

From behind the window shutters, Farquhar gazed into the dark street. He could see nothing untoward in the shadowy tenement closes or on the illuminated strips of narrow pavement below. No cars, no people. Nothing moved. He returned to his typewriter.

BARCELONA—HEARTS AND MINDS

One day, in the early part of that first summer, Laureano took me to a second-hand bookshop in the Carrer de Fontanella in the Raval district. It was also an ateneu. Walking through the door my first impression was of the comforting smell of old paper and leather. The shop was empty except for a young woman sitting behind the counter absorbed in a book. It was Lara, from the bar in Escudellers! My heart rate soared. She lowered her book, and our eyes met. She gave me such an enormous smile of recognition that my face must have blushed the colour of a joint of silverside in a butcher's window. Leaping out of her seat, she rushed over and gave me an enormous hug, kissing me on both cheeks. I was hoping for a kiss on the lips, but you have to start somewhere. I was slightly irritated to see she greeted Laureano the same way.

I was so taken aback at seeing Lara so unexpectedly, not to mention still reeling from her warm hug, that I found myself garbling inanities in pigeon Catalan and Spanish—Catish—about how pleased she must be to see me again. Laureano, blowing a friendly kiss to his young friend and laughing at my tongue-tied attempts at gallantry, gently propelled me between piles of precariously stacked books towards a curtained doorway behind a tall, glass-panelled bookcase at the rear of the shop.

'I think my Scottish brother has a soft spot for you, Lara!' he called. 'You'll have to watch your step!'

She laughed, such a gentle infectious laugh. I fell in love with her that instant. Looking back, I smiled and waved at her. Her laughing eyes followed me, playing havoc with my adolescent emotions. Old enough to be a man of mystery, I was old enough for love! And I would be back; neither the British nor the German secret services would stop me.

Passing through the curtained doorway we entered a long room with bare, unpolished wooden floorboards; chairs lined the walls. At the far end was a table behind which, pinned to the wall, was a large banner with the red and black diagonals of the CNT. Seated in the centre of the room, in a battered leather armchair, was an old gentleman in a shiny and thread-bare black suit with a trim salt-and-pepper beard in a style not unlike that sported by the late King Edward VII. His back was ramrod stiff. Around him in a semicircle sat an attentive group of perhaps twenty men and women of all ages, some on chairs, others cross-legged on the floor. Clearly he was a man of considerable dignity—and with the ability to hold an audi-ence's undivided attention. Known as Maestro Barba, he taught geography, history, and English in one of the few lay schools in the city, in the Carrer Tallers. Maestro Barba lived alone and dedicated his life to spreading the 'Knowledge' and the 'Idea'.

When he finished his lecture, which Laureano informed me was on Max Stirner's ideas on the individual and property, my friend introduced me to the old man. His friendly face creased into the warmest of smiles.

'At last,' he said, embracing me enthusiastically, 'I have someone with whom I can practise my English.'

I warmed to him immediately.

Maestro Barba held literacy classes at the ateneu most evenings. It was mainly for the local analphabets, the illiterates of the neighbourhood, of whom there were many. I asked if I could join his classes. It was the ideal way for me to learn Spanish and Catalan as I had the advantage of being able to read, an advantage most of the other pupils lacked. It was good for the both of us. He taught me the finer points of grammar and vocabulary, and I helped him with his spoken English and my vernacular. I also helped teach some of those who couldn't read. Maestro Barba was extraordinarily knowledgeable about world literature. It was a privilege to pass the time of day in his company. His idea of teaching wasn't simply imparting knowl-edge; he encouraged us to think for ourselves and to constantly push back the thresholds of our minds. Over the next few years Maestro Barba and I spent many pleasant hours together discussing life, art, ideas, and the writers he admired, particularly Shakespeare and Milton. Often since then I have recalled the much later words of Cory:

> ... I wept as I remember'd how often you and I
> Had tired the sun with talking and sent him down the sky.
> And now that thou art lying, my dear old Carian guest.
> A handful of grey ashes, long, long ago at rest.

Still are thy pleasant voices, thy nightingales awake:
For Death he taketh all away, but them he cannot take.

Maestro Barba was a living, breathing encyclopaedia, especially with regard to classical and contemporary Spanish literature and music. Whenever an opportunity presented itself he insisted on taking me to art exhibitions or to a concert, recital, opera, ballet, or *zarzuela* performance in one of Barcelona's twenty theatres. They changed their bills weekly in those days, with matinees beginning at five in the afternoon. Manuel de Falla's *Noches en los jardines de España* was Maestro Barba's favourite. I recall quite vividly the memorable production we saw together of Falla's *El sombrero de tres picos*, the one produced by Serge Diaghilev. Pablo Picasso designed both the set and costumes for that production.

My deep appreciation for culture in all its forms has been entirely due to Maestro Barba. His influence has remained with me throughout my life. Under his inspiring tutelage my spoken and written Spanish and Catalan improved in leaps and bounds—as indeed did my English. A born teacher, Maestro Barba was a true dominie: gentle, uncontentious, dignified, and saintly. Like the restive Abelard he taught me, 'wandering youth', many things I was unaware of about myself—or the world. Also, although he inspired and stimulated me and was intellectually exciting to be around, an added attraction to attending his classes was the possibility of seeing more of Lara. Now I only needed to conjure up her sweet face and body and my loins were on fire. I ached for her. I was eighteen years old and I had found my object of adolescent desire.

Grace was in all her steps, heaven in her eye,
In every gesture dignity and love.

In practice it wasn't so easy. Having met Maestro Barba, I began at once to attend his classes at the ateneu with great frequency, and I expected to meet Lara again very soon. But she was an elusive creature. Sometimes I would see her on the Ramblas with her friends, laughing and chatting gaily. Occasionally she would catch my eye and wave, but I was too shy to work out how to take matters further.

RECESSIONAL
Towards the end of that summer of 1918, with the Kaiser's War rumbling to its close, unemployment and inflation were taking their toll. Across the city, groups of angry people met in union halls, bars, street corners, and public squares to protest against the worsening economic crisis.

As France and Britain clawed back their foreign markets, Spain's banks, trading companies, and manufacturing industries began tumbling like a line of dominoes and workers were being laid off in their thousands.

The greedy and short-sighted employers often had only themselves to blame for the loss of their markets. At the height of the war, for example, Igualada, a town not far from Barcelona and an important centre of the Catalan leather industry, had won a massive order to supply boots to the French army. The employers thought they would boost their profit margins by cutting costs, and instead of using the traditional 'Moroccan' tanning process, which was difficult and time-consuming, they adopted a new 'rapid' system which took three weeks instead of the usual nine months. The problem was, this method meant the animal hides were not cured properly and the boots quickly fell apart in the muddy trenches of the Somme. Needless to say the contract wasn't renewed.

To make matters worse, apart from the disastrous economic plight of the country's deprived and undernourished workers, the scourge of the 'French' flu epidemic—which in fact originated with American soldiers from Kansas—was still decimating the population. I remember returning home from a union meeting in the narrow Carrer Mercaders and finding myself having to stand hard against the wall while a convoy of eight trucks laden with corpses trundled by. A few days later, while climbing the stairs to my apartment in the Carrer Carders, I was obliged to turn back to make way for a dozen or so undertakers bringing down six coffins from the upper landings.

Every morning I examined myself all over—and in the mirror—for the telltale signs of the virus.

OPENING SHOTS

The first indication that the employers had launched their new anti-labour offensive to prop up their declining industries was when new faces appeared in El Tastevins, people who weren't from the barri and who clearly hadn't come for the food, drink, or the banter. Why they were there we could only guess; they were outsiders, trying a bit too hard to strike up conversations with locals, which made everyone suspicious—and nervous.

As was the custom in Spain we dined late, around ten o'clock at night. Dinners in El Tastevins were communal affairs taken at a long table next to the door that opened on to the Carrer Matamoros. Ramón, José Figueras, Laureano, Andrés, Maria, and Maestro Barba were all there on that particular night, as was Lara, whom the Maestro, aware of my infatuation for her, had invited along. It was Maestro Barba's birthday, his *cumpleaños*.

Dinner usually consisted of liver and onions with chorizo, cheese, and bread—or, on special occasions, goat or chicken. A basket of oranges graced the centre of the table along with a couple of carafes of the patrón's wine, a pitcher of milk and a botijo of ice-cold water. The botijo was an unglazed earthenware container with a spout that you held above your head in both hands to allow a hard stream of water to pour into your mouth, as though from a fountain. The first few times I tried to use it I missed my mouth and drenched my face and my shirt and trousers, much to the amusement of everyone in the bar.

'He's either found a new way to wash his face or he's still practising his aim,' Lara said, grinning wickedly. 'There's always room for improvement!'

Halfway through the meal, one of the new 'faces' walked into the bar. Pausing at our table briefly, he tipped his hat and, with an oily smirk, wished us 'good appetite' before moving to the bar where he ordered a fino, which he downed quickly and then left, politely doffing his cap again to us on the way out. Five minutes or so later, Tirillas, one of the compañeros playing chess on the narrow pavement outside, suddenly jumped up—overturning the table where he sat, scattering his chess pieces onto the cobbled street—and ran into the bar shouting:

'Sometent! The Sometent!'

The Sometent, as I have already mentioned briefly, was an officially sanctioned parapolitical body of right-wing shopkeepers, bourgeois, and lumpen vigilantes trained by the military, licensed to carry arms, and deployed by the authorities as police auxiliaries in the battle against the 'red peril'. Suddenly, ten of these characters, dressed in dark suits with armbands, wearing bowler hats and fedoras, stormed in through the door and took up positions around the table, brandishing pistols, rifles, and shotguns.

'Everybody up!' ordered the one who appeared to be their leader, a brutal-looking character by the name of Cabaña, an 'off-duty' Guardia Civil corporal with a pockmarked mushroom-coloured face, a flat nose, and the fallen eyebrows of a circus pugilist, his black mouth lined by irregular yellow-grey teeth and contorted into a grimace that passed for a smile. He was a big man and must have weighed around eighteen stone.

I was completely taken aback by this turn of events. One moment we had been laughing and joking, the next the demons from hell had taken over the room. Suddenly I felt very afraid. Everyone rose to their feet, hands in the air, except Maestro Barba, who remained seated. The Sometent leader strode up to the elderly teacher, grabbed him roughly by the whiskers, and pulled him to his feet.

At this point Archs and José Figueras, unaware of what had happened, emerged from the back room where they'd been discussing some business with the patrón. José, who was standing behind Archs, slipped out, unseen, through the rear kitchen door to get help. Archs, however, reacted immediately when he saw Maestro Barba being manhandled and jumped on Cabaña, forcing him to release the teacher. The Sometent heavies closed in on him from all sides, and within seconds Archs was sprawling on the ground moaning in pain, his head and face bloodied by repeated kicks and blows from their gun butts. One of them picked up an overturned stool and brought it crashing down on Archs's head as he tried to rise. He fell to his knees, and then sank to the floor. Numbed and paralysed by the unexpected violence of the situation, I gazed in horror at the splintered blood-splattered stool and the unconscious Archs. María Antonia, however, didn't hesitate. Pushing her way through the group gathered around Archs on the floor, she pushed the Sometent leader off balance then punched him hard on his nose, which exploded in a cascade of blood. An ominous silence descended on the room.

Cabaña said nothing, dabbing at his nose and mouth with a handkerchief as he tried to stem the bleeding, then, raising his pistol, he pointed it at Maria Antonia's forehead. Her eyes, filled with contempt, bored into his, almost daring him to shoot.

By this time I had recovered some of my courage and composure, and I ran towards Cabaña shouting the Govan war cry, 'Ya bastard!' in the most aggressive Glaswegian accent I could muster, but the thug, still pointing his pistol in María Antonia's face, threw me off with a flick of his wrist while another Sometent seized me from behind. Enraged, I slipped from his grasp, grabbed an empty wine bottle from the table and smashed it over Cabaña's head as hard as I could. But he was a big man, with a neck like a tree trunk and the bottle simply bounced off his bowler. I hadn't cracked his skull, as I had hoped, but I did send him staggering.

Pulling himself up, Cabaña slipped his gun back into its holster, then reaching down drew a stiletto from a sheath strapped to his leg. Crooking his forefinger, he beckoned me forward. His face was expressionless. I was absolutely terrified to begin with, but then the adrenaline kicked in from somewhere and I began to relish the situation. It was almost a rite of passage; I had to prove myself. Smashing the bottle against a nearby table, I faced Cabaña, my arms slightly apart, crouching in a wrestler's pose. I'd never been involved in a fight before, certainly not one as life-threatening as this, but I had witnessed a few pitched battles between the Glasgow razor gangs on Sauchiehall Street that were particularly bloody—some of them remarkably balletic. I tried desperately to recall the moves and feints I'd seen. As he raised his blade, I leaped forward and we fell to the ground together, scattering the tables and chairs, but he was way too strong for me and broke free. Again and again he slashed out at me with the knife, while I jumped to the left or the right, trying to avoid coming to grips with him. Each jab of his blade stung my pride as well as my flesh. My only decent white shirt, the one my mum had bought me from the Co-op, was in tatters. That made me really angry.

I had to engage with him, but I was bleeding badly, and nipping from lots of small cuts. Just as I thought I was on the point of collapse and losing all self-control, Lara climbed onto a table, grabbed hold of a pitchfork decorating the wall, a memento of the patrón's family's bucolic past, and threw it to me. The tables had now turned in my favour, and with a cry of what I hoped sounded like animal like ferocity, I beckoned to the son-of-a-bitch before me to taste its four prongs. He backed away warily as I jabbed at him.

Advancing cautiously I tried to hold the fork steady, its prongs upwards, without taking my eyes off him for a moment. Why his friends didn't shoot me there and then I'll never know. Perhaps they were enjoying the gladiatorial spectacle too much, or maybe in their heart of hearts they wanted to see Cabañas get his comeuppance.

My adversary's eyes were glued to the four gleaming steel prongs waving before him. We were on more equal terms now. The way my feet were planted, carefully, as I advanced, ruled out any doubts about my resolve. Our heavy breathing punctuated the otherwise deathly silence. As he closed in, moving his stiletto from hand to hand, I tensed my muscles for the thrust. At that moment a commotion outside distracted me momentarily; Figueras had returned with a dozen or so compañeros from the local union hall. Some had pistols, others carried Catalan shillelaghs. A pitched battle broke out as they stormed through the door. The noise was deafening, but no strangely no shots were fired, presumably because it was at such close quarters and it would have ended in a massacre with both sides killing their own people.

At that moment Cabaña lunged at me, catching me in the arm. Just as he was about to deliver the coup de grâce to my chest, Archs suddenly appeared, swinging his arm in a low and sweeping arc, his fist clutching a stiletto. It struck upwards, deep into the bullnecked Sometent's groin. His grotesquely contorted face was a picture of agony and he let loose a howl of pure pain that reverberated through the bar and out into the street. Archs used to say that the cruellest way to send a man to his death was to give him a *cornada*—a goring—in the groin, the part of the body where the bull usually sinks his horn. It causes horrendous suffering, and even if it doesn't kill the victim it makes it difficult for them to pee standing up ever again. The Sometent fled, carrying their wounded with them. No doubt they'd be back at some point, but in the meantime they'd gone, leaving a trail of blood, bowlers, and fedoras in their wake.

What remained of my Co-op shirt was soaked in blood and sticking to my back. I had perhaps a dozen or more cuts, some of them quite deep, but surprisingly I felt no pain, probably due to adrenaline and the numbing effects of the euphoria and the fight. Lara came over and hugged me gingerly. I held her tight, savouring the moment.

'You saved me from a bit of a situation there, compañera,' I said, grinning ruefully.

'Now I'm going to save you from bleeding to death,' she retorted, dabbing at my wounds with a dainty, lace-trimmed handkerchief soaked in brandy. She grimaced as she examined a particularly large gash on my arm. It was deep enough for her to be able to lift up a tongue-sized flap of flesh. Splashing brandy over the wound, which made me leap from my chair and howl in pain, she disappeared into the kitchen and came back with a basin of hot water, a bottle of iodine and a cold, wet, towel. After cleaning and disinfecting the wound she bound and tied the towel tightly round my arm.

'I guess I'll live,' I said once I'd recovered my composure.

'I guess you will!' she replied.

Our eyes met. This time it was she who blushed.

Ramón Archs told me later he saw something of himself in me that night. Whatever it was, he and José Figueras decided to adopt Laureano and me as their protégés, to pass on to us some of the benefits of their experiences as activists. Figueras, a twenty-eight-year-old metalworker, served on his union's steering committee. He too had an interesting history. Having deserted from the Spanish army, Figueras had lived in exile in France for seven years before being expelled the previous year for his anarchist activities. His French police escort, sympathetic to the plight of their prisoner, didn't hand him over to the Guardia Civil but instead dropped him close to the frontier at La Junquera from where, somehow, he evaded the border patrols and made his way back to Barcelona through the Pyrenees via Manresa and Odena.

With help from Figueras, Archs, and Pestaña, Laureano and I were turning into serious revolutionaries. But I should stress that I have never regarded myself as being particularly courageous or temperamentally inclined towards violence. In fact I have always had an intense distaste for all forms of violence, physical and psychological, but, unfortunately, as a measure of last resort in brutal and undemocratic societies unable to distinguish between subversive radicalism, social legislation, and ameliorative reform it becomes, on occasion, a necessary evil.

UP THE AIRY MOUNTAIN . . .

After the Tastevins provocation it was clear the employers and their cohorts in the military establishment were escalating their offensive against organised labour, and were targeting the sindicato único in particular. We needed to learn how to resist, and not only for defensive reasons. The social revolution seemed imminent, and we had to be prepared. So, most Sundays for the remainder of that summer and autumn Laureano and I—together with half a dozen or so other young comrades, including Lara, from the metalworkers' union and the Raval ateneu—all took the train up to Vich where we spent the afternoons running up and down hills, and climbing three-metre-high sheer rock faces. It was good exercise and we laughed a lot, but I was never quite sure what we learned from it other than how to run up and down hills, which didn't require much intelligence or imagination, only a lot of puff, which I had in abundance in those days. However, these outings gave me plenty of opportunities to see more of Lara.

Something had happened between us during that memorable evening in the Tastevins—we learned we could trust each other—and being out in the country with her gave me my chance to get to know her better. After the energetic exercise, which appealed to her tomboyish nature, we would sit together, a little way off—*rancho aparte* ('all on our owney-oh') as the others teased—in the shade of a pine tree, sharing a picnic of bread, tomatoes, oil, and cheese, and watch flocks of cotton wool cumulous clouds drifting across the sky and eagles gliding the air currents, scanning the hills for a rabbit.

She told me about her upbringing, her parents, brothers and sisters, and the hardships they had endured. How they had encouraged her to come to Barcelona where her mother's sister lived, and where she could improve her education at the ateneus, while supporting herself by working. On one occasion we'd been for a walk and were sitting side by side in the long grass talking about this and that—she'd been reading poetry to me— when, suddenly, she jumped on top of me, mussing up my hair, laughing and giggling, her knees sticking in my stomach and her hands running over my body under my shirt. She was strong for a girl, but I managed to push her knees off me, grab her by the shoulders and pull her down on top of me. Neither of us said anything, we just lay there in the long grass, breathing hard and looking into each other's eyes. I could feel myself becoming aroused by the touch of her hands moving over my chest and by the natural perfume of her skin and hair. Embarrassed and slightly panic-stricken by the situation, I twisted myself awkwardly out from beneath her.

'Farquharo,' she said, pulling my face close to hers. 'I want you ... I want you ...' she said, savouring my now-obvious consternation with an infectious and coquettish laugh, '... to improve my English.' Pushing me back, she jumped up, grabbed my hands and pulled me to my feet, then, giving me a hug and a light kiss on the lips, she skipped back down the path through the woods towards the others who were waiting for us.

Relieved at having 'got out from under', so to speak, from what was for me an embarrassing situation, my spirits soared as I thought of the opportunities and all the possibilities of the syllabus I might offer her—when I was better prepared, obviously.

'*Estupendo!*' I said, running after her. 'I'd love to teach you, if you'll let me! Perhaps you could teach me a few things as well?' I added, with what I hoped was a roguish smile but probably looked more as though I'd had an attack of Bell's Palsy.

'Perhaps,' she said, returning my smile—more impishly than enigmatically.

I could hardly sleep that night. I lay on my back staring at the ceiling until the early hours of the morning, thinking of nothing but Lara and how much I desired her, trying to remember how it felt when she was straddling me with her thighs, and how the smell and touch of her hair brushing against my cheeks made my heart beat faster.

Archs and Figueras ran classes on unarmed combat and the use of knives, guns, and explosives. These were much more interesting than the fitness training exercises. They also talked about coping with police violence—at least theoretically—and described the sort of treatment to expect if we fell into the hands of the Guardia Civil or the Special Services Brigade.

'The crucial thing,' said Archs, 'is to try, if at all possible, to hold out for at least forty-eight hours. Screaming at the top of your voice might help you get through it, provided of course they don't gag you. Remember, the point of torture, in most cases, is to get you to talk, for you to give them the information they need, so they will need to remove the gag at some point. Torturers can be more fragile than their victims, so your screams may have an effect. Screaming helps you through the pain—but there is no guilt attached to talking under extreme interrogation, especially if your eyes are being singed with cigar ends, your fingernails and teeth are being torn out with pliers, your lungs are being pumped full of water, or your testicles—if you have any—are being crushed in a vice. Remember that you are psychologically and ethically vulnerable in these situations precisely because of your ideals, your conscience, and your belief in humanity. That vulnerability is in direct proportion to your nobility of spirit and generosity of heart. Unfortunately there's no advice we can give to help you in such situations, other than try to hang onto your integrity and dignity—because when they go, so do you!

'In 1912, when I was arrested for the Tous shooting, my door was kicked in at three thirty in the morning by six detectives of the Special Services Brigade who carted me off to the Atarazanas barracks where they made me strip off before starting their session. For over an hour three of them punched me in the stomach, chest, shoulders, and kidneys, after which they hung me on a horizontal bar through which they passed an electrical current. This went on until about nine o'clock. Every half hour or so they gave me a ten-minute break to restore my strength, but after several sessions on the horizontal bar, I couldn't stand. Around midday they took me down to the dungeons where I spent the next four or five hours. Later that evening I was brought back upstairs and again questioned intensively by four or five detectives who tried to get me to confess to killing Tous, and also asked questions about other compañeros, and the movement. They gave me what they called the 'genuflection', which involved being forced to my knees and pivoted on my toes for two hours.

'Next morning, about nine, they again hung me on the horizontal bar and tortured me until noon. Then they took me upstairs to their offices and tied me to a chair, punching me repeatedly in the stomach, kidneys, and wrists. This bout of questioning lasted until about eight o'clock when I was returned to the dungeons where I spent the rest of the night on a stone bench. Next morning the same detectives put me on the horizontal bar for the third time, and this time the procedure lasted, uninterrupted, for more than two hours. Afterwards they beat me with their fists and kicked me, not to mention the other methods they used: twisting my testicles, arms, and legs; one of them even stuck his fat, nicotine-stained finger up my arse. Nor was I given any food or drink for almost three days,

'Fortunately that was the end of the torture. Next day they sent me for more formal interrogation by an examining magistrate who refused to believe what they'd done to me. "Tut, tut," he said. "Don't sing me that old song. You lot, you're all the same."'

That particular talk made me feel distinctly uncomfortable, and I quickly put out of my mind the images and possibilities that Archs had conjured up for us in the hope that the interrogation he described would never happen to me. I certainly got that wrong!

...DOWN THE RUSHY GLEN...

Lara and I met regularly for 'English lessons'. The temperature in the city was so high that summer and autumn that whenever we could, she'd prepare a picnic of sausage and bread and a bottle of vino tinto, and we would take a short trip on the little train up to Vic, travelling in a third-class carriage with wooden benches, just the two of us, young and full of energy. From the station we would walk arm-in-arm up the winding paths through the forests, towards the open white cliff-tops where, on a clear day, we could see for miles. Occasionally, sitting under the green canopy, we could hear something rustling and crashing around in the undergrowth. 'Probably a wild boar,' she said, laughing at my face, a study in consternation, 'or maybe a tiger!' Once we were out of the forest, I got my revenge by terrifying her with stories of Sawney Bean, his cannibal family, and the wild haggis that stalked the Galloway hills preying on unsuspecting travellers!

I loved being in her company. We made each other laugh, and I felt completely at ease in her presence. There was also the possibility of more to come as we got to know each other better. We had a strong mutual physical attraction and I had to control my excitement, especially when I was close to her, or when she stood framed against the bright afternoon sun wearing a flimsy cotton frock with leaf dust swirling around her and a breeze lifting her skirts a little, exposing her baby-smooth brown thighs. I desperately wanted to take her in my arms and kiss her soft, sweet lips and hold her tightly, feel the warmth and softness of her skin, and gently squeeze her small, firm breasts. I knew she felt the same way, but we also both wanted to keep the friendship we had intact and didn't want to run the risk of spoiling things. We talked about everything under the sun: our lives, our families, the things we loved and hated, what we thought of politics and people we knew—and what we hoped life would be like after the war. We had so much to say. Our trips to the mountains were a wonderful panacea for the realities and uncertainties of everyday life in Barcelona.

But in the pit of my stomach a fear was growing; I knew I was getting in deep and I knew I couldn't take Lara with me.

JACA—A RAILWAY RUNS THROUGH IT

One evening that autumn, an excited Laureano rushed into the *Soli* office as we were putting the following day's issue to bed. He had just finished his shift at the RENFE marshalling yard. Pulling me to one side he said he had something to tell me and that we should go across to the bar for an aperitif. His excitement related to information he had picked up in the yard. The following Saturday the army garrison at Jaca, the ancient capital of Aragón, was due to receive an important shipment of rifles, small arms, ammunition, grenades and wages—by rail.

Located deep in the Aragón valley, in the north of Huesca Province, fifteen miles or so from the French border, Jaca is a Spanish sentry-post in the foothills of the central Pyrenees, a rugged and inhospitable mountain range whose grotesque, serrated spine spans the horizon with snow-covered, cloud-stabbing peaks. The opportunity was too good for the Defence Commission to miss. When we told Archs—a man of boundless energy but who only became truly alive when an action was in the offing—he immediately started putting together a plan. First we needed to reconnoitre the area, he said. So, early next morning, Archs, Figueras, and I met at the Estación del Norte and caught the eight o'clock train to Lérida, almost two hundred kilometres away—a three-and-a-half-hour journey through San Andrés, Tarrasa, Manresa, Cervera and Mollerusa. The train was packed and we were obliged to share our compartment with a party of rosary-fumbling monks, priests, and nuns mumbling their Hail Marys. In Lérida we made our way to a bar close to the station in the nearby Plaza de la Constitución, next to the old Romanesque Gothic cathedral, where we ordered some sandwiches while Archs went to borrow a lorry from a compañero who had a vegetable stall in the town market.

After our meal we headed north on the rutted and potholed Huesca road, across the arid plains of Aragón through Binéfar and Barbastro until eventually we reached Huesca, where we stopped for another quick bite to eat. Then, leaving the town by the Coso Alto, it was back on the road again, following the narrow-gauge railway track for most of the way as it weaved and meandered through the belly of those soaring mountains, occasionally cutting through tunnels, skirting cliffs and clinging to the sides of sheer drops. This boneshaker of a road bucked relentlessly and sickeningly as it climbed higher and higher, through Nueno, Jabarella, and

Sabiñanigo, negotiating sharp bends and unexpected gullies until, finally, through the gloaming, the twinkling lights of medieval Jaca glimmered in the valley below.

At the top of the pass we halted on a grassy verge to consider where best to ambush the train. By this time it was dark, and it didn't help that it was a moonless night, or that we were enclosed on all sides by black, snow-peaked mountains. Each time I breathed, the cold mountain air cut into my nostrils and hit the back of my head. After some discussion, Archs decided a place we had passed further back down the road looked to be the best spot to attack the train. It was a couple of miles out of Sabiñanigo, where the road and the track curve sharply through a narrow gorge. Beyond this point there was a steep incline where the road ran parallel with the railway track for about half a mile, with plenty of brush and tree cover on either side of the road and on the embankment. We drove back down the road to watch and wait. Eventually, in the distance, we heard—then saw—a small goods train huff and puff and coil and twist its way around the bend like a caterpillar suspended from a lettuce leaf, until it finally lumbered slowly past us, pulled by a straining locomotive, steam hissing noisily from its great pistons.

With the location agreed upon and mapped out, we drove back to Huesca in the early hours of the morning where we breakfasted on a big bowl of *café con leche* (café au lait) and freshly fried *churros* before freshening up in a bar and driving on to Lérida to return the lorry and catch the two o'clock train back to Barcelona. It had been a gruelling twenty-four hours and my eyes were stinging with tiredness.

THE AMBUSH

It was Saturday, and the predawn eastern sky was beginning to glow pinky-red behind the Pyrenean mountain peaks. Some of the nine compañeros lying near me in the brush along the embankment watched me closely, smiling to themselves while an anxiety knot the size of a clove hitched P&O mooring line tightened in my belly. I was on tenterhooks, filled with an acute sense of foreboding about what was about to take place and worried that I might make a mess of things. In the heightened psychological atmosphere of the action all my senses suddenly switched into hyperacute mode: touch, hearing, smell, taste, and sight. From not being able to see well in the dawn's early light, I could now see just fine. I also needed to pee and I suspected from the clawing sensation in my stomach that my bowels were about to liquefy.

In the distance I heard the faint chuffing sound of a locomotive as it emerged suddenly from the tunnel, belching and wheezing its way up the valley towards us. It seemed unusually slow, yet in no time at all it was bearing down on us—its wagons clattering past, directly above my head. It was now or never. As the train rumbled through the gloaming, Archs stood up and shouted 'Now!' at the top of his voice. Almost as one, the men rose up from their hiding-places in the brush and began running along-side the wagons, searching for footholds in the beast's armour. Following Archs's example I leapt onto the swaying footboard behind him. He turned and grabbed me by the arm, holding me firm until I could secure a grip on the stair rail.

We worked in two-man teams, each allocated one of the four wagons. Hanging on to the side doors for grim life they set to work with crow-bars, quickly forcing open the bolts and padlocks. I followed Archs and Figueras onto the wagon roof, slowly edging our way along the top of the train, leaping from wagon to wagon, towards the guard's van at the rear. Their task was the most dangerous of all—preventing the sentries in the guard's van from raising the alarm. Meanwhile, the compañeros emptied the wagons, throwing boxes, sacks, and parcels down the embankment where two RENFE lorries were parked.

Clinging to the ventilation ports on top of the last carriage as it lurched its way to the top of the valley, I peered down through the window of the guard's van where the faint glow of an oil lamp was visible. Inside I could see the lolling head of a soldier, fast asleep, a rifle by his side. Archs and Figueras clambered down the ladder onto the open veranda platform. All the while my peripheral vision was registering boxes tumbling along the trackside and shadowy figures scurrying to gather them up. Occasionally the half-light of the early morning would be momentarily illuminated by the flash of sparks on a curve. 'By Jove!' I thought to myself, 'this is some high jinks I've got myself involved in here! If the boys in Govan could only see me now!'

Kicking open the door of the guard's van, Archs and Figueras rushed inside, waking the two sleeping soldiers, little more than boys, whose mud-dled senses gave them no time to register anything. I hoped Archs and Figueras wouldn't have to kill or injure them.

'If the guard is wearing a helmet and you have to work in silence,' Archs had said in his briefing prior to the ambush, 'use your knife!' Walking behind me, he unexpectedly grabbed my hair and pulled my head back to illustrate his point. 'Sink your fingers into his eye sockets then jerk the head back towards you,' he said. 'Then, press against the side of the wind-pipe, just below the jaw, and draw the cutting edge of your knife across his throat . . . a single stroke . . . just like that,' he said, pushing me away. 'Then let the body slump forward. That way you avoid getting covered in blood. The gypsies who taught me to use a knife claim that when the carotid artery is severed in this way death is quick and painless.'

Massaging my scalp where he'd pulled my hair, I wondered how the gypsies were so sure this particular death was painless; it sounded pretty painful to me; Archs pulling my hair was bad enough. But my worries were unfounded. Archs knew I was squeamish in these matters, so I sus-pect they were having a joke at my expense.

Not that he couldn't or wouldn't have killed had it been necessary; Archs and Figueras were battle-hardened compañeros but, fortunately, it didn't come to killing. The young soldiers were terrified and made no attempt to fire their weapons or pull the communication cord. Figueras pressed the point of his knife to one of the soldiers' throats, pricking him slightly, while Archs bound, gagged and blindfolded his companion—then repeated the process with the other. With the soldiers taken care of, they dragged the strongbox out onto the veranda and called me down from the roof.

'You're going to have to jump now,' said Archs. 'Focus on the tracks. When a telegraph pole comes into sight, throw yourself towards it, but keep your elbows tucked in and roll yourself up into a ball before you land. Don't worry, you won't hit a pole. In fact, it's the only sure way to avoid hitting it.'

The two men manoeuvred the strongbox to the edge of the veranda platform and pushed it into the void, watching it tumble, bounce, and roll into the shadows. Then they jumped, first one and then the other, leaving me staring down at the tracks, hypnotised by the sleepers flashing by and trying to shrug off the fear. Taking a deep breath I launched myself into space, hitting the ground with a painful thump before rolling, spinning, and bouncing until my body eventually lost inertia and I slid to a stand-still—winded, disoriented, bruised, and grazed.

I sat up, aching all over and feeling nauseous. Along the embankment compañeros were busy loading the boxes onto the waiting lorries. Archs and Figueras emerged out of the darkness, grabbed me by the armpits and pulled me to my feet, hugging me roughly. Only then did I realise I was wounded. A sticky liquid felt tacky on my cheek. It was my blood . . . shed in action for the first time, apart from the barroom brawl with the Sometent. I felt an inexplicable sense of elation, and then vomited.

Euphoric with success, we sang and joked nervously most of the drive back to Huesca, constantly aware we could run into a Guardia Civil road-block at any moment. We hoped it would be at least six hours before news of the attack on the train got out, but we still faced a long journey down a rough, potholed road.

We had a head start though, having cut the telegraph wires at various points between Huesca and Jaca while other comrades, including some sympathetic soldiers from the local garrison, had cut all the other main telegraph lines out of the town.

We stored the weapons in a blacksmith's forge in Huesca, a temporary arms dump until the Defence Commission could organise its network of caches across Aragón, Catalonia, León, Asturias, and the Basque Country.

Most of the compañeros involved in that morning's action were locals—Aragóneses—who could return to their homes without anyone other than their partners knowing they had been away. Archs, Figueras, Laureano, and I, however, weren't locals and couldn't risk travelling by road or rail beyond Huesca to Zaragoza or anywhere else. Once news of the train robbery broke, the Guardia Civil would have roadblocks set up on every conceivable route out of the region. They would also have men on every train and rail station, with patrols combing the countryside, villages, and towns to hunt us down.

Every traveller in the area would be stopped and searched; but we had anticipated this. After returning the 'borrowed' lorries to the compañeros at the Huesca RENFE marshalling yard, we made our way to a 'safe' house, the home of a retired professor from Salamanca University where we stayed for four days. During that time I received the silent ministrations of the professor's housekeeper, an elderly gypsy woman whose archaic and mysterious medicines soon had my cuts, bruises, and strains attended to. Within a week we were all safely back in Barcelona by way of Sariñena, Caspe, and Vandellós. The army, the Guardia Civil and the Special Services Brigade went berserk. Not only had we stolen the Jaca garrison's arms—rifles, pistols, and ammunition—and some emergency rations, but we had also taken 200,000 pesetas, the garrison's wages for the month, money which went straight into the defence fund to support prisoners' families and their legal fees.

SIGNS AND PORTENTS

By the end of 1918, three autocratic European empires—the Austro-Hungarian, the German and the Russian—had disappeared into the midden of history. Austria-Hungary's declaration of war against Serbia, originally meant to reassert its position as an independent Great Power, had led, instead, to the break up of the Habsburg Empire, while in Russia, Lenin's Bolsheviks replaced the Romanovs, and Kaiser Wilhelm II, the last German emperor and king of Prussia, had fled into exile in Holland.

> The tumult and the shouting dies;
> The captains and the kings depart . . .

Most of Europe's currencies were now worthless, and the continent was in the grip of famine and the so-called 'French' or 'American' influenza pandemic. For the superstitious and gullible, the signs and portents that the Millennium was at hand were everywhere. The Four Horsemen of the Apocalypse were bearing down on us, fast:

> And I looked, and behold a pale horse: and his name that sat on
> him was Death, and Hell followed with him. And power was given
> unto them over the fourth part of the earth, to kill with sword, and
> with hunger, and with death, and with the beasts of the earth.

Inflation, misery, poverty, and widespread anger over the lack of basic commodities were leading to demonstrations and riots across Europe. Street disturbances were an everyday occurrence in most cities. In rural areas, the day labourers who survived did so on pittance wages, unhealthy diets, and short-term jobs.

Working for *Soli* I learned a lot about what was happening inside Germany, mainly from army and Imperial Fleet deserters who escaped to Spain where the CNT locals and the *Soli* office tended to be their first port of call in town. Nodding acquaintances of mine at the time included two young English-speaking able-seamen, Walter and Karl, who had served on the battleship *Thüringen* at Wilhelmshaven and Kiel. Their accounts of conditions inside wartime Germany were horrific. People were living off turnips, mouldy bread, and—if they were very lucky—potatoes. Both lads belonged to the Spartakus Jugend and the anarcho-syndicalist Freie Vereinigung deutscher Gewerkschaften (FVdG) (the Free Association of German Unions). And by jings, did they hate their officers. It was almost visceral, and no wonder. While the Kulies of the fleet, the matelots, existed on starvation rations, the officer squirearchy from the great landowning families east of the Elbe tucked into butter, white bread, and champagne. What finally pushed them to desert was the Kaiser's order that the High Seas Fleet was to make a final suicide attack; all hands were expected to go down with their ship to save Germany's honour.

One of them, Walter, said: 'The mood on the *Thüringen* that night was ominous. The atmosphere was like inside a prison the night before a hanging. The officers got drunk, but we, the sailors, didn't relish the idea of mass suicide so we mutinied and took over many of the ships, including the German navy's other big battleship, the *Helgoland*. The stokers doused the fires in the boilers and killed the steam, after which we dropped anchor and locked all the officers below decks, much to the relief of most of them I imagine.

'When we did return to port, 580 of us were arrested and packed into the holds like salted herrings in a barrel. But, when the dockers heard this they stormed the ships, seized the bridges and armouries—and released us. On the *Helgoland*, one brave young lad, a stoker called Ernst Wolwebberand, climbed the main mast, hauled down the Kaiser's flag and raised the red flag in its place. By 7 November the entire German fleet, led by Kiel sailors, was in revolt and the movement had spread south. Bremen and Hamburg, the most radical towns in Germany, declared themselves Soviet Republics. So did Munich. In Prussia the government collapsed.'

With Armageddon over, the apocalypse was now at hand. The 11 November armistice was signed at a time of greater than usual social upheaval in Spain; it also coincided with the fall of the government of the arch-reactionary Prime Minister Antonio Maura. He was replaced by a minority Liberal government led by the Conde de Romanones, who promptly announced that he would force through an autonomy statute for Catalonia. This was a blatantly opportunistic manoeuvre intended to reintegrate the disenchanted Catalan urban middle classes into the Spanish system, a proposal rejected outright by the Catalanistas who promptly walked out of the Cortes in protest.

SOWING THE WIND . . .

A few days after the Armistice, their work in Spain completed, the Cairo Gang were ordered to Damascus, shipping out discreetly in the dead of night on Alf Mason's yacht. I hadn't seen much of any of them since the end of June, and it was only by chance I heard they were leaving when I ran into Mason's skipper, 'Hurricane Jack' Maclachlan, on the Ramblas. We went for a farewell dram in a bar close to the docks. All he knew was the boat was sailing that night under sealed orders for somewhere 'east of Suez'.

I learned later from Marshall, whom I met weekly for my small 'stipend' which was paid up until the week after the Armistice, that their orders were to 'neutralise' suspected Arab terrorists and Turkish agents of the Ottoman general Kakhro Pasha who was refusing to accept defeat and was fighting on after the armistice. Pasha and his colleagues were furious that Syria had been presented to France in the postwar carve up, and that British-ruled Palestine was being gifted to the Jews following the Anglo-French Declaration. Arabs everywhere were outraged at Britain's treachery in failing to keep its promise to grant them an enormous area of Ottoman territory stretching from the Arabian peninsula, through modern Israel, Palestine, Jordan, Syria, Lebanon, and Iraq. It was to have been their reward for supporting General Allenby against the Ottoman Turks.

The British government had been caught out in their lies, hence the problems which the Cairo Gang were off to 'sort out' on behalf of their imperial masters. They failed, of course, and in the process succeeded only in aggravating an already inflamed situation and radicalising a whole new generation of Arab nationalists and Mussulman fanatics. The Cairo Gang were finally pulled out of Damascus early in 1920 and sent back to Britain to 'attend to matters' in Ireland—where many of them were murdered by the IRA on Sunday 21 November 1921. But that is another story. Nor was the subject of my repatriation brought up again. I suspect it all got lost in the postbellum shuffle. Either that or Marshall buried it in the hope I would prove useful to him in the future.

BRAVO PORTILLO—PALADIN!

With the end of the Great European War and the spectre of revolution looming over Europe, Barcelona's angst-ridden bourgeois establishment, the 'men of order', the *'gent d'ordre'*, needed to find someone capable of restoring their authority and rolling back an increasingly radicalised labour movement led by the sindicato único. Their Paladin—their modern El Cid Campeador—was Don Manuel Bravo Portillo, the 'disgraced' former chief superintendent of the 'Special Services Brigade,' who had been released on bail on 6 December. A week later, at the Barcelona High Court, all outstanding charges against him—espionage and conspiracy to murder the manufacturer Josep Barret—were dropped, without explanation. In spite of the fact that the prosecution had presented what appeared to be unassailable documentary and graphological evidence that it was his handwriting on the incriminating letters, Bravo Portillo stuck to his guns and firmly denied it, claiming he was the victim of an international anarchist Masonic plot to frame him. More importantly, the murder of Royo de San Martín, the main prosecution witness, and the fact that other witnesses were refusing to testify meant there was insufficient evidence to proceed against him or Bellés. Or so they claimed. The case never came to court so the evidence was never tested.

The decision not to prosecute Bravo Portillo provoked widespread public outrage, triggering riots and mass demonstrations that were ferociously put down by the Guardia Civil with 'sabre and revolver'.

That the authorities dropped the case against Bravo Portillo should have surprised no one. The former chief superintendent knew exactly where all the bodies were buried—it was he, after all, who had buried them! To put him on the stand would have been too risky. With his connections, experience, knowledge, and personal dossiers he really was untouchable, but it was still a scandalous, embarrassing, and provocative subversion of justice. Nor had it gone unnoticed that, less than a week after Bravo Portillo's initial arrest, Interior Minister García Prieto made an unscheduled visit to Barcelona, on 30 June, for urgent top-level and secret meetings with the province's political and administrative leaders. No one was in any doubt as to what had been top of the agenda that day.

Despite the dropping of all charges against him, and the support of a powerful Catalanista lobby, Bravo was not reinstated as head of Barcelona's Special Services Brigade. Madrid's new Liberal government instructed the captain-general, Joaquín Milans del Bosch, that under no circumstances was Bravo Portillo to be reemployed in the police department or appointed to any other position in the city administration.

But the captain-general, a long-standing friend of Bravo Portillo, had been complicit in all of his protégé's covert activities, and although he wasn't prepared to disobey a direct order, he was able to sidestep the problem with the help of his influential and scheming friends in the Patronal, Josep Bertrán i Musito and Joan Miró i Trepat, who came up with an 'elegant' solution to the problem by inventing and bankrolling a position for the disgraced former chief superintendent as a 'security contractor' with his own parallel and nonattributable private 'security service'.

MURDER INCORPORATED

Operating covertly and answerable exclusively to Milans del Bosch, Bravo Portillo's parapolitical operation quickly became an integral part of the strikebreaking apparatus of the captain-general's office. Its existence was kept secret even from Barcelona's police commissioner, whom Milans distrusted, convinced his department was riddled with freemasons and liberals. It was the military-industrial oligarchs' 'elegant solution' to the perennial question: 'who will do the dirty work?'—because in the complicated world of big business and international capitalism, there is always dirty work to be done. Bravo Portillo's 'deniable' and 'nonattributable' parallel detective agency was to become Milans del Bosch's personal death squad for the elimination of troublesome union organisers.

Manuel Bravo Portillo's role-model was Alan Pinkerton, the renegade Chartist and national disgrace to Scotland whose detective agency in the United States was the forerunner of the FBI and the US Secret Service. Like Pinkerton, Bravo Portillo's employees included not only well-connected military, police, and secret service officers, but also ideologically driven ultra-conservative Carlists, integrist ultra-Papists and lumpen proletarian thugs recruited from Barcelona's demimonde—the criminal gangs and their police cohorts who ran protection, prostitution, and drug rackets, and who murdered to order on behalf of anyone prepared to pay the going rate.

One of Bravo Portillo's main subcontractors was another detective agency run by a sinister scoundrel and master of deceit who went by the name of Baron de Koenig, and whose network of agents, mercenaries, low-life informers, spies, intriguers, bribe-givers, and professional strike-breakers operated from a former Sometent office at number 214 Carrer Diputación. Bravo Portillo's contractual relationship with the so-called 'Baron', however, was a secret known only to his patron, Miró i Trepat.

Bravo Portillo, a man with a chip and a grudge, now had a licence to kill. Driven by an all-consuming desire for revenge, the focus of his unremitting and all-consuming hatred were Barcelona's two prominent cenetistas, Ángel Pestaña and Salvador Segui, whom he believed were personally responsible for his downfall. The name on the shingle of his new company, 'Nemesis—The Great Private Detective Company', was a clear indicator as to his agenda

BARCELONA, HOGMANAY 1918

After almost sixty years my memories of that first Hogmanay in Barcelona remain unusually vivid. It was the last day of 1918, a truly momentous year. After a festive dinner, Laureano, Lara, and I relaxed over *carajillos* at a terrace café, the Liceu, on the Rambla de los Caputxins, near the entrance to the Plaça Reial. Our shared experiences over the last eight months had bonded us in a way that nothing else could have done. The streets were crowded with people talking, laughing, and arguing; horse-drawn carts rumbled by, tramcars and buses clanked and rattled along, and buses and sleek, shiny cars—De Dion Boutons, Léon Bollés, and Panhard-Levassors—driven by Catalan Mr Toads honked loudly, demanding passage.

A procession of shadowy figures passed to and fro beneath the tracery of the bare branches of the lime trees that arched across the Ramblas. The tree trunks formed a colonnaded avenue as far as the eye could see, all the way up to the brightly illuminated Plaça de Catalunya where flashing coloured electric lights hung from their branches in strings of Christmas motifs: bows, crowns, and stars. Around us workers with jobs hurried home to their barris, while rich and middling bourgeois gentlemen, dressed in their Sunday best, enjoyed a final evening stroll, arm in arm with their wives, friends, or mistresses before returning home to celebrate Año Nuevo in their large, comfortable apartments. As they passed, they greeted each other with a flourish of hats and nods of acknowledgement. Lovers, holding hands, strolled along oblivious to the rest of the world, their eyes only for each other. Also among this milling crowd were the angry dispossessed—wretched, unskilled, and impoverished casual day-labourers with their gaunt, unshaven faces, collarless shirts or blue overalls—drawn into the city centre from the dirt-poor areas, the *barris bajos*, trying to forget the misery of their existence. It was a Manet painting brought to life.

My mind wound back to the previous year's Hogmanay, standing on Woodlands Hill in Glasgow's West End. The memories were crystal clear, yet an eternity away. Wandering along Park Terrace's genteel Florentine Renaissance-style crescent on my way to a New Year party in Woodside Road, I remembered leaning over the balustrades to take in the view over Kelvingrove Park, the Art Galleries, the University, and the cityscape beyond, a living, three-dimensional Toytown with grimy tenements, church spires, and factory and foundry chimneys pumping dark smoke into the evening sky.

In my mind's eye I could see the sun in the distance, low in the western sky—furnace-red through the haze of smoke, steam and smog and haze—sinking slowly behind the Renfrewshire hills. Around me, in the background, the noises of the city vibrated and thrummed through the swirling reek and rosy purple glow still lingering above the horizon: a distant orchestra of shipyard drills, turbines, and dynamos in power stations, locomotives whistling and shrieking, and tramcars rattling and whining along Sauchiehall Street. Glasgow may have been a city of mean streets of ignorant, tarnished, or cowed men and women, but there were many others, people of integrity, honour, principle, steadfast of character, with a rude, sharp wit and a sense of the grotesque and the ironic, a distaste for sham, and a contempt for pettiness. Above all, it was home: my birth-place, a place of memories, ties, traditions, the community that gave me my sense of status ...

Unfortunately, we cannot live our lives according to the moral and reli-gious convictions or petrified dogmas of our forebears. We have an obliga-tion to live by our own faith, forever renewing the traditions of the past and adapting them to the demands of own time and place.

Lara roused me from my melancholic reverie with a friendly shove and gentle banter, thrusting a large brandy into my hand:

'*Oye, hombre! Basta con el duende! Mañana es año nuevo y el futuro es nuestro!*'

We raised our glasses in a toast to the New Year and the prospect of 'La Revolución Social!' We were on the threshold of a new age, a new Enlightenment, a new human adventure; we were, indeed, the first of the 'moderns'—or so we believed at the time. I mused to myself, how strange it was that my life, my expectations—and my prospects—had changed so dramatically, by chance and accident, over the course of a few months.

But it wasn't only the passing of the old year and the prospect of a new world we were celebrating. That morning I had received a letter confirm-ing that my application had been accepted for a job as an engineer with the Sociedad Anónima de Riegos y Fuerzas del Ebro (the Ebro Irrigation and Power Company). I was to report for work the following Monday at the company's electricity generating plant in the Avenida del Paral·lel, just a quarter of an hour's walk from where I was living.

'A peseta for your thoughts, Farqhuaro?'

I looked into Lara's dark El Greco eyes for a long moment and a surge of happiness dispersed any remaining shards of unease. I lifted her and spun her laughing and giggling in my arms; she held me tightly, her arms around my neck. I kissed her on the cheek, then our lips touched, very lightly. I kissed her again, delicately, first on her cheeks, then her eyes, and her ear-lobes. Finally, our lips met. As I pulled her into my arms, she gave herself completely to me, pushing her body upwards against mine.

I was in heaven. This city, this country, these comrades, this special girl, they were my home and family now. The scales of past and future had tipped in the balance. What fresh adventures would the New Year bring? Little did I know the extraordinary surprises dame Fortuna held in store for me—a Caledonian Candide in Catalonia—and for all of us. Tomorrow was, after all, another year.

Belleville, Paris 1976

Farquhar McHarg pushed back his typewriter and took off his spectacles, wiping his tired eyes with the back of his hand. There had been tears. It was so vivid, this personal history he had revisited, a time-traveller in the sweet and now distant land of his youth. He rose again, the window drawing him like a magnet. How long would it be before they found him? By now 'they'—whoever 'they' were, the pistoleros *of the Hiéron du Val d'Or, the heritors of Bravo Portillo and de Koenig, now calling themselves Los Guerrilleros de Cristo Rey, 'Warriors of Christ the King'—would know that Laureano's personal and police files, with their damning evidence of fifty years of criminal intrigue, treachery, and murder, were to be released to him. His old friend had passed him the Black Spot.*

Out of nowhere, Dan Macphail's words came back to him:

I live and know not how long, I travel and know not whither.

Clippings and Photos, 1918

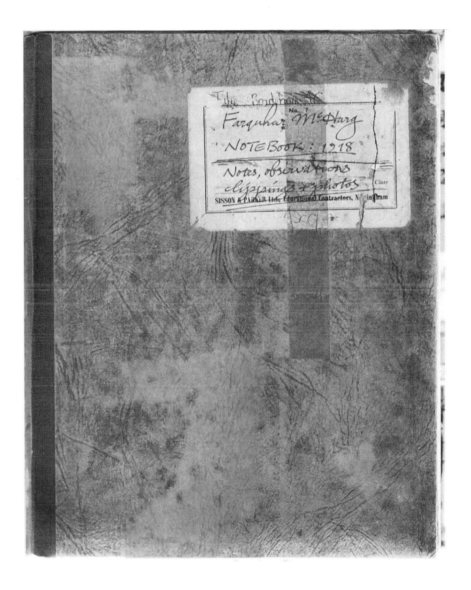

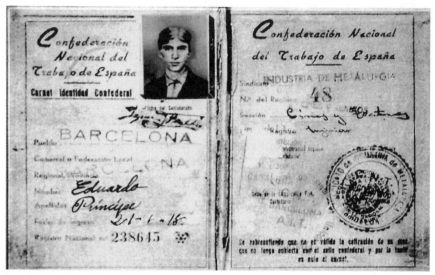

Farquhar McHarg/ Eduardo Principe's Confederación Regional de Trabajo (de Cataluña) membership card (metalworkers' union), 1918.

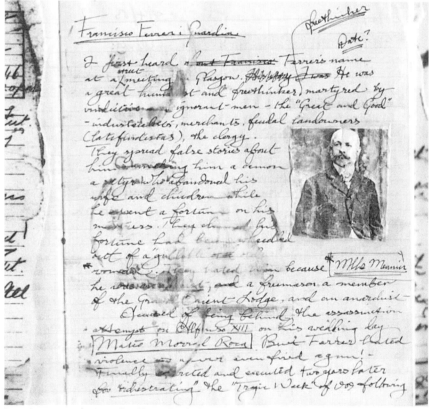

Page from contemporary (1918) notebook/diary.

The River Clyde with Govan on the left bank, Partick on the right, and Whiteinch, Clydebank, and Bowling further downriver towards the Firth of Clyde. Inset: Howden's advertising leaflet.

The Broomielaw, River Clyde, Glasgow, March 1918.

Glasgow, 1915: Highland Light Infantry (HLI) recruiting for 'The Big Picnic' (below).

Political and religious debate on Glasgow Green on a Sunday evening in the late nineteenth century.

Guy Aldred.

Glasgow Anarchist Group, 1916.

Barcelona harbour with Montjuïc fortress dominating the city.

The Paseo de Colón, looking south to the Columbus Monument and Montjuïc beyond.

The hill and fortress of Montjuïc.

Port stevedores.

Barcelona port (from Miramar).

El Paral·lel.

Nou Paral·lel.

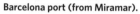

Bar La Tranquilidad; El Café Español; Paral·lel (Marqués del Duero); Columbus Monument; Escudellers.

Plaça Reial.

The Flower Market in the Rambla de San José.

Carrer Escudellers.

Guardia Civil.

The Columbus Monument.

Arco de Triunfo.

Calles Pelayo y Balmes.

Plaça de Catalunya.

Via Layetana (HQ of the Patronal—Employers' Association).

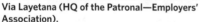

Rambla de Centro.

Calle Ramon i Cajal (Tastavins sign on right).

Ronda de San Pedro.

Llano de Boquería.

Jaca—close to the ambush point.

Jaca, Aragón Valley, Huesca Province.

Barcelona skyline.

Calle Marqués del Duero —El Paral·lel.

Tibidabo Funicular.

Barcelona from Tibidabo.

Plaça d'Espanya.

Arco de Triunfo and El Salon de Garcia Heran.

Carcel Modelo (Model Prison).

Las Ramblas.

Café Español, exterior

Café Español, interior

Left: Café La Tranquilidad, Paral·lel.
Below: Teatro Apolo.

Crowds gather in the Paral·lel in the wake of one of Joan Rull's police-sponsored bombing provocations, 1907.

El Raval, located in the medieval city quarter of Barcelona, at the time one of the most densely populated urban areas in the world.

At home with the Foixes' in-laws.

A woman of Escudellers.

Street scene: Govan, Belleville, or the Raval, not much difference.

Street meeting.

The final straw: the sinking of French-registered vessel the *Provence* by the Croatia-based *U-35*.

U-boat mother ship *SS Vulkan* off Cartagena.

U-14 also photographed off Cartagena.

OPDR Line—
Oldenburg
Portugiesische
Dampfschiffs-
Rhederei. Front
company for German Naval Intelligence
Special Command—*Etappendienst*—headed by
Kapitänleutnant Wilhelm Canaris.

Cartagena: operational HQ of German Naval
Intelligence Special Command—*Etappendienst*.

Barrels of submarine diesel and boxes of
anthrax and glanders microbes are landed from
the *Ganeko* and hidden in a cave near Palamos.

Here's tae us! Mason's farewell to Barcelona
(with the *Privet* in the background).

U-34 (off Barcelona), later sunk by Mason's
Privet near Gibraltar on 9 November 1918.

Solidaridad Obrera breaks
the news that the head of
Barcelona's secret police, Bravo Portillo (right)
is a German agent responsible for the loss of
the Spanish ship *SS Joaquin Mumbrú*.

TRANSPORTE

CNT Maritime
Workers'
Union.

Juan March Ordinas—
pirate, gangster, and
German double agent.

Last moments of *The Covenant*.

U-boat intercepts Spanish mail ship off Cadiz.

SS Joaquin Mumbrú: sunk by U-boat, January 1918.

U-boat interior.

Cutaway of a German U-boat.

U-boat photographed close to Barcelona port.

U-35 Captain Lothar Arnauld de la Perière.

U-35, commanded by Captain Lothar Arnauld de la Perière, photographed in Cartagena harbour.

Microbiological terrorism: von Krohn commissioned a professor Kleine to manufacture gelatinised cholera and typhus cultures to dump in rivers along the Portuguese border.

Marthe Richard, 'mistress' of German spymaster von Krohn, French double agent, and anarchist sympathiser.

The CNT Maritime Workers' Union lost more than forty members due to German sabotage operations in ports and docks (Helios Gómez).

Queen Mother: Austrian Archduchess María Cristina, pro-Axis facilitator.

God's Sword: Kaiser Wilhelm II.

Ferdinand of Bavaria, Queen Victoria Eugenia, Alfonso XIII, Vicenti, Queen Mother María Cristina.

Junker warlords: the Kaiser (centre) with von Hindenburg (left) and General Ludendorff.

Prime Minister Count Romanones.

Asesinato de un patrono

A última hora de ayer tarde se registró en esta ciudad un nuevo atentado, que viene á aumentar la ya larga serie de los cometidos desde hace algún tiempo contra patronos y encargados de fábricas ó talleres. A la hora en que escribimos estas líneas no conocemos detalles del execrable suceso; sólo tenemos noticia sucinta de la brutal agresión que ha causado la muerte á un honrado, inteligente y trabajador industrial.

9 Jan 1918: murder of industrialist Josep Barret.

Vapor español torpedeado

A primeras horas de la mañana circuló con insistencia, entre la gente de mar, una noticia funesta para la matrícula de Barcelona.
Relacionábase con el torpedeamiento de un vapor de alto bordo, de está inscripción. Después de las averiguaciones correspondientes...

13 Jan 1918: torpedoing of the *SS Joaquín Mumbrú*.

LOS ATENTADOS CONTRA LOS PATRONOS

Descubrimiento de los autores

La serie de atentados cometidos en esta capital contra patronos y encargados de fábricas y la impunidad en que casi siempre quedaban sus autores, había originado justificada alarma y dado ocasión á las más acerbas censuras contra los encargados, por su...

13 Feb 1918: Bravo Portillo frames and arrests CNT activists Joaquín and Pedro Vandellós Romero, Pedro Boada, Valero and Carlos Anglés, and Juan Soler for the murders of Josep Barret and Sr Pastor.

Solidaridad Obrera

EL ESPIONAJE ALEMÁN EN BARCELONA

DOCUMENTOS IMPORTANTISIMOS

El torpedeamiento del Joaquín Mumbrú se realiza de acuerdo con Brabo Portillo.
La opinión pública debe intervenir. Nosotros denunciamos los hechos. Que obre quien le interese.

9 Jun 1918: *Solidaridad Obrera* breaks the news that Superintendent Bravo Portillo is responsible for passing information to the German secret services that led to the sinking of the *SS Joaquín Mumbrú*.

EN EL JUZGADO

Detención de Brabo Portillo

Como dijimos en nuestra edición anterior, los peritos calígrafos señores Bofarull y Pabeja, designados por el Juzgado especial que entiende en el asunto promovido por la publicación de los facsímiles de dos cartas que se atribuían al comisario de policía señor Brabo Portillo en varios periódicos locales y relacionadas con la salida del vapor *Joaquín Mumbrú*, que fué torpedeado, han informado en el sentido de que, á pesar de las retiradas negativas del señor Brabo, la letra y firma de las expresadas cartas son realmente de su puño y letra. Después de haber estudiado detenidamente este dictamen, el juez especial, la...

22 June 1918: Police Superintendent Manuel Bravo Portillo, head of the 'Special Services Brigade' is arrested and charged with espionage.

EN EL PUERTO DE BARCELONA

Un submarino alemán

Ayer mañana circuló la noticia de que había entrado un submarino alemán en nuestro puerto. La noticia se extendió con gran rapidez y adornada con diversidad de detalles, desprovistos la mayor parte de fundamento, pero que no obstante eran acep...

22 June 1918: German submarine enters Barcelona harbour, allegedly to take Bravo Portillo to Germany.

EL ASUNTO BRABO PORTILLO

Dos detenciones importantes

Con motivo de la detención de dos conocidos individuos, Mariano Conde y Tomás Bernardini (a) *Tomasito*, empleado este último en la sección de recreos de Novedades, vuelve á adquirir interés el asunto Brabo Portillo, por las aseveraciones de uno de los detenidos.
Parece ser—pues informes oficiales es imposible adquirirlos por guardar el juzgado

6 Dec 1918: Superintendent Manuel Bravo Portillo is released on bail and, within a week, all outstanding charges against him—espionage and conspiracy to murder the manufacturer Barret—are inexplicably dropped by the Barcelona High Court.
The prosecution presents what appears to be unassailable graphological evidence, but Bravo sticks to his story that the handwriting is not his and that he is the victim of an anarchist plot to frame him.

Conferencia

Acerca del asunto de Brabo Portillo, han celebrado una conferencia los señores conde de Romanones, Jimeno y el presidente de la Audiencia de Barcelona, que se encuentra en Madrid.

13 Dec 1918: Bravo Portillo is summoned to Madrid.

Anoche en el expreso salió para Madrid el comisario de policía señor Bravo Portillo.

10 Dec 1918: Cabinet meets to discuss Bravo case.

El gobernador civil

Anoche el gobernador civil mostrábase profundamente afectado por los sucesos ocurridos. Manifestó que había dispuesto que inmediatamente fuesen retiradas las carabinas que se habían entregado á los guardias de seguridad y con el anuncio de que se proyectaba celebrar á toda costa la manifestación para pedir el encarcelamiento de Bravo Portillo.

16 Dec 1918: civil governor González Rothwos orders police and Guardia Civil to suppress with 'sabre and revolver' the growing number of demonstrations calling for the rearrest and trial of Bravo Portillo.

The 'Cairo Gang': British Secret Service 'licensed to kill'.

Chain of Command: Field Marshal Sir Henry Hughes Wilson (Chief of the British imperial General Staff).

General John Charteris: Wilson's chief of intelligence

Searching for the 'Hidden Hand': Lloyd George and Winston Churchill.

Victims: John S. Clarke's pamphlet on the Alice Wheelden conspiracy.

Captains George Bruce and George Marshall of the British Secret Service Bureau, 1918.

Lord Curzon, leader of the House of Lords.

MI-5 head: Vernon George Waldergrave Kell.

Captain Francis Cromie RN, naval attaché and intelligence officer.

Only known photo of Lt-Col Keyes.

Lieutenant Colonel Terence Keyes, Secret Service officer in Russia until August 1918 when he was deported for funding the anti-Leninist Volunteer Army. Also involved with Cromie in plotting the escape of the Russian royal family—and Lenin's assassination. Adviser on Russia and second-in-charge of Oriental Section of the UK's Ministry of Information.

Sidney Reilly, British special services officer in Russia.

Pravda editor and British agent Roman Malinovsky.

Scotland Yard Special Branch chief, Assistant Commissioner Basil Thomson.

Edinburgh, May 1918: John Maclean tried for promoting mutiny and sedition; Special Branch claimed he was a Leninist agent.

Solidaridad Obrera editor José Borobio spent most evenings on stage under the name 'Jean Kiss'.

Eduardo Dato's government attempted to control the press scandals by means of an Espionage Bill.

Ramón Archs.

Inspector Jean Belin of the Sûreté Nationale (right) interrogates a station-master during the hunt for Ramón Archs.

Roadblocks.

Salvador Seguí (a.k.a. el 'Noi del Sucre). Charismatic public speaker, secretary of the Catalan CNT and member of the 1917 strike committee.

Ángel Pestaña, journalist, watchmaker, and one of the most outstanding figures of Spanish anarcho-syndicalism.

Ángel Pestaña, Salvador Seguí, and Molins discuss strike strategy, August 1917.

Meeting of the Catalan Regional Committee of the CNT with Simó Piera between Pestaña and Seguí.

Laureano Cerrada Santos was to become one of the most skilled and successful forgers in Europe.

Eduardo Principe's (Farquhar McHarg) confederal union card.

Café Royale, Rambla de Estudios (where Royo de San Martín regularly met Bravo Portillo).

Anarchist bookshop and *ateneu* in the Calle de Fontanella (behind the horse and trap).

Courtyard view from McHarg's rear window in Escudellers.

Tomás Herreros's bookshop in Atarazanas, a central anarchist rendezvous point in Barcelona from 1918 to 1923.

Francisco Ferrer i Guardia.

56 Carrer Bailén, la Escuela Moderna
(1901–1906).

Corpse of Mateo Morral.

Mateo Morral, teacher.

EM Bulletin.

Barcelona, July 1909: (above and below) angry
demonstrations against the war in Morocco
erupt into insurrection (above right).

Barcelona, 26 July 1919: antiwar protestors set
fire to the convento de los Escolapias.

The Notebooks

FRANCISCO FERRER I GUARDIA

I first heard Ferrer's name during an anarchist street-corner meeting in Glasgow, and was deeply moved by the story of how this secular intellectual had been martyred by vindictive and ignorant men. His enemies were the so-called 'great and the good' of Spain's capitalist bourgeoisie: the manufacturers and merchants; the feudal landowners—the *latifundistas*—and the clergy, the Roman Catholic Church. They all spread scurrilous stories about Ferrer, painting him as a demonic and selfish satyr who cruelly abandoned his wife and children, leaving them to starve, while he spent vast sums of money on his mistress. His fortune, they claimed, had been wheedled out of a 'gullible old woman', Ernestine Meunier, by hypocrisy and 'disguised philanthropy'. What clinched Ferrer's badness for them wasn't just that he was a proselytising atheist, educationalist, and freethinker, but that he was also a freemason, a member of the Grand Orient Lodge—and a 'self-confessed' anarchist!

In their attempts to rid themselves of this troublesome teacher who had defied and undermined the Church's control of education, taught children to 'deny God' and 'defy the State', Spain's 'men of order'—enthusiastically supported by the country's newspaper barons and oligarchs of the dynastic parties that alternated in power in Madrid—accused Ferrer of being the *éminence grise* behind the 1906 assassination attempt on King Alfonso XIII and his new Queen on their wedding day. Although it is possible Ferrer may have funded the assassination attempt, the evidence against him was entirely circumstantial. The would-be assassin, a young anarchist, Mateo Morral Roca, had worked as a teacher and librarian at Ferrer's Modern School in Barcelona's Carrer Bailen. An unfortunate coincidence for Ferrer.

As far as Spain's antidemocratic governing classes were concerned, Ferrer's 'atheist' schools were the root cause of the country's social dissatisfaction. The fact that he had never planned or committed an act of violence, fired a pistol, or made or thrown a bomb was irrelevant; as far as the ruling classes were concerned he was guilty of the 'corruption of young

minds'. As the writer Anatole France described it: 'His crime was founding schools.' In so doing he had opened Pandora's Box and released the evil
consequences of knowledge on a benighted working class, thereby raising
unmeetable hopes and expectations for a more equitable and just world!

After the attempt on Alfonso XIII, the elderly teacher was charged with
conspiracy to murder, and taken to Madrid where he was held on remand
in the Modelo prison for over a year before facing a court-martial in 1907.
Only then did it become clear there was no case to answer and the state
was forced to release him.

The 'crime' for which Ferrer was finally convicted and executed occurred
two years later—the alleged 'orchestration' of the insurrectionary events
of Barcelona's so-called 'Tragic Week' of July 1909. This followed a campaign of vilification by the national press, which relentlessly pursued and
portrayed him as the 'mastermind' and 'instigator in chief of the rebellion'.
What began as an angry popular protest movement against the selective
and arbitrary call-up of working-class Catalan reservists to fight in Spain's
unpopular colonial war in Morocco—a war clearly designed to defend the
property interests of the mine owners whose majority shareholders were
leading members of the political elite and the Jesuits—was quickly transformed into a full-scale urban uprising and was on the verge of triggering a
revolution. The popular anger that exploded that week led to a hundred and
four deaths, with many more injured, eighty religious buildings put to the
torch and unprecedented havoc on the streets of Barcelona. It also led to the
arrest of around two thousand people of whom six hundred were convicted.
Fifty-nine of these were sentenced to life imprisonment and seventeen to
death, five of whom were executed. Only one of the five, Miguel Baró, was
involved in leading the popular movement. On 17 August he was the first
to face the firing squad in the moat of the fortress of Montjuïc. The last to
die was Francisco Ferrer, on 13 October. In Ferrer's indictment the prosecution ludicrously claimed that he had provoked the disturbances and blood-
shed in a calculated attempt to manipulate the Madrid stock exchange for
the benefit of his personal investment folio!

Taking the traditional precepts of modern education outlined by Jean-
Jacques Rousseau in the eighteenth century—targeting authority and organised religion—he adapted these to the wave of revolutionary ideas being
propounded by anarchists and secular freethinkers in the industrialised and
urbanised society of the late nineteenth and early twentieth centuries.

Ferrer abhorred violence—and those who advocated it. The idea of
employing violence for personal gain was anathema to him. His life's aim was

1907, Madrid: Francisco Ferrer (top) arrives for his court-martial —'consejo de guerra' (below) for his alleged role in the attempt on the life of King Alfonso XIII.

Madrid, 31 May 1906.

EL ATENTADO CONTRA LOS REYES

El presunto autor del atentado

Por más que, como pudieron observar nuestros lectores, en la información que ayer dimos no apuntábamos el nombre del supuesto autor del atentado de Madrid, ni indicábamos la población de donde es natural, con el objeto de no estorbar la acción de la justicia, sacrificando así los datos y antecedentes que teníamos á la discreción necesaria en casos como el presente, nos vemos obligados hoy á romper el silencio, debido á que la pista que se sigue ya no resulta secreta.

El supuesto autor del horrendo crimen cometido en Madrid, ó por lo menos el individuo

La Vanguardia, 3 June 1906 (Morral's arrest).

simple: to transform the world by regenerating it through free, rational, secular, and egalitarian education, by persuasion and eliminating ignorance, prejudice, credulity, and coercion. His crime was breaking the Catholic Church's
monopoly over schools and bringing dogma-free education, also promoting
self-help, anticlericalism and antimilitarism. In a priest-, officer-, and land-
lord-ridden country that maintained the children of its poor in ignorance,
poverty, and squalor. In Ferrer's own words, the Modern School looked to
reason and science for 'the antidotes to all dogma'.

Roman Catholic schools relied on violence and fear, punishment, and
humiliation to instil obedience and respect in the children of the working classes. Nor did they teach children to read and write in those days.
Schooling consisted of sewing, Bible stories, and reciting the rosary and 'The
Catechism'—which was compulsory in all Church schools. A million children
were buried in darkness there, learning the rotes of the fourteenth century.

I remember the shock I felt when shown a children's history of the world
that began with Adam and Eve's expulsion from the Garden of Eden. Not
only was the omnicompetent Spanish Roman Catholic Church—Europe's
oldest continuous institution and divinely established repository of eternal
values—determined to cling to its immutable dictum, 'semper eadem' ('No
change!'); it refused even to consider adapting its message to the evolving needs of the modern world. To men and women like Ferrer who challenged the Roman Church's spiritual and temporal power, it was a powerful, implacable, and malevolent enemy.

The Church in Spain focused its attention primarily on the children of
the middle and upper classes, with the Jesuit and Augustinian establish-
ments responsible for educating the children of the country's elite. Their
institutions were modelled closely on British public schools—at least in
terms of imposing what they described as 'good order and discipline' on
their pupils. As far as Spanish Roman Catholic education was concerned,
the verb 'to educate' was a misnomer. As the Liberal Conde de Mortera
observed: 'Jesuits don't educate, they domesticate.'

Even as late as 1918, the Catholic Church in Spain was still reeling from
the aftershock of the Protestant Reformation, the French Revolution with its
cry of 'Reason!' and the then ongoing persecution of the Jesuits in France.
To them all these events were clear evidence of a mounting pattern, proof
of an intelligent and secret design linking, in one great conspiracy, all the
symptoms of social discontent and the main inspiration for the perversion of
western civilisation and values. It was for these reasons, especially in Spain,
that the Catholic Church, the grandees, and the political elite were so hostile

The 'black crows'.

Roman Catholic school.

Secular school.

to the idea of an educated working class. Not only were the Rationalist and Modern School Movements heretical, inasmuch as they propagated an anticlerical culture that challenged obscurantist Church education; they also encouraged individual and collective activism, and eroded the respect that children, labourers, and 'social inferiors' owed their masters or their betters.

Subjects not taught in Catholic schools included science, mathematics, agriculture, and political economy; these were considered dangerous for anyone other than trained theologians. Nor were Jesuits keen on history and literature, offering as they did too many negative role-models and bad examples to the young and credulous.

The only practical subjects that could be studied at university were law, technology, and engineering. Medicine was taught but subject to the suppression of the 'erroneous Lutheran notion' of the circulation of the blood. As for physics, even in 1918 the Copernican system was still considered suspect by the Holy Office of the Inquisition. And when it came to intellectuals—that is, people who use their brains rather than follow their emotions and instincts—the Church's attitude was encapsulated in the University of Cervera's infamous address to Ferdinand VII: 'Far be from us the dangerous novelty of thinking'. But that was possibly an attempt at irony or sarcasm.

There was little to choose between Church schools and State schools, other than their approach to politics—liberal politics that is. Children attending Church schools were taught that associating with liberals encouraged individualism, egalitarianism, freethinking, and antireligious enlightenment and was a fast track to perdition. For the faithful, the Church catechism posited questions on a range of subjects that they then proceeded to answer themselves, reserving their particular hostility for those of a liberal persuasion, a description considered synonymous with 'malefactors' and 'cosmopolitans':

> What does Liberalism teach? That the State is independent of the Church, but the State must be subject to the Church as the body is to the soul, and the temporal to the eternal . . . the false liberties of Liberalism are: liberty of conscience, of education, of propaganda and of meeting. These are heretical!

It continues:

> What kind of sin is Liberalism?—It is a most grievous sin against faith.
>
> Why?—Because it consists of a collection of heresies condemned by the Church.

Barcelona: 26 July 1909 (view from Montjuïc): antiwar demonstrators are fired upon by monks of the Patronato Obrero de San Jose, a Sacred Heart of Mary sect funded by the marqués de Comillas, an action that triggers the burning of many of the city's convents and monasteries.

The Army occupies the Plaça de Catalunya during 'Tragic Week'.

July 1909: neighbourhood barricades.

July 1909: protestors halt a tram and (below) turn it into a barricade.

July 1909: barricade in Gran Carrer, Gracia; below, barricade in la Ronda de San Antoni.

Is it a sin for a Catholic to read a Liberal newspaper? 'He may read the *Stock Exchange News.*

What sin is committed by him who votes for a Liberal candidate?' —Generally a mortal sin.

Although Ferrer's benefactor, Mlle Meunier, the so-called 'gullible' old woman referred to by the priests, press, and prosecutors, was a great admirer of the gentle anarchist, she remained a staunch Roman Catholic. When she died, however, she bequeathed to Ferrer a substantial legacy in her Parisian properties, the sale of which provided the revolutionary teacher with a remarkable fortune that allowed him to open his school and put his educational theories into practice. He was a generous benefactor, who used his newfound wealth to fund many other radical activities such as workers' *ateneus,* cooperatives, journals, books, and newspapers. Who knows, he may even, perhaps, have sponsored Mateo Morral.

Unlike the dominies in my Govan schools, Ferrer treated his pupils as valued friends, teaching by example and not precept. 'Children should be treated with respect', he wrote. If a child behaved badly, he would hold out his hand and tell the child to smack him, saying, 'I am the one at fault here, not you; I clearly have been unable to inspire in you the necessary self-discipline'. Mind you, the sense of guilt this induced in his pupils was probably worse than anything corporal punishment could achieve. Even so, according to all his students I spoke to, Ferrer's classes were exceptionally well-behaved.

Playtime and physical exercise were as important in the Modern School curriculum as book learning and intellectual exercise. Equally revolutionary was his advocacy of coeducation: 'Let humanity, male and female, mingle from childhood onwards.' This was revolutionary stuff. Another feature of Ferrer's classes was the seminar-type 'conversation' in which he would suggest a subject for discussion and use it to tease out the children's views on all manner of subjects. His aim was to teach them things that would help orient them in their world and, hopefully, show them that anything was possible and they should always aspire to the highest goal when they saw it. The Modern School was where children would investigate 'the underlying causes of popular ignorance' and become acquainted with 'the origin of all the conventions that sustain the current dog-eat-dog regime.' It was hardly surprising that the Catholic Church and Spain's 'men of order' should choose him as their scapegoat.

Barcelona: July 1909: Guardia Civil and soldiers escort trams driven by scabs.

Barricade in the Calle Nueva.

Having seized the barricades, soldiers begin the hunt for militant workers (below left/right).

August 1909: workers imprisoned in Montjuïc.

Days of Vengeance — Montjuïc, August 1909: state repression claimed the lives of 104 strikers during 'Tragic Week', with 6,000 imprisoned in Barcelona alone and 2,000 more imprisoned elsewhere in Spain. There were 216 courts-martial held, which passed 5 death sentences and sentenced 60 workers to life imprisonment.

Fusilan a Francesc Ferrer i Guàrdia en los fosos del castillo de Montjuïc

Educationalists like Ferrer were far from unusual in the socialist movement. There were many like him: 'tradition bearers', older men and women
who saw it their duty to pass on to others the benefits of their life experiences and their insights into literature, politics, science, and philosophy.
As with the zealous Presbyterian colporteurs who travelled the length and
breadth of Scotland selling religious tracts, it was never enough just to 'know'
about a subject; the information had to be discussed, debated, and communicated. It was how I acquired much of my own political education attending the Sunday morning open-air meetings held at the corner of Shamrock
Street, New City Road, and on Glasgow Green. These open-ended lectures,
debates, and discussions could run from ten in the morning until late at night,
with speakers on every subject imaginable—from Kant, Hume, Hegel, and
Nietzsche to sexual hygiene and contraception.

KROPOTKIN'S *MUTUAL AID*
Kropotkin's book *Mutual Aid* was another strong influence on me. Mutual
aid, he argued—which involved voluntary cooperation, mutual depend-
ency, and reciprocity—was the decisive factor and inherent in all social
beings who depend on group life for survival. A group of individuals acting
together without compulsion is, after all, a more effective way of dealing
with danger than acting alone. Grooming, too, is nicer with someone there
to help. Reciprocity is yet another aspect of mutual aid—the idea that I will
help you if I can count on you to help me. In fact, morality itself is grounded
in reciprocity and mutual dependence, although I can't help point out that
on its own doesn't leave much place for those who need most help, and who
may never be in a position to repay. Compassion, therefore, is an equally
important element in the idea of 'morality', in other words, 'Love thy neighbour as thyself.' It's unconditional.

THE GENERAL STRIKE, AUGUST 1917
In the summer of 1917, the socialists and their trade union affiliates, liberals,
and Republicans, the unenfranchised professional classes, and the politically excluded wartime nouveaux riches joined forces in an attempt to free
the economy from elite aristocratic and landed interests and turn Spain into
a social-democratic republic. The means by which this was to be achieved
was the general strike, and the introduction of a new party more representative of the middle-classes into Spain's musical chairs system of government. It was the most serious frontal challenge to the repressive constitutional monarchy since the short-lived First Spanish Republic in 1873.

Death of Francisco Ferrer i Guardia, Montjuïc, 13 October 1909 (Flavio Costantini).

Francisco Ferrer.

Alfonso XIII confirms death sentence.

Il Corriere della Sera.

The police hunt for Ferrer began on 7 August. Unable to locate him, they arrested and exiled his entire family. Ferrer was finally arrested by Sometent vigilantes on 31 August; court-

Sometent vigilantes who captured Ferrer.

martialed on 9 October, he was sentenced to death by firing squad and judicially murdered in Montjuïc on 13 October 1909.

Since the collapse of the First Republic in December of 1874, the Liberal and Conservative parties had, by mutual agreement, alternated in power by a process known as the Restoration System. The glue that held these parties together wasn't a shared ideology or attachment to principle—it was support for a particular party boss, and the prospect of office. It was about personality and power—acquiring it, keeping it, and getting rich by it—not policy. The mutual interest in maintaining the status quo, and ensuring that power remained firmly in the hands of the privileged elite, had kept the old bipartisan system in finely tuned balance for forty-three years. In Spain this system was known as 'el turno político'; in Britain it was known as 'Buggins's Turn'—'el turno Buggins'!

The strike, planned for August 1917, was a half-baked attempt by an unlikely coalition of middle-class professionals and social democrat trade union leaders to provoke the bourgeois democratic revolution that Spain had never had, and to reshape Spain's quasi-feudal state to serve their class interests. They wanted power transferred from the landed aristocracy to the political leadership of the professional classes—themselves. Both groups were privileged elites, separated from the wider population by class, cultural formation, status, and organisation and, like ruling classes everywhere, they wanted the monopoly on political decision-making.

Social revolution was the furthest thing from the minds of the reformist Socialist Party and UGT union leaders. They didn't want to overthrow the state, they wanted to 'control it' with their particular brand of conservative social democracy—to make it more decorous, a state as seen by the reactionary Edmund Burke in the 'Glorious Revolution' of 1688–89, or even one formed after the Kerensky model of February 1917 in Petrograd. Not for them confronting the repressive forces of capitalism on the barricades, or seizing factories and workshops, land, public buildings, abolishing property rights, and declaring libertarian communism in the hope of making the earth a common treasury for all. No, their modus operandi was compromise, negotiation, and political restraint. That is all very well if you live in a civilised, fair, just, and relatively equitably structured society in which everyone is equal before the law—but was no answer to the brutal and grindingly repressive, poverty-led, capitalist or feudal capitalist society that was Borbón Spain—and the rest of the world!—in 1917.

For the liberal and Republican bourgeoisie, the general strike was an opportunity to call a mass nationwide protest against the rising cost of living caused by the fast-shrinking economic benefits of the war, and to demand political reform and a new parliamentary assembly. For the strike to be effective, however, they needed the CNT on board and so, after much discussion, the national and regional committees of the CNT agreed to support the strike. The anarcho-syndicalists, however, had their own agenda, one they didn't share with the socialists. The strike was to be the signal for full-fledged revolutionary insurrection.

As the date for the August 1917 uprising approached, the socialists grew increasingly worried about the consequences of their pact with the CNT, whose militants were committed to the idea of a social general strike, an insurrection. Were they about to open a Pandora's box, as had happened with the Bolsheviks in Russia? In July 1917, just a month before the general strike, Pablo Iglesias, the 'grand old man' of the Spanish Socialist Party, rushed—if he could be said to rush anywhere!—to Barcelona to discuss strategy with the Catalan Regional Committee, hoping to dampen the CNT's revolutionary ardour and expectations.

'His arrogant and patronising manner didn't win him any friends—nor did it get him very far,' observed Salvador Segui.

'It's easy for you manual workers to defend violent methods,' said Iglesias, 'but it's different for us intellectuals.' The cheeky bastard continued: 'This is not the time for heroic deeds that would unleash who-knows what sort of violence.' He went on: 'We will bring about radical change, not by bloody revolution, but from within, through incremental change and piecemeal reform. Remember, the person who takes one step ahead of the others is a leader. The person who takes three steps ahead is a martyr.'

A few days later the CNT's Catalan Regional Committee had another visitor. This time the Socialist Party leader himself, Largo Caballero, who met them secretly at Valvidria in the mountains outside Barcelona, in a last-ditch attempt to try to contain the worryingly enthusiastic anarcho-syndicalists with sugary promises about the benefits that Caballero's socialist government would bring to Catalonia.

'His face drained when he met Pestaña, Peiro and myself at the rendezvous,' Segui told me later, 'along with about fifty fired-up compañeros, all armed to the teeth and ready to declare libertarian communism there and then. His paranoia went into overdrive. I've never seen anyone's face drain to grey so quickly. He had to sit down.

'Even though we have a large membership,' continued Segui, 'we knew we couldn't carry it off on our own. We were gambling that our actions would rouse the oppressed masses and trigger a wider popular movement—

and that the soldiers would join us, as they had done with the protestors in Russia in March. It seemed the only way to move things forward.

'We have no other way of protesting against persecution and suffering, or of resolving working-class grievances. As far as the bosses and the political elites are concerned labour protests are a law-and-order issue, and they deal with them accordingly. By taking the struggle onto the streets we at least preserved our dignity. The choice is simple: passive obedience in the face of oppression—or direct economic and armed resistance.

'When it became apparent last year that capitalism was fallible and failing we felt an almost tangible sense of euphoria. It seemed like one of those pivotal moments in history when it might just be possible to recreate the world anew. The oligarchs felt it too, but they sensed dread and foreboding. All we needed was a helpful push,' said Segui. 'People must have felt like that during the early days of the Paris Commune, or in the Easter Rising of 1916 in Dublin, when eight hundred poorly armed Irishmen held out for a week against almost six thousand British troops, or last year in Petrograd when the Russian workers seized the Winter Palace.'

BETRAYAL AND DEFEAT

But the strike plans were betrayed. It wasn't surprising, really; it was such a poorly kept secret, a joke in fact. Everyone and their grannies seem to have known about it beforehand. The moment the strike was declared on 14 August the entire strike committee in Madrid was arrested in an apartment in the aptly named Calle Desengaño (Disillusion Street). When the Special Services Brigade raided the flat, they found the strike committee hiding in wardrobes, under the bed and even inside a couple of large Ali Baba-type pots on the veranda. The Socialist Party and UGT leaders completely lost their nerve and within two days the strike throughout the central region—the UGT's stronghold—had collapsed, leaving the CNT everywhere else high and dry. We should have known better than trust the *políticos*, but to be fair we hadn't told them everything. In fact, we told them nothing of importance, certainly not that we intended launching an insurrection and had made plans to seize the telephone exchanges, telegraph offices, the public transport system, and public buildings and turn the national general strike into a revolution.

The Defence Commission estimated it would involve at least a week of street fighting and had put a lot of time, effort, and money into the plan. In fact, the CNT spent every last peseta it had on guns, ammunition, and explosives. As they say, God laughs at those who make plans. At least we lasted

El Turno politico —'Buggins' (Romanones) Turn': the procedure by which Spain's ruling elites retained power.

Francisco Largo Caballero (UGT).

Pablo Iglesias: PSOE/UGT.

'The King' by Helios Gómez.

SOLIDARIDAD OBRERA

El gran conflicto obrero

Las huelgas: El Arte Textil y Fabril. Los trabajadores del e
La huelga de los ferroviarios

ESTADO GENERAL DEL MOVIMIENTO OBRERO

La huelga ferroviaria

13 August 1917: martial law declared in the Catalan capital.

Army and Civil Guard (above) occupy the Plaça de Catalunya.

Madrid, August 1917: arrest of a striker (1).

Madrid, August 1917: arrest of a striker (2).

Madrid, August 1917: arrest of a striker (3).

Madrid, August 1917: strike by rail workers triggers the General Strike of 1917.

August 1917: Prime Minister Maura briefs King Alfonso XIII on the strike's latest developments.

Maura's Cabinet, August 1917.

Funeral, August 1917: not even the undertakers work during the General Strike.

Valencia, 13 August 1917: proclamation of military law.

Arrest of an anarchist.

Machine guns in Madrid's Cuatro Caminos.

Barcelona: army deploy canons in Plaça de Catalunya.

Montjuïc: imprisoned strikers.

Madrid, 13 August 1917: troops protect scab tram workers.

Sabadell: the army closes the local CNT premises.

Terrassa: strike committee (water branch).

Sabre charge against strikers in Madrid's Gran Via.

longer than the UGT, but the outcome was disastrous for us. In Barcelona, Zaragoza, Valencia, Bilbao, Santiago, and all the major industrial cities where the CNT had deep roots in the community, barricade committees held key points in the working-class *barris*. But there was no way our people could hold out on their own for any length of time against seasoned troops and the Guardia Civil, especially once the UGT called off its rail strike.

Amazingly—or perhaps not—the UGT, our fellow unionists, following orders from their Socialist Party masters, authorised their members to drive the troop trains carrying reinforcements for the military garrisons we were besieging in the north. This proved to be the fatal blow to our plans; the railway workers were a crucial source of direct power. All the lessons were there. In Russia, just six months earlier, during the uncertain period after the so-called 'bourgeois February revolution', it had been the railway work-ers' union, the Vikzhel (the All Russian Committee of the Union of Railroad Employees) that proved decisive in defeating General Kornilov's putsch by refusing to carry soldiers to Petrograd. Again, in October, when Kerensky fled from Petrograd seeking refuge with Krasnov's army after Lenin's coup, he was defeated by the Vikzhel threat to leave the troops stranded unless he, Kerensky, negotiated peacefully with the Bolsheviks, which of course he had no intention of doing. So this was in effect a demand for uncondi-tional surrender.

Ultimately, the August 1917 strike failed because Spain's middle-class socialists, Republicans, liberals, and the compromised UGT trade union leadership were more afraid of unleashing workers' power than they were of asserting their own democratic political rights against the conservative and traditionalist politicians and landowners who controlled the country, and who were determined to keep power out of the hands of the middle classes as well as those of the workers.

The strike was a fiasco and ended with an abject surrender by the workers' organisations to the army, handing total victory to the Employers' Federation. It proved to be another traumatic and humiliating event— alongside that of the Tragic Week of 1909—to be engraved in the collec-tive memory of the Spanish labour movement. It was a humiliation that we either had to live with for the rest of our lives—or seek to avenge. The fact was that apart from the removal of the government the CNT had nothing in common with the UGT who wanted to progress to a liberal/social dem-ocratic republic. The CNT, on the other hand, expected to install libertarian communism, taking over all productive and public wealth under workers' self-management with distribution according to need, leaving the capital-

ist with only three choices, abandoning class privilege, joining the opportunist gangs of armed bohemians to fight the workers' militias in order to
regain it, or fleeing to an uncertain future in exile.

AFTERMATH...

The repression that followed the general strike was barbaric. Spain's manufacturers, midlevel civil servants and middle classes were the loudest in
demanding that the military be called in to break the strike. Paradoxically,
these were the very people who, according to the classic Marxist model, were
supposed to be responsible for toppling the *ancien régime*, not bolstering it.

In Barcelona, thirty-seven people were killed and hundreds wounded.
Some working-class barris were taken only after days of street fighting. CNT
sharpshooters held off the army and Guardia Civil from rooftops, windows,
balconies, and barricades, but it was hopeless against the heavy artillery they
brought in. Most of the CNT halls, such as those in Sabadell and Manresa,
which were the centres of neighbourhood resistance, were reduced to piles
of dust and rubble.

By the time the dust had settled, across Spain a total of 250 people
were dead, 700 wounded, and over six thousand in police custody, most of
them anarchists and cenetistas. Many of these prisoners were manacled in
chains and leg-irons and marched across the country to prisons in Galicia
and the Basque country. As these columns of prisoners—'strings' they were
called—wound their way through the villages and towns of the northeast,
they were forced to pass crowds of spitting, jeering, and abusive right-wingers—Catholics, manic Carlists and ultra-*Catalanistas*. Women clutching rosa-
ries would run out and hit the manacled prisoners as they filed through the
streets. Militants, identified by priests and secret policemen located at regular intervals along this *via dolorosa*, were dragged from the 'string', stripped,
and publicly beaten with batons and belts by uniformed and plainclothes
policemen. All this had happened only eight months before I arrived, and
with many compañeros languishing in prison, bitter feelings still ran high.

It's impossible to say how many of those who took part in the uprising thought it would be successful, but everyone—including me—was convinced that the fall of capitalism was imminent. We just got our dates wrong!

FIRST PRINCIPLES!

Socialist theories of revolution conflict directly with the fundamental anarchist tenet that the central problem of human society is power. For anarchists, power is the beating heart of the State and government, and can

only be superseded by a mutualist society based on voluntary organisations. Marxists claim that history is rooted solely in the class struggle between the property-owners and the dispossessed. It isn't! Power is much more than mere economics and motivation; it is also a struggle between governors and subjects, between freedom and authority.

Anarchism's guiding principle has always been rooted in the idea that the principles of 'liberty' and 'justice' cannot be upheld through state power or by any authority principle—even with the most enlightened and liberal political leadership, including that of people claiming to be anarchists. This view was clearly spelled out at the first major anarchist congress held at St Imier, in September 1872:

> Being of the view that all political organisation cannot be anything other than the organisation of the rule of one class to the detriment of the masses, and that the proletariat, were it to attain power, would itself change into a ruling, exploiting class, Congress declares 1)—the destruction of all political power is the first duty of the proletariat 2)—any organisation of a political power styling itself provisional and revolutionary with that destruction as its objective can only be one more trick, thereby being as dangerous to the proletariat as every government presently in existence . . .

The experience of centuries shows only too clearly that whenever people entrust their fate to a central authority, that authority will always end up enslaving them. It is ironic how anarchists are often accused of having too optimistic and rosy a view of human nature when in fact they are the ones who understand that nature. They know only too well the immanent dangers of the drive for power—and the need to curtail it.

THE CNT AND ANARCHO-SYNDICALISM

The Confederación Nacional del Trabajo (CNT—National Confederation of Labour) was a national anticapitalist and aggressively revolutionary-syndicalist labour union founded in Barcelona in 1910. Its foundations had been laid in 1907 with the formation of Workers' Solidarity (Solidaridad Obrera), a citywide federation of socialist and anarchist labour unions firmly rooted in the informal but finely meshed social networks of the barris.

Directly democratic in structure, the union had no apparatus or bureaucracy that could be taken over by power-hungry factions. And although set up and guided by an anarchist and anarcho-syndicalist rank and file whose fundamental tenets were working-class solidarity, direct democracy, and direct action, the CNT was always a pluralist, nonsectarian body that welcomed members from across the political spectrum regardless of creed and politics. Membership encompassed socialists, Republicans, Marxists, trade unionists, Roman Catholics—and even Carlists.

As committed anarcho-syndicalists in an industry-based, early capitalist society, our political centre of gravity was the union, as opposed to political parties, parliamentary politics, or the state. The barri, the shop floor, and the economy were our battlefields, direct action our strategy of choice, and self-managed labour associations our preferred agencies for implementing workers' power. We organised by industry rather than craft or trade and didn't believe in concepts such as 'shared class interests'. To us class interests were irreconcilable. Our creed was the inescapability of the class struggle, that the state was a destructive force, that power corrupted—and that submission to force; manipulation or arbitrary authority was servitude.

While our short-term objectives were improving wages and conditions, our other immediate and long-term goal was to provide the collective organisation that would allow us to overthrow capitalism, outflank the state, and replace them with worker managed industries and directly democratic local and national councils—what we called libertarian or anarchist communism. The tension between these two objectives, however, created serious ongoing problems for the union, and for years the role of anarchists in unions had been a subject of heated debate between anarchist-communists and anarcho-syndicalists. Some anarchist groups, such as those affiliated to Barcelona's Bandera Negra Federation, weren't interested in the workers' struggle; instead they focused their energies into organising discussion groups and corresponding nationally and internationally with like-minded groups on every subject under the sun—except the class struggle. Actively hostile to labour unions, especially to the anarcho syndicalist CNT, their argument was that militants shouldn't involve themselves in movements for social reform or improving wages and working conditions. The anarchist's role, they insisted, was to promote the spirit of individual and collective revolt by constantly challenging and attacking the employers and the state through education, direct action, and propaganda of the deed.

'Reform is a function of the ruling class,' they argued, 'not something with which anarchists should concern themselves. The union's role is to ameliorate capitalism by seeking for its members immediate and partial improvements in pay and working conditions—which makes them complicit in maintaining the existing economic system, in all its manifestations and relations. Joining a union means entering into a mutually supportive partnership with capitalists, the privileged classes, and the state; it leads the unions into functioning as custodians and guardians of the organised working class.'

The Bandera Roja Federation of anarchist groups, on the other hand, supported revolutionary-syndicalism and anarcho-syndicalism, and its members, all of whom were affiliated to the CNT, played an important part in imbuing the union with anarchist values.

Despite the mutually contradictory goals, we believed that unions could defend and improve workers' rights, provide the means of overthrowing capitalism and, at the same time, prepare the workers intellectually for the revolutionary general strike as well as providing the framework for worker self-management in the new society. We hoped to achieve this through education, union organisation, and working-class solidarity, helping to over-come people's natural psychological fear of acting against those in power, with the result of the facing down of intransigent employers to the point where the whole immoral system that buttressed both state and capital-ism would collapse.

But we were also obliged to remember fundamental first principles! As anarchists outside the union, we had to act as anarchists inside the organ-isation. We could never be part of the leadership or assume any responsi-bility for administering the union, a contradictory position that created seri-ous problems when it came to choosing the best candidates for positions of responsibility within the organisation. Because we rejected power we had no choice but to leave the mechanics of it to others; all we could do was keep an ever-vigilant eye on our prominent committee members, marking their cards or revoking their mandates as necessary, while rotating offices as was practically possible without compromising effectiveness beyond the bounds of reason, in order to ensure they did not turn into 'Grand Inquisitors' or characters such as Dostoevsky's Pyotr Stepanovich Verkhovensky. As Plato observed in *The Republic*:

> Good men refuse to govern . . . I think that if ever there should exist
> a state exclusively of good men they would seek as much not to
> govern, as there are some now anxious to govern.

Hence the constant and unavoidable tension between, on the one hand, the militant rank and file and, on the other, the prominent union activists, pragmatic, utilitarian men like Segui, Pestaña, and many others, all honour-able men whose inborn charisma, organisational skills, and moral author-ity led them into positions of natural leadership. But no matter how radical or honourable they may have been, if they weren't 'reformist' to begin with, they inevitably became so; not because they had lost their belief in the Idea or the values of libertarian communism. No, they still clung fast to those values, at least philosophically. The issue was how to put those ideas into practice. Even the best-prepared compañeros fail to fully appreciate just how insidiously accommodating, seductive, and corrupting capitalism—and power—can be.

But 'notable' and competent militants such as Segui and Pestaña weren't the only ones drawn into the committees; there were others who had compromised with reality, the accommodations idealistic people often make, as they get older and lose faith in their ability to effect wholesale change—and when they need to pay their bills and feed their families. There were also those of considerably lesser moral fibre who actively sought positions of 'responsibility' and 'influence' within the union, men with 'administrative' or reformist mental processes but devoid of principles and with a hunger for office and power.

SANTS—A TURNING POINT

One problem facing the CNT in mid-1918 was that only a fifth or so of Spanish workers were involved in industry or commerce, and that considerably less than half the population could read or write. In the rural communities and adobe townships of Andalusia and Extremadura, the priests and landowners' agents, the *caciques*—Spain's mandarin class—acted like feudal overlords, ruling their great estates like personal fiefdoms, through fear, ignorance, intimidation, and violence. Life for agricultural day labourers was indistinguishable from serfdom, and woe betide any union organiser found on their land. To the *caciques*, labour unions were the agencies of the Beast, and union organisers were his earthly emissaries to be cast out like demons.

The Sants Regional Congress of the CNT, held over the weekend of 28 June to 1 July 1918 in the Rationalist Athenaeum at 12 Calle de Vallespir, in the southwesterly working-class suburb of Sants, coincided with the height of the 'American' influenza pandemic. The authorities tried to sabotage the event by flooding the streets around the ateneu with uniformed police and Guardia Civil in an attempt to intimidate delegates. Informers and secret policemen of the Special Services Brigade were also out and about, identifying and arresting known militants on trumped-up charges. Among those arrested was Pedro Vandellós, a close friend of Ramón Archs, and a defence groups coordinator. Vandellós was one of Bravo Portillo's particular bogeymen. The previous January Bravo Portillo had tried—and failed—to frame him for the murders of Barret and Pastor. It had been a thinly disguised attempt to cover Bravo Portillo's own involvement in the murders and lay the blame for the killings at the door of the anarcho-syndicalists, but with no real evidence the court had had to acquit Vandellós.

The Sants Congress was a great success, particularly with regard to the overwhelming acceptance by the members of the new anarcho-syndicalist *sindicatos únicos*, industrial unions modelled along the lines of the North American Wobblies. By establishing grassroots *comités de barriada* (neighbourhood committees)—community-based unions and groups that were the eyes and ears of the union in every neighbourhood, and the principal point of contact between the barris and the local federation, which determined union strategy—the new structure strengthened the union and made it much more effective at city level. And by making full use of improvements in the means of communication—the municipal transport system, the greater availability of bicycles and *Solidaridad Obrera*'s enormous circulation—the local federation could quickly advertise meetings, and receive feedback from and send instructions to the neighbourhood committees. This enabled the sindicatos únicos to respond rapidly to events on the ground, allowing them to mount a more sustained and coordinated opposition to capitalism.

The CNT's strategy to deal with the new world order that would emerge from the Great European War had been the collective brainchild of Salvador Segui, Ángel Pestaña, and Evelio Boal, who convinced the membership to adopt the idea of a confederation of industrial unions—as opposed to individual trade unions. The woodworkers' and the foodworkers' unions had already taken on board the One Big Union idea and had become the standard-bearers of the new sindicatos únicos.

SINDICATOS ÚNICOS AND INDUSTRIAL UNIONS

After Sants, the sindicato único—the local union branch—became the basic unit of the CNT. It was divided into sections by trade, and linked within a local or provincial federation; the local and provincial federations of each region being linked through their respective CRT, or Regional Confederation of Labour. The idea was to unite all skilled and unskilled workers in any particular industry, thereby breaking down the old craft and trade divisions that had previously weakened working-class solidarity. The únicos were decentralized, self-contained organisations based on the principles of direct democracy as practised in large, open, rank-and-file assemblies—the opposite of the hierarchical and centralised socialist labour unions.

Above: Sometent auxilliaries on patrol and right, Sometent Feast Day in the Plaça de Catalunya.

Sometent church parade, San Bois.

'El Sometent' by Helios Gómez.

Left: CNT founding Congress, 1910. Below: Eusebio C. Carbó, Simó Piera, and Balbina Pi, well-known militants and public speakers, were imprisoned on many occasions over the years. Carbó, for example, was arrested more than sixty times. Salvador Quemades, a member of the Catalan Regional Committee of the CNT, was also a public speaker of considerable note. Evelio Boal and Manuel Buenacasa were general secretaries of the CNT.

Eusebio C. Carbó.

Evelio Boal.

Salvador Seguí.

Ángel Pestaña.

Salvador Quemades.

Manuel Buenacasa.

Bruno Lladó.

Balbina Pi.

Each sindicato único elected a section or administrative committee responsible for issues specific to the union. For areas broader than the sindicato único, there were to be regular congresses attended by a delegate from each member organisation. National congresses were to be held every year, but because of the sustained repression this proved to be rarely possible. These national congresses took decisions on matters of national interest, organisational structure, international relations, and, of course, Confederation policy.

Decisions taken by a national congress, where voting power depended on the number of members of each union, could only be overturned by another national congress. However, because of the difficulties and dangers associated with holding regional and national congresses, plenums were often held instead. These regional meetings could be attended only by delegates from the different local or regional federations, while only regional committee delegates could attend national plenums.

Also, conscious of the dangers of bureaucratisation, reformism, and parliamentarianism, the únicos refused to amass strike funds, preferring instead direct action, class solidarity, and strike actions based on direct and secondary picketing, as well as collective actions such as boycotts. And although each único was sovereign, there was total solidarity between the various únicos in different industries, especially during strikes and industrial disputes. In areas where there wasn't much industry or where the CNT had a limited presence, one único brought together all cenetistas in the area under one umbrella. It was a loose structure designed to allow the unions to resist employer intimidation and state repression.

Whenever a strike committee member was arrested, as was almost inevitable, other activists were always ready to step in to take their place, wave after wave of them. The shop steward—the *delegado del taller*—was the key person in the único as he was the only one authorised to call a stoppage whenever asked to do so by the membership.

Each único elected a sectional committee and delegated a representative to the local federation, which became the main discussion forum for all CNT unions in any particular town or city. Local federations reported to a regional committee, the final level before the national committee itself. Most importantly of all, the higher committees had no direct control over the shop stewards, who were answerable only to the union rank and file at shop floor level. Industrial unions embraced all workers in different jobs in a given area—but in the same industry.

After Sants, CNT membership was divided between thirteen industrial branches, or *ramos*. While the number of strikes could be reduced, the disputes could also be longer and the movement's strength greater. Almost overnight, the CNT became imbued with a revolutionary fervour that transformed it from a collection of weak and disunited unions sustained by small groups of activists into a powerful mass organisation.

REBIRTH OF THE CNT

Among the many resolutions passed at Sants, perhaps the most important was the decision to launch a nationwide propaganda and recruitment drive targeting Spain's agricultural workers. And when the congress ended—on a euphoric high given that everyone was convinced capitalism was on its last legs and the final struggle was at hand—the finest and most inspiring speakers in the anarchist and anarcho-syndicalist movement went off to organise in the most out-of-the-way corners of the peninsula.

The focus of this CNT road show was the agrarian south, mainly because of the regional congresses of agricultural workers taking place that summer and autumn. In Catalonia itself the recruitment drive proved particularly successful, with most unions in the region queuing to affiliate to Spain's new One Big Union.

It was the extraordinarily rapid growth of the Catalan Regional Committee of the CNT, better known as the Catalan Confederación Regional del Trabajo (CRT)—from a relatively insignificant union of around 15,000 in 1915 to its 1918 size of 74,000—55,000 of whom came from Barcelona itself—that had necessitated the organisational restructuring. By the end of September 1918, CNT membership in Catalonia had increased to 114,000, with over 70,000 paid-up members in Barcelona alone. Within a year, national membership was well over 800,000 and the sindicato único had replaced the reformist UGT as the workingman's union of choice.

By October 1918, the question of the CNT's political orientation had become so important that the Spanish anarchist groups convened a national conference to thrash out their divided attitudes towards the union. Some of those generally thought of as 'ideologically purist' anarchists—such as the writer Joan Montseny (better known by his pen name Federico Urales) and his daughter Federica, labelled as 'liberals' by their opponents—disliked the CNT intensely and denounced anarcho-syndicalism as 'deviationism'. Fortunately, wiser counsels prevailed, mainly through the support of veteran anarchist and revolutionary syndicalists such as Manuel Buenacasa—who was also the secretary of the CNT National Committee—which led to most anarchist workers joining the union. Many of these comrades tended to be influenced by insurrectionary 'Malatestan' or 'Galleanisti' ideas and were firm supporters of 'propaganda by the deed', tending to focus on forming defence groups, the affinity or action groups within the CNT—in other words, ad-hoc urban guerrillas.

Meanwhile, labour associations and federations across the country were affiliating en masse to the CNT. Indeed, so successful was the union's recruitment drive that the government tried to disrupt the campaign by introducing internment without trial—*detención gubernativa*—which gave the police the power to arrest and hold anyone without charge for up to fifteen days on the say-so of the civil governor. The police could apply and reapply for extension orders at the end of every fifteen-day period, which meant that activists could be held for months and even years without trial.

Delegates at the Sants Congress also unanimously endorsed, as the new editor of *Solidaridad Obrera*, Ángel Pestaña whose closing speech reflected the revolutionary mood of the times:

> After this Congress it is not just bread we shall be demanding from the capitalist system. From now on we demand justice, equality— and control of the means of production and distribution. We do not deny anyone the right to life, but neither will we accept that this right should be denied to us.

THE LEEDS CONFERENCE

Sants was similar in many ways to a revolutionary socialist conference at Leeds in Britain, in June 1917, the previous year. The agenda there had also been dominated by discussions on workers' control, industrial democracy, syndicalism, and the destruction of capitalism—with delegates urged to promote the organisation of workers' and soldiers' committees, similar to those that had emerged earlier that year in Russia, and on the Eastern Front. Another proposal had been to divide Britain into thirteen Soviets coordinated by a self-appointed Central Committee.

The Leeds Conference struck the fear of God into the British Cabinet and the British Secret Service Bureau, who chose to believe that the exaggerated revolutionary rhetoric of some of the delegates represented the majority view of popular working-class opinion—which I suppose it did to some extent, certainly within the organised labour movement.

The February Revolution in Russia that year came as a bolt from the blue to the British Cabinet. Now, with the tumultuous events of the 'July Days' in Russia, there was real fear that revolution would spread to Britain. Lord Curzon, the insufferably arrogant and patronising former viceroy of

India and the new leader of the House of Lords, had completely misjudged the situation in Russia. A few days before the February Revolution he presented a report to Lloyd George's War Cabinet, stressing the 'childlike nature of the Russians', arguing that they too were the victims of the German 'hidden hand':

> That class [referring to the workers] is very much perturbed in mind at the moment. It is very restless and easily swayed, and is exposed to German and pro-German influences at every point of the compass, some open, many clandestine. The Tsar will remain in power, and as far as the purely political aspect of the matter is concerned, I have formed the opinion that the talk of army disloyalty is greatly exaggerated. The autocracy is the only sector holding Russia together, and it will take at least a generation to organise anything in its place. The danger currently threatening Russia is not so much deliberate revolution as chaos!

NATIONAL PROPAGANDA, THE NAVY LEAGUE, THE ANTISOCIALIST UNION

Curzon couldn't have been more wrong. The British Central Committee met only twice. Its first meeting was well attended by trade union and women delegates sent by their various organisations to find out what the Committee was about. The meeting was attacked and broken up by a mob of vigilantes incited to violence by the *Daily Express* and members of various proto-Fascist National Propaganda-led networks of imperialist and private right-wing groups such as the Navy League, the Anti-Socialist Union, and the British Empire Union.

National Propaganda, the lead mover in all these machinations, was a cabal of influential extreme right-wing Conservatives, obsessed with the threat of revolution and the prospect of a 'left-wing' postwar parliament elected by radicalised and disenchanted ex-servicemen looking to the Russian Revolution for inspiration.

National Propaganda, which acted as a central coordinating body for a multitude of covert and extralegal operations, had two objectives: according to its publicly stated position, its primary role was to educate British workers on the dangers of socialism, but its real—albeit covert—aim was to set up the framework of a parallel secret state, one that was beyond parliamentary and governmental control. It was no longer a question of protecting elite government from the people; the state itself now had to be protected from a 'left-wing' government. Other National Propaganda sidelines included providing a domestic strikebreaking organisation and a 'counter-subversion' intelligence-gathering operation that was much bigger and more efficient than that of the state.

VERNON KELL AND 'THE DIEHARDS'

Sir Vernon George Waldegrave Kell, then head of MI5, was another 'superior person' who shared George Curzon's view of the working class as naïve simpletons. Briefing the British Cabinet on the subject, the security service chief spelled out his views on the radicalisation of British workers:

> Socialism is a movement of poor and illiterate people corrupted and
> taken over by militants. They are also malleable, fickle and easy prey
> for German spies and provocateurs fomenting industrial unrest.

This narrow vision of the shallow character of the British working class was also held by Kell's other intelligence services colleagues, all of them members of the Conservative Party's 'Diehards', groups of radical right-wingers: his boss, General Sir George McDonough; Director of British Intelligence, Sir George Cockerill; Director of Special Intelligence of the General Staff of the British War Office, Sir William 'Blinker' Hall; Director of Naval Intelligence, Admiral Sir Hugh 'Quex' Sinclair of the Special Intelligence Service [MO5(a)]; and the totally paranoid and off-the-wall ultra-reactionary Basil Thomson, head of Scotland Yard's Special Branch. Thomson was so obsessed by the threat from organised labour and the possibility of revolution prior to the Kaiser's War, that he actually argued, in 1913, that a European war was the only way to avoid revolution. If he thought like that in 1913, you can imagine how he felt in 1918. Addressing one meeting of the Diehards, he said:

> The only way to deal with the rabble is to suppress and repress them.
> A single fox will clear out a hen roost while it is cackling its indigna-
> tion to the skies. Just think, if Louis the Sixteenth had mounted his
> horse and charged the mob there might have been no Thermidor.

THE 'HIDDEN HAND'

Formed in 1916 to combat suspected German sabotage in the munitions industries, the Department of Intelligence and Statistics of the British Ministry of Munitions (MMDIS), like Topsy, was one of those organisations that just grew and kept on growing.

William Melville, cofounder of British Secret Service Bureau.

Sir Arthur Henry Hardinge, British ambassador to Spain 1913–1919.

Captain Sir Mansfield Smith Cumming RN, first head of MI6.

Sants Regional Congress of the Confederación Regional del Trabajo (CRT-CNT): 28 June–1 July 1918.

Top and below: after Sants, the agricultural workers' unions of Andalusia increasingly federated with the CNT's sindicatos únicos as anarchist influence grew. In Córdoba Province alone there were 184 strikes during 1918.

Following a series of explosions in a number of munitions factories in the UK, some of which, if not all, were potentially accidental, Churchill and Lloyd George played the 'enemy within' card, and claimed it was the work of what they called the German 'hidden hand'. Of this no evidence was ever found. So, in order to prove its efficiency and value as a spy-catcher, MMDIS gave up trying to find German saboteurs by 1917, and focused instead on easier targets. Home-grown subversives, such as radical shop stewards, became the real enemy. When questions began to be asked about the agency's illegal and extralegal tactics MMDIS changed its name to the more reassuring-sounding Parliamentary Military Section 2, or PMS2 for short.

MMDIS and PMS2's spies and provocateurs were mainly military personnel or lowlifes recruited through the right-wing strikebreaking organisation National Propaganda. For a body allegedly sworn to uphold the law, PMS2's methods were not only immoral, shameful, and malign; they were downright illegal. Unable to identify, much less capture any German agents, or expose any organised revolutionary threat in Britain, they manufactured their own by concocting a plot to kill Lloyd George and one of his ministers, Arthur Henderson. The conspiracy was exposed and the agency was quietly disbanded and reabsorbed into the security service, MI5. Their plan had been to frame a radical socialist suffragette by the name of Alice Wheeldon by entrapping her into sending curare through the post to the two politicians. The plot was the brainchild of PMS2 supremo Colonel Frederick Labouchère, his deputy, Major William Lauriston Melville Lee, and two of their top agents—William Rickard, also known as 'Alex Gordon' and Herbert Booth. Wheeldon, their victim, spent years in prison, as did her daughter and son-in-law before they were eventually released following a series of hunger strikes. Wheeldon died soon after her release from prison.

John S. Clarke, the socialist writer and agitator, openly accused Lloyd George of responsibility for her death:

> There are a number of ways of murdering our valiant women comrades. There is the straightforward, brutal way of sheer murder, such as that which killed Rosa Luxembourg . . . the other is the more secret, sinister, cowardly and slower method such as that which Lloyd George used to kill Mrs Wheeldon.

THE OLIGARCHS TREMBLE...

Just as the British Cabinet had been shaken by the industrial unionism and revolutionary ideas discussed at the 1917 Leeds Conference, the Spanish employers' federation, the Fomento Nacional del Trabajo, was horrified by the rapid growth of the reorganised and reinvigorated CNT of 1918. Equally fearful were Spain's arrogant and brutal aristocrats, its venal Church prelates, the talentless incompetents of the officer class who owed their rank solely to birth or their family's ability to buy promotion, the bourgeois Catalan nationalists of the Lliga, the militant Carlist zealots, the Sometent and all the other so-called 'vital forces' that constituted the Catalan and Spanish haute monde.

Bloody revolution threatened, and the sindicatos únicos of the CNT were the enemy at the gate. To defeat them they had no choice but to put aside their internal squabbles and differences. And although there was never any violence or intimidation in any of the CNT's recruitment campaigns, the employers opted for draconian counterrevolutionary police measures, treating union membership as a matter of law and order, rather than engaging politically with the union.

For the oligarchs there could be no compromise, no surrender—the sindicatos únicos had to be destroyed. And behind every act of public violence, every move to curtail liberty, every judicial murder, there stood a bishop, who either in his pastoral role or as a leader-writer in the Catholic 'yellow' press, showed his approval—and called for more!

THE CNT DEFENCE GROUPS

The CNT defence groups—the autonomous action groups—usually consisted of around five of six friends, sometimes more, sometimes less, but all of them well known to each other and trusted. They were almost impossible to infiltrate. An important function of these informally structured groups was to defend the economic and social interests of fellow union members and the barris, by taking up grievances and resisting acts of injustice, usually by robust and clandestine means but always through direct action. Their other, more general objective was spreading the Idea through education, but always working to undermine Spain's neo-feudal capitalist regime and replace it with a society founded on federalist and self-management principles of libertarian communism.

The men and women involved in these groups bore no resemblance whatsoever to the ludicrous, fanatical, rootless, and burning-eyed bohemian caricatures portrayed by Dostoevsky in *The Possessed*, Conrad in *The Secret Agent*, G.K. Chesterton in *The Man Who Was Thursday*, or Henry James in *The Princess Casamassima*. Nor were they professional déclassé agitators like Adam Weishaupt, Philippe Buonarroti, Louis Auguste Blanqui, Lenin, or Trotsky, or even fanciful literary demons such as Dostoevky's Nikolai Stavrogin or Conrad's Mr Verloc. They were pragmatic, ordinary people who worked hard for a living, and who believed, passionately, that a better world was not only possible but also achievable, and—in the face of so much misery, corruption, and injustice—urgently needed. They were decent human beings—idealists, in the truest sense of the word—people who understood the ethics of ends and means, embraced humanitarian ideals of solidarity with enthusiasm, and valued actions that would both deepen the understanding among the oppressed of the nature of the social problem and increase their confidence in their ability to solve it themselves through collective action.

They also believed in actions that confronted the state and capitalism. I don't think I came across one politically aware worker who didn't applaud the actions carried out by the defence groups in those years. In fact they looked upon them almost with a degree of class pride as proletarian avengers. Direct action was, in effect, the only means by which ordinary workers could meaningfully engage in a political process sustained by courts-martial, brutal repression 'legitimised' by regularly declared states of emergency, the suspension of constitutional rights and 'judicial' or 'executive' murder. Short of the general strike, direct action was the only way workers could hold to account a murderous clericalism, an arrogant officer class, corrupt politicians, reactionary self-replacing governments, and a brutal, malign state run unashamedly in the interests of the country's ruthless and ludicrously short-sighted capitalist and land-owning elites. As Welsh miners' leader and workers' control advocate Noah Ablett said regarding direct action: 'Why cross the river to fill the bucket?' Nor was parliament a check on public abuses. It was the façade behind which corrupted politicians bowed to expediency and ran their scams with impunity.

> Only by making the ruling few uneasy can the oppressed obtain a particle of relief.

With a few notable exceptions, the defence groups had strong roots in their local communities. Members tended to belong to the same union branch or ateneu and kept themselves to themselves, rarely crossing barri boundaries. This made them, in effect, impenetrable in organisation and inscrutable in motivation, at least to the ruling classes. A long time ago Sun Tzu noted: 'If you do not know who the enemy is, you cannot win the war.' They were also 100 percent working-class. Students, in those days, were drawn almost entirely from the privileged classes and were, on the whole, as in

Glasgow, right-wing conservatives who not only played no part in the movement, but also were actively hostile to it. In fact, until the big tertiary education changes of the early 1960s, most students I encountered were out-
and-out reactionaries who were affiliated to the Sometent, Carlists, Catholic
Integrists, or some other royalist, nationalist, or separatist movement. As
Friedrich Paulson, a late nineteenth-century German professor of education observed: 'It is only in unhealthy societies that students take the lead
in political agitation'—not that Castilian or Catalan bourgeois society could
in any way have been described as 'healthy'.

Of the two dozen or so action groups operating in Barcelona during
that period, the 'Calle Toledo' and the 'Metal' groups were the most active.
Members of the different groups tended not to know each other; the only
people with links to most of the key activists in the groups—of whom there
were about two hundred at the time—were Archs and Vandellós, and that
was on a purely informal and personal basis because of their role on the CNT
Defence Commission. In Spain's deep south, however, the Andalusian action
groups in the adobe townships where the priest was king organised themselves differently, forming shadowy guerrilla armies of the disaffected to
protect the ruthlessly exploited landless agricultural day labourers—'village
Hamdens' and 'inglorious Miltons' championing the oppressed against local
feudal tyrants—against the terratenientes, landlords' bailiffs, the caciques,
and venal ecclesiastics. They were similar in many ways to the shadowy
'Horseman's Grip' society, a loose-knit body of agricultural day labourers
who operated across rural Scotland around the same time, burning hayricks
and barns, and generally putting the fear of God into the big landowners.

LAWYERS AND POLITICIANS

Perhaps the most distinguishing features of revolutionary syndicalism were
its commitment to direct democracy and its rejection of power politics, parliamentarianism, and those political parties who claimed to speak for the
workers. Direct democracy has nothing to do with 'liberal' or 'parliamentary' democracy; in fact it is the exact opposite. Like the Presbyterian and
Covenanting tradition in which I had been brought up, direct democracy
functioned without intermediaries such as politicians, priests, and prelates; all mandated delegates were subject to instant recall should they act
against the people's will.

Revolutionary syndicalism's greatest significance derived from the clear
way in which it recognised the oligarchic dangers of all institutionalised
power structures: power exercised by the State, as Goethe said in one of

his commentaries, can never be anything more than power exercised by a minority:

> Nothing is more odious than the majority, for it consists of a few powerful leaders, a certain number of accommodating scoundrels and submissive weaklings, and a mass of men who trudge after them without thinking, or knowing their own minds.

The refusal to negotiate or collaborate with the State or political parties reflected the revolutionary syndicalist rejection of the orthodox Marxist position adopted by the social democratic parties of the Second International before the Kaiser's War. As Bakunin pointed out, any workers joining a revolutionary government would, de facto, become ex-workers. It was the focus on politics that led to socialist movements and labour parties everywhere being dominated by a middle-class elite who lacked any working-class connections, from high-minded elitists and sordid careerists to cunning scoundrels and opportunistic rascals—journalists, lawyers, intellectuals, would-be professional politicians who wanted working people to delegate power to them—on the strength of a promise to act in their 'best interests'. As a result they succeeded in imposing a centralised, bureaucratic, and ultimately passive mentality on the socialist movement, corrupting, suborning, and subjugating it to their own selfish interests. It was precisely to thwart—or at least hinder—the creation of such elites that the CNT adopted its horizontal organisational structure, as opposed to the more traditional pyramid structure, in which individual unions maintained independence of action and decision-making on issues directly affecting them. The decision-making process moved along through the Organisation as opposed to being dictated from above.

There were many anarcho-syndicalist and revolutionary syndicalist organisations around the world at that time. Some, such as the French Confédération Générale du Travail (CGT), claimed to be politically neutral, leaving it to individual members to act according to their political beliefs—but always outside the framework of the union. The CNT, however, was specifically anarcho-syndicalist inasmuch as it was apolitical, antiparliamentarian, libertarian, and committed to overthrowing capitalism and the State. Above all, its rank-and-file militants understood the fundamentally conservative nature of power and constantly tried to guard against the political dynamic by which all organisations move from being a means to an end to becoming an end in themselves. It was for precisely this reason that the anarchist founders of the CNT insisted on not having full-time or paid officials.

The influence and watchfulness of the anarchist rank and file meant a high degree of awareness of the hierarchical and oligarchic consequences of organisation—even within the most anarchistic, socialistic, and idealistic of bodies. Like some hands-on Greek chorus, much of our time was spent guarding against the dangers of power, and checking oligarchic tendencies and the formation of elites within our ranks, at least until late 1936 when the struggle against Fascism and the political machinations of the Stalinists unleashed the demons of opportunism in the shallow souls of those compañeros who thought they could be government ministers and remain anarchists.

Even so, despite emphasising the equality of all CNT members, the same names kept reappearing on the regional and national committees. The reality of the situation was that although, theoretically, all members had an equal say in union policy, some people—because of their charisma, experience, drive, intellect, or whatever—were consistently more active and exerted more moral authority than others.

Again, it was the Ulsterman Wee John McAra who explained the process to me. We had been discussing the then recently published book *Political Parties*, by the German political sociologist Robert Michels, about how democracy functions within large-scale organisations and institutions:

'Michels argues that it is organisation that gives rise to the power of the elected over the electors, and of the delegates over the delegators. When you say organisation, you say oligarchy. The problem,' he continued, 'is that the oligarchic dangers of democracy can never be entirely avoided; even so, we have always to choose democracy as the lesser of all political evils. Our role as anarchists, however, must always be that of the outsider—questioning, criticising, or challenging the power and the decisions of all political leaders, bureaucracies, and authority figures   constantly pushing back the boundaries of the possible.'

Although the anarcho-syndicalists were the moral driving force within the CNT, far from all its 250,000 members at the time were committed anarcho-syndicalists. In fact the number of activists was relatively small; many were merely sympathetic to anarchism, but most were content to let the militants play the dominant role in the decision-making process, letting them stick their heads above the parapet. Others—the Marxists, social democrats, Catholics and Carlists in the CNT—were hostile and resistant to anarchist influence, wanting that influence for themselves. But they also operated on the principle of 'least said, soonest mended' and tended to keep their opinions to themselves, biding their time for the most propitious moment to make their moves. Even so, the wide readership of the confederal press, the size of audiences at its public meetings and the support for the strike actions it organised showed that a large percentage of CNT members were genuinely interested in the outcomes of the debates.

Remember, too, that although anarcho-syndicalist militants were highly respected members of the community with significant moral authority and influence in the barris and the union locals, it would have been impossible for their ideas to predominate without support from the wider membership, something the minority factions within the CNT—those who wanted the union to be 'independent' of anarchist influence as well as that of other political groups (i.e., to control it themselves!)—never achieved.

RAMÓN ARCHS SERRA

Ramón Archs Serra, a former secretary of the CNT's Metalworkers' Union, had been an active unionist and revolutionary since his teens. He was one of that breed who always returned to revolutionary activity, no matter what the certainty of exposure and punishment. Ramón was just seven years old when his father, Manuel Archs, also an anarchist, was executed by firing squad in the trench at Montjuïc on 18 May 1894, framed for his alleged role in the 1893 bombing of the Liceo Theatre—a 'settling of accounts' by Salvador Franch for the massacre of Jerez peasants—and an assassination attempt on General Martínez Campos. Manuel Archs was executed alongside Paulíno Pallás, Cerezuela, and Bernat Sirerol.

Archs's first experience of prison was in 1908 as a result of a labour dispute at Hispano-Suiza's Rablons factory. Arrested again the following year during Barcelona's Tragic Week, he was charged with attempted murder but the case was dropped for lack of evidence. In 1910 he was accused of shooting a member of the Employers' Federation who had been bussing in scabs during a strike against the powerful Mateu family, owners of a huge foundry who dominated the Catalan iron industry. Archs believed the quickest way to settle the strike was to get rid of the company's recalcitrant 'diehard' manager, which was why he and two compañeros walked into the administration building of the Maquinista Terrestre y Maritima factory and shot and wounded the managing director, Tous.

Arrested and charged with this shooting in mid-1912, Archs was tried and acquitted, but with the CNT again outlawed and knowing the police would be looking for any opportunity to arrest or kill him, he decided discretion was the better part of valour and moved to Paris. There he regularly attended the lectures given by the anarchist encyclopaedist Sébastien

Faure, whom he admired enormously. It was at these meetings and social gatherings that he linked up with the survivors of the notorious French and Belgian 'illegalist' anarchist groups, including former members of the Bonnot Gang and Marius Jacob's 'Night Workers', the hundred-plus strong band of anarchists known as Les Travailleurs de la Nuit credited with burgling at least 150 churches and homes of prominent members of the French and Belgian haut monde. (Jacob became the model for Maurice Leblanc's fictional character Arsène Lupin.)

In 1915, the French police issued a warrant for Archs's arrest in connection with the assassination of a particularly brutal Sometent leader during a visit to Paris. The vigilante in question was a truly evil piece of work. With his gang of Carlist thugs he had broken into the apartment of a prominent CNT militant in Manresa in the early hours of the morning, hauled the sleeping man from his bed, tied him to their car, and dragged him through the streets to the outskirts of the town where they used his body for target practice.

As the gendarmes forced their way through Archs's apartment door in Paris, he escaped through the back window, shinning down a drainpipe, and caught the first train from the Gare de Lyon to Marseilles where he took a taxi to the Saint Nicolas fortress and joined the French Foreign Legion, the then newly formed Régiment de Marche de la Légion Etrangèr (RMLE), with which he served three years. He fought at Verdun and was involved in the 1917 Luffaux mutiny over officer incompetence and the impossible battles they were expected to fight. Pushed to the limits of their endurance, he and the other men in his company finally decided they'd had enough and refused to return to the front line. The punishment for this act of mutiny was decimation, the execution by firing squad of every tenth man—*pour encourager les autres!* Archs was lucky to survive, but by the beginning of 1918 he had had enough and settled accounts, at least partially, by shooting dead the colonel responsible for suppressing the 'antiwar soldiers' council' set up the previous June by a French infantry regiment in the town of Missy aux Bois.

Escaping from the French military police, again with only minutes to spare, Archs returned to Spain with the help of the French and Belgian anarchist networks. Although he had only been back in Barcelona a few months when I came on the scene that April, he was already one of the leading lights in the Metalworkers' Union, a coordinator—with Simó Piera and Pedro Vandellós—of the CNT's ad-hoc defence groups.

Although diplomacy, negotiation, and compromise were never Ramón Archs's strong points, he was careful, prudent, and imaginative when it came to organising actions. Stories about his exploits were legion. One of his more spectacular coups occurred during the preparations for the Sometent militia's feast day. An altar had been set up to celebrate Mass in the Plaça de Catalunya with a review stand at the junction between the Paseo de Gracia and the Gran Via, where the Sometent bigwigs were assembled, including most of the general staff from the Barcelona garrison along with ranking members of Catalonia's civil and ecclesiastical establishment. Suddenly, a driverless car with a brick on the accelerator and a tied steering wheel careered down the Calle Corts towards the stand and crashed into a lamppost, sending the cream of Catalan society running for their lives. Inside the wreck of the car they found a two-foot-tall brass bell packed with explosives that had failed to detonate.

SALVADOR SEGUI RUBINAT

Salvador Segui was, arguably, the most astute and popular Spanish labour leader of his time. A painter by trade, he was the fighting sage of the movement: secretary of the Barcelona CNT's Construction Workers' Union, and a founder member of both the forerunner of the CNT, Solidaridad Obrera, and the Ateneu Sindicalista, a labour union education centre. He possessed, usually, a great gift for rational judgment and was a firm believer in what he called 'principled compromise' in the interests of working-class unity. His blind spot was the flawed assumption that the UGT and Socialist Party leaders were equally honourable and principled men. Segui had supported the CNT/UGT socialist alliance in 1910 and, in spite of their repeated betrayals, continued to broker agreements between the two unions in 1916 and again in 1917. He remained adamant, however, that the CNT should remain independent of all political parties and organisations, including anarchist groups, even though he described himself as a committed anarchist.

Born in 1887 in Lérida, a northern province adjoining Andorra, he was very young when his family moved to Barcelona where, as a twelve-year-old apprentice painter, he was drawn to the ideas of anarchism. First convicted at the age of fifteen during a metalworkers' strike, by the time he was seventeen, Segui—whose byname was 'El noi del sucre' ('Sugar Boy')—had become a 'weel kent' face in the local police stations, magistrates courts, and in many of Barcelona's working-class barris. The 'Sugar Boy' sobriquet had nothing to do with any predilection he may have had for sweeties and the good life, but because he had worked, briefly, in a sugar mill before learning his trade as a 'painter with a large brush'.

Like many young men across the generations, Segui had been a delinquent in his adolescent years, one of the estimated eight to ten thousand *trinxeraires* (street gang members) in the city at the time. Later in life he was haunted by the ghosts of what he felt was a shameful period in his 'incorrigible' youth, especially his involvement, as a fourteen-year-old, with one of the most notorious gangs, a *pandilla* called 'Els fills de putas' ('The Sons of Bitches') who roamed the streets like the Golden Horde, looking for trouble. These volatile, unruly and unbiddable Barcelonan teenagers, like gangs in Govan and everywhere, had their own dress codes, rituals, street corners, and territory centred around the bars and cafés near the Theatre Arch in Barcelona's notorious Fifth Quarter—an area well-known for its villains and lowlifes. There they threatened all and sundry with the slogan: 'We're the Sons of Bitches! Who dares take us on?'

Always ready to fight to defend their status, they never accepted 'no' for an answer and set upon anyone they believed to be disrespectful or who challenged their authority, stabbing them or beating them senseless. Definitely not the sort of testosterone-driven characters you would choose to sit next to on the top deck of a tram. One of the gang's more positive political pastimes, however, was baiting the poisonous Republican demagogue Alexander Lerroux: heckling and shouting abuse at him, breaking up his public meetings, accusing him of being an agent provocateur—which was true, but Lerroux wasn't used to having his own tactics turned against himself.

Ironically, it was Lerroux's rhetorical techniques and use of emotive language to persuade—'false rhetoric' as Segui described it—that fascinated the future union leader and made him determined to become a master of the spoken word; not with a view to obfuscation or manipulating his audience as Lerroux did, but to enlighten and persuade. Segui travelled great distances to listen and learn from the great orators and debaters of the day: on street corners and in political and cultural *tertúlius* (gatherings) in bars, cafés, and ateneus or in people's front rooms.

Inspired by the great Roman writers, Quintilian and Cicero, Segui read everything he could on the subject, and in his *tertúlias*, Segui often quoted from Cicero's *De Oratore*:

> The man who can hold forth on every matter under debate in two contradictory ways of pleading, or can argue for and against every proposition that can be laid down—such a man is the true, the complete, and the only orator.

I remember hearing that a young Guy Aldred did exactly this, after he had abandoned being a boy preacher. The subject—unsurprisingly—was the existence of God.

Segui, however, was a true rhetor, a master of eloquence, mainly as a protest against the example provided by Alexander Lerroux, whose language was always exceptionally abusive and provocative. Lerroux was a nasty, mean, arrogant, podgy demagogue with an enormous walrus moustache who employed his undoubted oratorical talents to harangue and bully his ignorant, lumpen listeners to 'take to the streets' and 'man the barricades'— but with no other purpose than diverting working-class people away from the real social and economic issues of the day. He wasn't interested in engaging in public debate or shining a light on the contentious issues of the day; it was mob manipulation at its most blatant. He was good at pandering to the popular hatred of the Church, ranting at audiences with his grating voice, urging them to vent their fury by sacking and burning the churches, convents and monasteries, murdering the priests and monks—and raping nuns to 'raise them to the status of mothers'! His tactics were much the same as those used against the Jews by a later Austrian demagogue. Lerroux specialised in generating and manipulating hatred, and always ended his contrived rants with the extraordinary exhortation: '. . . Fight! Kill! Die!'

Tellingly, in spite of his regular public incitements to violence, the police never arrested Lerroux or broke up or banned his meetings. There was a good reason for this: Lerroux was a personal friend of the captain-general, Milans del Bosch, and was on first-name terms with most of the Barcelona General Staff. He was, in fact, a government agent, bought and paid for by the Madrid politicians Segismundo Moret and José Canalejos. His tactics were to 'out-radical the radicals'. As for 'Left Republicans', I didn't need anyone to warn me against them, I knew enough about them and their role in Irish history from Wee John McAra in Glasgow: 'Left Republicanism may seem an easy short cut to socialism,' he told me once, 'but it would be a structure built on sand. Republicanism's weakness isn't due to its failures, but to its successes. Success requires nationalist unity, be it military or political, and the price of national unity is always the same, the elimination of any suggestion of class struggle or social revolution from the political agenda. Republicanism has nothing to do with class issues such as education, bread, or freedom. If we want real freedom we need to break with nationalist class alliances and look instead to international social revolution. Bakunin's dictum described it so elegantly: "Liberty without socialism is inequality and injustice; socialism without liberty is brutality and slavery". A week before the Easter rising of 1916 James Connolly, the revolutionary syndicalist, addressed a rally of the Irish Citizens' Army in Dublin saying: "If we win, hold on to your rifles, because the Volunteers have a different agenda. Remember, we seek not only political liberty, but economic liberty as well!" Mark my words, Farquhar, he'll be proved right yet.'

SEGUI'S POLITICAL EDUCATION

Segui's youthful dalliance with the Sons of Bitches gang was always held against him by some sections of the movement. It was the albatross he carried around his neck, but Segui was a person who learned from his mistakes and who genuinely tried to atone for his 'misspent youth', if indeed that is what it was, even before his youth was over. He spent most evenings and weekends at meetings in the ateneus and union halls, listening, debating, and acquiring powerful oratorical and rhetorical skills. A voracious reader, he was, unusually for an anarchist, particularly fond of quoting the German thinker, Nietzsche. All things considered, he turned out well, given his background—a thoughtful, considerate, and capable man who rose well above his circumstances.

Segui was both passionate and spontaneous, which may explain his bohemianism—that and the fact that he could never settle—or never was allowed to settle—into a regular job. A popular speaker, he was in great demand for public meetings, rallies, or picket lines. The Brigada de Servicios Especiales, the Spanish secret police, kept him under constant surveillance and whenever he managed to find work at his trade as a housepainter, their officers would have a 'quiet' word with potential employers advising them he was a 'dangerous man' and that it would be 'disadvantageous' to employ him. The intimidation never ceased.

As a result, often when Segui turned up for work, his erstwhile employers would tell him they couldn't risk taking him onto their books, but they would pay him for two days' or a week's wages. Even so, Sugar Boy managed to earn a living from friends and comrades who found him work painting and decorating their homes, union halls, or ateneus.

Segui had been a union delegate at the first Congress of Solidaridad Obrera—the forerunner of the CNT—in Barcelona in 1907 and was out on the streets during Barcelona's Tragic Week in 1909, the events for which Francisco Ferrer was executed. As a result he was forced to escape to Gualva.

A delegate at the founding conference of the Catalan CNT in 1910, he was later at the forefront of the protest campaign to prevent the deportation of American anarchists, and played a leading role in the 1911 general strike, as well as in the 1914 hunger riots. As president of the Barcelona Construction Union and secretary of the Catalan Regional Committee of the CNT, he served on the 1917 strike committee. By mid-1918, he had acquired

near-legendary status as a public speaker, attracting mass audiences wherever he went. Crowds flocked from miles around to hear his rich, deep, bar-
itone voice, and his clear and concise arguments as to why anarcho-syndicalism was the only viable solution to the poverty, injustice, and illiteracy
keeping the Spanish working class in thrall.

But Segui was also a pragmatist, a 'gritty realist' as he described himself, who was often only too willing to take a utilitarian approach and compromise or embark on joint initiatives with nonlibertarian socialists and
Republicans in the hope of resolving union members' day-to-day problems.
Too often, however, this flexibility of mind and readiness to accommodate
parliamentary politicos backfired on him—and on the CNT—and he was
forever arguing with the more ideologically inflexible anarchists, such as
Federico Urales, who accused him of being 'too political'.

Segui's *charlas*—impromptu talks—in the Café Español were highly popular occasions, and the men and women surrounding him listened avidly
to his lively and thought-provoking dissertations on a wide range of subjects from free love to Darwin's theory of evolution. When he moved these
charlas to the Café Tupinamba in the Plaça de la Universidad his audience
became more distinctly middle-class—students, lawyers, writers, and teach-
ers. I'm told these occasions never compared in enthusiasm with those of
his Café Español days.

SEGUI AND JOAN RULL

Another former member of the Sons of Bitches, with whom Segui didn't get
on, was a youth by the name of Joan Rull Queralt. Both left the gang around
the same time in 1903, with Rull joining the Centro Obrero de Estudios
Sociales, the anarchist Workers' Social Studies Centre. It wasn't entirely
coincidental that around this time a bomb exploded at the Barcelona Opera
House, an event that marked the start of a random terror campaign lasting
almost four years, until July 1907.

Rull, the main suspect, was arrested and charged with the bombings,
but was acquitted at his trial in 1906. During his time in prison, however,
he cultivated a friendship with the prison director to whom he claimed to
have seen the light. Renouncing his 'anarchism' he offered his services as
an informer to the then civil governor, who employed him not only to infiltrate the Barcelona anarchist movement, but also to act as an agent provocateur. His handler was a police inspector by the name of Momento.

Most of Barcelona's anarchists, however, distrusted Rull, knowing him
to be a *confidente*; they avoided him like a plague carrier, so the information

he fed to his employers was either fabricated or extravagantly exaggerated gossip recycled to enhance his own standing and credibility. The bombing campaign that fed public hysteria almost daily for the next three years was in fact the work of the entire Rull family: his father, Josep Rull i Lladó; his mother, Maria Queraltó i Gatell; and his brother. Rull turned terrorism into a family business with the complicity, of course, of Inspector Momento, a company of Jesuits, the civil governor, the Duke of Bivona and who knows how many others from the police department and among the city fathers.

The purpose of Rull's 'false-flag' terror campaign of random bomb attacks in public places targeting innocent passers-by—later known as the 'Strategy of Tension'—was to discredit the anarchists and the Liberals by creating a climate of emotional stress through fear and uncertainty. Thus Rull's immediate victims weren't the real target; the bombs were aimed at the wider public, the physically unharmed but emotionally distressed survivors who were too terrified to leave their own homes. This has now become a psychological warfare strategy favoured by agents of the state or by mercenaries contracted by great political, corporate, or religious institutions. It is employed to subvert social reform or agitation that harms or threatens to harm the status quo. Through manipulating the emotions and behaviour of the wider population the instigators of the bombings seek to promote conservative, reactionary social and political tendencies. And—above all—they aim to create a near-hysterical desire in the man on the street for a return to order, tradition, certainty—and strong central government.

Rull's mother, Maria Queraltó, who collected the explosives and planted many of the bombs, was a devout and simpleminded Catholic woman who believed she was doing God's work, helping to make the world 'a holier place'. Her belief that she was serving the Lord's purpose was reinforced by the fact that she collected the infernal devices from a Jesuit seminary which bore the ubiquitous AMDG (*Ad Majorem Dei Gloriam*, To the Greater Glory of God) inscribed in gilt above the door and, on the door handle, the letters of the Jesuit Trinity, JMJ. It was here the bombs were manufactured along with other more commercial articles of corporal mortification. In addition to an artisanal sideline in infernal devices, this particular Sacred Heart seminary produced Alices: barbed, belt-like contraptions worn around the thighs of the self indulgently sanctimonious to induce self-inflicted pain, or 'express spiritual devotion' as the promotional literature had it. This same Company of Jesus also manufactured and sold knouts, knotted rope flays known to the faithful as 'the discipline'.

When his mother returned to the family home at 26 Carrer del Foment with the explosives, Rull would prime the devices and tell her where they were to be planted. Ma Rull then carried them around town in her wicker shopping basket like some diabolical Old Mother Reilly, planting them in public lavatories, doorways, or newspaper kiosks. Occasionally Rull's father and brother planted the bombs.

Things began to go wrong for the Rulls in January 1907 with the appointment of a new liberal civil governor, Angel Osorio y Gallardo, who was determined to stamp out terrorism and police corruption. Rull made the mistake of approaching the governor and demanding more money from the authorities 'to put a stop to the bombings', which he began escalating in April 1907. A few months later, in July 1907, governor Osorio y Gallardo had Rull and his family arrested. The first to break was the old mother, after which the rest of the family agreed to testify against Rull. His terror campaign had lasted from early 1904 until July 1907, during which time he had injured and killed scores of innocent victims, actions that had been blamed on anarchists.

The governor's investigation into the Rull case was initially kept secret to prevent interference by corrupt police officers, magistrates, and officials complicit in Rull's conspiracy. The investigation and arrests were entrusted to a police inspector by the name of Tressolo, a liberal and a freemason. When confronted with irrefutable evidence and the witness statements, the surprised and highly embarrassed police commissioner had no choice but to allow Rull to be charged, especially when the case had been authorised by the civil governor—and at the highest levels in Madrid.

Tressolo's arrests of the Rull family coincided with the arrival in Barcelona of Chief Inspector Charles John Arrow, a former Scotland Yard detective who had been headhunted by the civil governor to set up Barcelona's newly formed Criminal Investigation Bureau. The appointment of the forty-six-year-old English policeman created a lot of interest in the Catalan press. It was at a time when the figure of 'the detective' was becoming increasingly popular owing to the recent publication in Spanish of Conan Doyle's Sherlock Holmes stories.

Chief Inspector Arrow's arrival, with his wife and son, in Barcelona on 21 July 1907 also coincided with a massive debate in the newspapers over the city's ineffectual, incompetent, anti-labour, and anti-Republican police force. There were also hostile references to the fact that Arrow and his family had been installed in a luxury suite at the Ranzini Hotel, overlooking the Plaça de la Constitución, directly opposite the Town Hall. Chief among those stirring up antipathy to Arrow's appointment was Alexander Lerroux,

Rull Gang: Joan Rull, Josep Rull.

José Perelló.

Maria Queraltó.

Joan Rull arriving at court.

Maria Queraltó, Rull's mother, arriving at court.

Joan Rull being escorted to the courtroom.

Joan Rull, police agent, provocateur, and 'strategist of tension'.

Below: police cart used to remove Rull's devices to safety.

Rull home at 26 Carrer de Foment.

Los Sucesos, illustrated magazine (Madrid).

Maurice Bernardon, explosives expert.

Model Prison, Barcelona.

a particularly corrupt politician with much to fear from a 'new CID broom' in police headquarters.

Concern about the extent of police corruption and the lack of progress in the bombing investigation provided the civil governor Osorio y Gallardo with the impetus to establish a new detective bureau. He had long suspected that the bombs were somehow connected with an ultra-right-wing Catholic cabal seeking to manipulate Catalan public opinion and political agenda.

It was George Smithers, the British vice-consul in Barcelona, a fellow freemason (of the British Grand Lodge, not the European Grand Orient Lodge) who recommended Chief Inspector Arrow to Osorio y Gallardo as a good policeman and a reliable brother freemason. Although Arrow's appointment coincided with Rull's arrest, he had nothing to do with the investigation. It was no coincidence, however, that Rull's arrest had been timed to ensure the investigation, and the subsequent trial were not interfered with by police officers complicit in the affair. Even so, in an attempt to muddy the waters, the Special Services Brigade, the Borbón secret police, pulled in many anarchists for questioning, including Salvador Segui who, when questioned by the examining magistrate about the bombings, told him, angrily:

'Fuck off! Of course I'm a revolutionary, but we do not believe in killing innocent people in random street bombings.'

'What about your connections with Rull, then? He has revolutionary ideas, like yours, and you've seen where it led him.'

Offended by the comparison, Segui began maligning Rull: 'If Rull planted those bombs he's a vile and despicable excuse for a human being . . . Rull would do anything for money.'

Segui continued in this vein for some time, calling his former fellow gang member all the abusive names under the sun, at which point the Examining Magistrate signalled to a detective at the far end of the room who pulled back a curtain—and there was Rull, in handcuffs and leg irons. Staring hard at Sugar Boy, Rull said: 'The same to you, Segui, the same to you . . .'

Seguí and the other anarchists were eventually released, but he never forgot that depressing moment when confronted with Rull. It gnawed at his conscience. Since then, if Sugar Boy thought someone was being overly judgmental he would interrupt, exclaiming, 'No! No! Let's pause and consider. Let's think about this!' then he'd explain about the Rull incident.

'Dammit!' he swore. 'Even if a man's a total arsehole, I'll never bad-mouth anyone again! That moment will live with me for the rest of my life!' said Sugar Boy when he told me the story later.

The Rull trial lasted a fortnight, and although his family turned state's evidence and testified against him, Rull steadfastly refused to make any statement or name his powerful backers. He remained convinced, right to the end, that they would come to his aid and he would be granted clemency. Under cross-examination Rull, however, did admit that for the four years of his career as a police confidente he received regular monthly sums of 200 pesetas from his handler, Inspector Momento. Clearly the money was payment for the bombings, but this was never admitted or proven, nor was Momento charged with conspiracy.

In his evidence to the court, Inspector Tressolo said: 'I have absolutely no doubts Rull was responsible for the bombing campaign, but I must also state—clearly and unequivocally—that I am equally convinced he is merely the instrument of a terrorism with which the anarchists are in no way associated or involved. The men behind Rull—who are not beside him in the dock today—are not anarchists. They are influential, high-ranking individuals who will, no doubt, for reasons of state, go unpunished, because they are too important. To indict them would be to indict the state itself.'

No national newspapers published Tressolo's statement about Rull's 'high-ranking' protectors or the 'important figures of state' implicated in his terror campaign. According to Arrow and Tressolo these included not only senior figures in Barcelona's security apparatus and the city's 'men of order', but also national political, ecclesiastical, and business figures such as the civil and military governors, the Duque de Bivona, and even the Interior Minister, Juan de la Cierva. Antonio Maura—the prime minister—also came into the frame. All were complicit, to a greater or lesser extent, in Rull's mindless, visceral outrages in their attempts to justify their bloody repression of the organised labour movements and their programme of antiliberal legislation.

Rull told Tressolo that the purpose of the bombing campaign had been to spread the maximum amount of fear by creating a situation in which nobody knew what meaningless outrage would occur next or why, or who would be killed.

'I attacked ordinary, unknown people—innocent men, women, and children—people with no involvement in political life—in order to promote a sense of fear and chaos that would convince the populace to turn first to the State for security, order, and discipline, and to the Church for spiritual reassurance and comfort. Under cover of anarchist and antireligious activities, our purpose was to undermine the very structure of society to discredit these people. We have people infiltrated into the groups, and my actions were tailored to the ethos of their milieu: "propaganda by deed", to make it appear to the wider public that they were carried out by anarchists. We needed to create feelings of hostility and anger towards the satanic forces that are jeopardising the peace and undermining the spiritual and moral fabric of our society. The end result of this crisis was to be the Phoenix-like emergence of a popular movement that would champion the citizenry against the social disintegration currently being brought about by Godless anarchists, freethinking liberals, and freemasons.'

In effect, Rull's terror campaign was intended to provide the pretext to trash what passed for habeas corpus by suspending constitutional rights and civil liberties, justifying the introduction of martial law and the indefinite imprisonment of 'suspects' without trial for anyone opposing the government: liberals, anticlerical freethinkers, socialists, Republicans, anarchists, and freemasons. By demonising the anarchists, the manipulative plotters hoped—under the pretext of a 'war on terror'—to justify extending executive power and ensuring the passage through parliament of anti-labour and anti-Liberal legislation.

Hoisted by their own petard, as it were, the corrupt Maura government found the revelations that emerged during the Rull trial backfiring on them, and the concerted opposition of liberals, Republicans, socialists, and anarchists led to the withdrawal of the proposed draconian antiterrorist law. As for Rull, the fall guy for Barcelona's 'Merchant Venturers', he met his end in the yard of Barcelona's recently opened Model Prison on 8 August 1908. His was the first execution carried out in the prison. Until the last moment, when the iron collar of the *garrote-vil* was being strapped around his neck, Rull was convinced his powerful backers would come to his rescue, that he would be granted clemency and acclaimed as a hero in the struggle against the forces of Godless anarchism. His father, mother, and brother all received life sentences.

CHIEF INSPECTOR CHARLES JOHN ARROW

On 16 April 1907 Barcelona's city fathers had hired Charles John Arrow, formerly of Scotland Yard, to organise and head up a new Detective Bureau and improve the force's efficiency. Barcelona's constabulary was small by European standards, with a ratio of one policeman to every thousand inhabitants. Pay was poor, as was morale. Management was bad and corruption was widespread.

Arrow formally took up his post on 23 July 1907, having signed a three-year contract. His first year's salary of £800 rose to £900 in the second year, and to £1,000 in his third and final year. He had at his disposal a secret expense fund of £2,000 for informers and 'special payments'. He was also tasked with setting up a Catalan Special Branch 'for the investigation of terrorist offences', which was in effect an anti-anarchist, anti-Republican and anti-dissident police force.

In his first six-month confidential report to his political masters in the Mixed Commission of employers and union leaders, Arrow stated that they were 'compiling a file on a large number of known anarchists who "may come to this country". These names have been supplied to me by Scotland Yard, and I am also in correspondence with the Paris prefecture with regard to certain anarchists known to them . . .' At the same time, in a secret briefing to the British ambassador in Madrid, Maurice de Bunsen, Arrow estimated the number of 'dangerous anarchists' in Barcelona at around five hundred. He also said that he was 'greatly struck by the extreme bitterness obtaining between Catalans and Castilians', likening it to the attitude of Irish Fenians towards the English.

Arrow's second memorandum to his masters, dated 21 July 1908, covered his first full year in the job:

> You may wish to know that after having been in place for twelve months, I have a lead on the perpetrators of the latest outrages. All I can say at the moment is that the Bureau has assembled a huge amount of information on a number of people who will prove to be important—but on whom we lack definitive evidence. If we can find that evidence it may prove the connection between many suspicious events, each of which, on its own, is a trifling matter—but when tied together by credible intelligence, may prove to be of major importance. This is the sort of intelligence that results from the public positing of a definite regard for information (as I have several times urged the Most Illustrious Mixed Commission to do) from the use of secret agents and from the comprehensive exploitation of secret intelligence.

But city hall politics, bitter disagreements with his chef de bureau—appointed over his head and by the King, against his contractual agreement—plus public hostility and lack of support from his staff and his employers, led to Arrow's increasing disenchantment with the job. On 10 August 1909, a little over two years after his appointment, he was formally dismissed as 'chief consultant' to Barcelona's Criminal Investigation Bureau. The reason offered for his dismissal was 'failing to perform his duties'! Tellingly, he was sacked in the immediate aftermath of the Tragic Week, the popular insurrection that rocked Barcelona and other Catalan cities from 26 July to 2 August 1909.

ÁNGEL PESTAÑA

Like Segui, Ángel Pestaña was dynamic, strong willed, highly intelligent and imaginative, but whereas Segui and Archs were intuitive, extroverted, and flamboyant, Pestaña was more of a loner who preferred, where possible, to remain in the background.

In 1914 Pestaña moved to Barcelona where he befriended Anselmo Lorenzo, the 'grandfather' of Spanish anarchism, shortly before the latter's death. Laureano and Pestaña had met, briefly, in 1915 while Pestaña was working as a proof-reader in Tomás Herreros's printshop. Pestaña then moved to Algeria for a year, returning to Barcelona towards the end of 1916. It was in Sidi bel Abbés, in Algeria, where he met and struck up a close friendship with Ramón Archs, who was then still in the French Foreign Legion.

In Barcelona Pestaña became involved with the anarchist First of May Group who published their journal *Tierra y Libertad!* from premises in the Calle Cadena. A talented all-rounder—writer, orator, and a resourceful campaigner—Pestaña was soon appointed editor of *Tierra y Libertad!* and was widely respected within both the anarchist and union movements.

Depressed by the failure of the general strike of August 1917—or, more accurately, by the treachery of the socialists and their trade union partners of the UGT—Pestaña shifted his politics from intransigent 'purist' anarchism to more union-oriented anarcho-syndicalism, a drift in opinion that wasn't unusual among veteran working-class anarchists. Building and maintaining a mass labour organisation—however inspired it might be by the organisation's charismatic leaders—brought with it the practical problems of managing and coordinating a large membership with widely varying levels of commitment among both its anarchist and nonanarchist affiliates. The latter viewed the present as the culmination of a long series of determining events, whereas Pestaña, like most activist anarchists, looked on the present as an opportunity for a new beginning. There were also the political difficulties of maintaining union independence and wielding authoritative leverage amid the Machiavellian power struggles of the regime's contending political parties and power groupings, as well as dealing with a competing mass union movement—the socialist UGT—and to do all this without corrupting the antistatist nature of the anarchist ideal and practice.

Other dangers that came with the territory were institutional bureaucratisation and a defensive leadership style. But these were still the early days of the CNT when the leadership and direction still came from the rank and file.

On his return to Barcelona Pestaña dedicated himself, as a journalist, to building up his already extensive network of contacts. His subtle and sharp intellect, forceful personality, and good organising and negotiating abilities made a positive impression on most people he met, and as a strategist and negotiator he was also sensitive to the hidden barbs in employers' proposals before anyone else. Wherever he travelled, Pestaña made a point of doing an audit of local knowledge and networks, culling as much information as he could from local militants about who and what they knew—information that he classified and logged away for future use. Whenever possible he personally interviewed compañeros recently released from custody, militants who had gone through hell and who, on the whole, had emerged, tougher and even more committed to the Idea. He knew that these men would have acquired skills, knowledge, and friendship networks in prison that might one day prove useful. They were also perhaps privy to information that could identify possible informers or their handlers.

As a student of historical and contemporary revolutionary movements, Pestaña could 'read the political runes'. He was a walking encyclopaedia of the mistakes of the insurrections of antiquity, from the days of Spartacus through to Blanqui and onwards. He believed firmly that the fundamental reason most revolutionary movements failed was because of manipulation by spies, agent provocateurs or, more often than not, ordinary people who had been compromised in some way by the secret police and coerced into selling out their friends, colleagues, or neighbours. But he also knew there was no such thing as a treason-proof organisation.

This problem with spies and provocateurs was a global one that bedevilled all revolutionary movements. Wee John McAra often talked about the problems they caused the Clyde Workers' Committee in Glasgow. During the war the shop floors of Britain's munitions factories were choc-a-bloc with these maleficent characters, planted by a host of government and private security agencies and far-right 'private enterprise' foundations—paid informers out to entrap the unwary and the gullible.

In Britain, after 8 August 1914, anyone suspected of being an industrial agitator or expressing opinions critical of the government or the war soon found themselves targeted by either the State or the employers, or both, and sacked or even deported under the Defence of the Realm Act (DORA). But in Spain, in 1918, the political situation was quite different from that in Britain. In Spain the CNT was a social revolutionary organisation with a declared and unambiguous objective of libertarian communism that called for the complete reshaping of society through federally linked, self-governing communities embodying popular consumer and producer power—as opposed to political parties exercising centralised state authority. At the time there were no other options open to the Spanish working classes. Politically and socially the country remained firmly stuck in the Middle Ages, having had no Protestant Reformation or bourgeois political revolution to ease the workers' situation; the only way social conflict could be resolved was by social revolution.

In Britain, as in other industrialised countries, labour unions were led by social democrats and evolutionaries, elitists hostile to structural change. They believed in political revolution, i.e. acquiring state power by means of a coup d'état—à la Napoleon III, the master conspirator and usurper—or by persuading the upper classes the socialist-led trade unions didn't constitute a threat to their class interests, and convincing them either to step aside, voluntarily, or adapt to the needs of the emerging middle-class professionals, artisans, and workers.

Pestaña believed in the importance of timely and appropriate information—and action, up to a point anyway. The union's 'influential leaders' were, above all, pragmatists who knew the Organisation had little hope of achieving its revolutionary ends until it had its own intelligence and direct action service in place, which is what Archs, Piera, and Vandellós were in the process of setting up. And although they were also idealists, they weren't dreamers. Their idealism was firmly grounded in reality, i.e. on what was possible, focusing always on facts and never allowing themselves to get carried away by the dense haze of abstract, faith-based ideological and aspirational rhetoric as some compañeros were wont to do.

One role of the CNT's Defence Commission was to provide an efficient security and intelligence gathering body for the unions. Wherever there was information to be had—bars, restaurants, post offices, sorting offices, buses, trains, ships, schools, brothels, army barracks, and naval bases—the Defence Commission had its sources. Some of the most useful agents were compañeras employed as confidential typists in embassies and consulates, in national and local government ministries and departments with access to secret and confidential files. But these sources were few and far between.

Dockers and sailors were also important Defence Commission assets, as it was through them that matériel and people could be brought in and out of the country under the noses of the police and customs officers.

PESTAÑA ON 'PROPAGANDA BY DEED'

Pestaña's views on direct action, propaganda by deed, and *ajusticiamentos*—'account settling'—fluctuated over the years. But, as he pointed out, responsibility for most of the *atentados personales* of the time wasn't down to *cenetistas* so much as to the local groups of mainly young, action-oriented anarchists, who believed that the only way to resist the gross injustices of the time was by targeting those responsible, the factory-owners and managers, especially those of the big manufacturing concerns.

The activists did not think of their actions as being a substitute for mass collective action and protest, which, of course, was illegal and brutally and violently repressed. They saw them as a tactical means of resisting, and a way to settle accounts with brutal and intransigent employers, showing them that their arbitrary and oppressive actions did not have abstract consequences, but direct, immediate ones.

Dissent always finds ways to express itself, and 'direct actions' were particularly effective in 'shaking the scenery' as it were. We knew the odds were stacked against us and that we would probably end up dead or in jail, but at least we were hurting the regime at its roots and helping to corrode and destroy the myth of absolute authority in the process.

However, as most of us also knew intuitively—and Pestaña and Segui never tired of repeating, as did Archs—another likely consequence of violent actions was the legitimisation and escalation of oppression and repressive legislation, the polarising of public opinion and, ultimately, the movement becoming increasingly dependent on a small and ever diminishing core of militants for whom violence and clandestinity would increasingly become the only form of politics. Militants who would alienate themselves from the working class whose interests they claimed to be defending. For the individuals in groups like these, the means would inevitably become the self-perpetuating ends, and when that happened they would find themselves locked in a military confrontation with the state that was virtually impossible for them to win.

It was a dilemma. Most of us are brought up to believe that vengeance is wrong and primitive, but the fact remains that the desire for revenge is one of the strongest of human emotions—along with anger, grief, fear, and love—and equally binding. Bourgeois jurists tell us that only the state can exact revenge and administer justice on our behalf, but even in the most democratic societies where a genuine rule of law exists—which most certainly was not the case in Barcelona in 1918—anyone passing up the opportunity for vengeance lives to regret it. Of course it would be impossible for people to coexist peacefully if everyone had a right to exact personal vengeance on their fellow citizens. We would be living in a state of constant warfare and blood feuds, but the fact remains that ordinary law-abiding people do pay a terrible personal price in regret and guilt for leaving vengeance to the state. But what options are available when it is a cruel and oppressive state itself that deprives you of justice, or fails it so shamefully?

It was almost impossible, however, to distinguish between the actions of the anarchist groups and the CNT defence groups, who were interchangeable and indistinguishable. Most, if not all of the more dynamic CNT members were young working-class anarchists who belonged to local affinity groups that also doubled up as ad-hoc 'defence commissions' when it came to protecting union interests. Many armed themselves with pistols, mainly the easy to obtain Star automatics, which became known as 'sindicalistas'. These defence groups, however, were completely independent and informal bodies answerable to nobody but themselves—and certainly not to any of the CNT's 'higher' committees, including the Defence Commission.

PESTAÑA AND BRAVO PORTILLO

Pestaña publicly identified Barret's killers in *Solidaridad Obrera*, but in spite of being named they certainly weren't shamed—or even arrested or questioned. Bellés was suspended, briefly, then released after the intervention of his boss, Chief Superintendent Manuel Bravo Portillo.

Born on the Spanish colonial island of Guam in the Pacific, Bravo Portillo, a former Special Forces officer who headed up an antiguerrilla unit during the Spanish-American War of 1898, had served in the uniformed branch of the Barcelona police force for ten years. Promoted to inspector, then chief inspector, he commanded a number of police stations around the city: Atarazanas, Audiencia, Universidad, Lonja, Sur, and Hospital. He subsequently transferred to plainclothes work in the 'entertainment' squad, a euphemism for the vice squad, in which he spent a year, before being promoted to superintendent in overall charge of the Barcelona CID where he cultivated many useful political friends and contacts. His next move, to security headquarters in Madrid's Puerta del Sol, was a short one, after only a month he returned to Barcelona, in December 1917, to take over command of the Special Services Brigade from Chief Superintendent Riquelme.

Bravo Portillo, a stockily built man, was a bully and a misogynist who had acquired a reputation for beating up women, especially those arrested during the food riots of January 1918. Insecure and quick to take offence, he was always sensitive to real or imaginary slights, and had men tortured and killed on the slightest perceived provocation. Foppish in dress, he sported a meticulously groomed ambassadorial handlebar moustache and a comb-over that was more a cry for help than a fashion statement. None of his family, friends, or colleagues had had the cojones to say to him: 'Hey Superintendent, what's with the hair?' Perhaps if they had things might have turned out differently.

His particular bogeymen were anarchists and anarcho-syndicalists, whom he hated with a vengeance, showing them no mercy when they fell into his clutches. Whenever an opportunity presented itself he would have them murdered rather than arrested and charged. Many he shot personally.

Between 1916 and 1918, Bravo Portillo was the spider at the centre of Germany and Austria's espionage and special services network in Catalonia; he was the facilitator and mastermind of the terrorist strategy that targeted anarchists and pro-Entente-Cordiale manufacturers alike. The fact that the victims were some of the region's biggest employers—and managers—meant suspicion automatically fell on the CNT and the anarchist groups, a suspicion that Bravo Portillo did everything in his power to foster and encourage.

THE ARREST OF BRAVO PORTILLO

Although Carbonell led the investigation into Bravo Portillo's espionage activities with great diligence, higher authorities intervened and it was over a week before the police forensic experts confirmed that Bravo Portillo had indeed written the damning letters. *Soli*'s public exposure of the police superintendent's activities left the authorities with no choice but to arrest and charge their star secret policeman, and bring him before an examining magistrate. Even so, they did everything in their power to undermine the case against him. The judge in the case, Sr Echevarri, for example, insisted that before he could proceed with the case, the publisher of *Solidaridad Obrera*—who had made the allegation and presented the letters in Bravo Portillo's handwriting—was required to deposit 5,000 pesetas to cover legal administrative fees. A popular subscription campaign quickly raised the amount. Even so, Bravo Portillo's powerful patrons refused to allow Inspector Carbonell to formally arrest and charge him until Saturday 22 June, giving the police chief more than enough time to destroy any other compromising papers he may have had. So convinced were the authorities that the charges against their man would not be upheld they refused to appoint another superintendent to head up the Special Services Brigade. The post was given, provisionally, to one of his deputies, Inspector Santamaría.

Intriguingly, the morning Bravo Portillo was formally arrested, a German submarine surfaced in Barcelona harbour close to the cruiser *Princesa de Asturias*, where it remained on the surface for most of the day. The reason for this extraordinarily blatant breach of Spain's veneer of neutrality remains unknown to this day, but one story that gained credence at the time was that they had come to intimidate the authorities into releasing Bravo Portillo and take him out of harm's way to Germany.

The Madrid authorities were seriously embarrassed by the bad publicity following Bravo Portillo's arrest, exposing as it did the extent to which powerful elements within the administration had been colluding with the German secret services. It also undermined Spain's claims to neutrality. In addition to passing on information about the movement of merchant ships and their cargoes for German submarines to sink, stories were now openly circulating about Bravo Portillo's involvement in the Barret murders and his responsibility for running an extensive network of indigenous agents tasked with disrupting production in Spanish factories producing war matériel for the Entente. These agents, many of them serving or retired police officers, were responsible for a large part of Germany's sabotage and subversion operations in Catalonia and the Levante.

Arrested at the same time as Bravo Portillo were Guillermo Bellés, a former Special Services Brigade officer and José Ezcurra, a Civil Guard lieutenant, the police superintendent's liaison with German naval intelligence officers in the Canary Islands.

With the war reaching its crucial phase, Bravo Portillo's handler, Albert Honnermann, the head of Germany's Secret Service Department IIIb in Catalonia, kept pressuring him for more drastic measures, and ordered Barret's murder. For his services, Bravo Portillo was paid an honorarium of fifty pesetas a day plus large bonuses and expenses, slightly more than that given to Judas.

Honnermann, a forty-year-old career secret policeman in Department 1A of the Prussian state police in prewar Berlin—and later a founder of the Gestapo—was the protégé of his immediate boss, Rudolf Diels, who considered him to be a 'reliable pair of hands' and who regularly gave him the bloodiest tasks. Honnermann was one of Germany's two top agent-handlers in Barcelona, the other being Frederick Ruggeberg.

Short and stocky, with an large and closely shaven square head and no visible neck, Honnermann's jowly face, which looked as though it had been chipped out of pumice, and wouldn't have seemed out of place as a grotesque on the walls of Notre Dame. He could have been the model for the IWW cartoon caricature 'Mr Block'. He was a spectacularly unpleasant character with overdeveloped shoulders whose arms hung awkwardly—slightly forward and away from his body. He walked with the gait of a silverback gorilla. Enormously strong, his ham-sized hands looked as though they could smash through an oak door or kill a man with a single blow. They had! Ruthless and amoral, Honnermann had no regard for human life and killed without remorse or compunction. A true sociopath, he was totally indifferent to the means by which he obtained his ends. Archetypically Prussian in culture and discipline, he obeyed his masters without question or hesitation. 'What I did in Barcelona I did for my country, in good faith,' he wrote later in his memoirs. 'Even those things I didn't enjoy. One must never regret anything accomplished in the line of duty.'

Fearing for his life and hoping for a lighter sentence, Royo de San Martín, Bravo Portillo's confidente and liaison person with German Naval Intelligence, turned state's evidence. In addition to Bravo Portillo's terrorist networks, he said the former vice squad chief had been running gambling, extortion, and blackmail rackets, and was planning to assassinate the French ambassador to Spain.

Royo was right to be afraid. Nine days after his arrest, the star prosecution witness in the case against Bravo Portillo was found dead in his isolation cell in Barcelona's Modelo Prison. He had been poisoned. Again Bravo Portillo proved himself 'untouchable'.

Subsequent press investigations produced a welter of scandalous stories highlighting the endemic corruption and demoralisation that permeated the entire Barcelona police force. Most of them, including those in senior ranks, held part-time jobs, many of which conflicted with their everyday police tasks. An editorial in *La Policía Española*, the professional journal of Spain's national police force, commented bluntly that the Barcelona constabulary's main preoccupation was the 'framing' of innocent citizens, and that 'the only way to reduce crime in the city is to lock up all its policemen.' It later emerged that at least two previous civil governors and the military governor were aware of Bravo Portillo's espionage and terrorist activities and at best ignored the information or else had been complicit in his activities. Bravo Portillo was an *enchufado*, a man well connected in top military and Germanophile circles: his brother commanded the Barcelona garrison, while he himself was the son-in-law of a vice admiral and had been adjutant to the notoriously pro-German General 'Butcher' Weyler, the most senior officer in the Spanish army during the latter's reign of terror in Cuba.

JOSEP BARRET—INDUSTRIALIST

Josep Barret, the Catalan arms manufacturer, had a reputation as a bad employer whose arrogance and controlling behaviour towards his thousand or so workers verged on the tyrannical, but at the time of his murder things were relatively quiet on the industrial front. I must stress, however, that it was never CNT policy to murder employers, not even the most intransigent or reactionary ones. According to the contemporary police and newspaper reports, filed and fed mainly by Manuel Bravo Portillo, the killers were anarchists within the CNT, working for the German secret services to sabotage Entente supply lines, and to intimidate, terrorise, and kill Catalan manufacturers supplying war matériel, goods, and food to the Allies—which is what most of the Special Services Brigade were doing. It was a bonus for the police and the employers to be able to blame the sindicato único and the anarchists for the outrages they themselves had committed, but the awkward and embarrassing fact was that rogue, suborned "cenetistas" had indeed acted as proxies of the German secret services and Bravo Portillo's Special Services Brigade.

INSPECTOR GUILLERMO BELLÉS AND THE CONFIDENTE FERRER

Police Inspector Guillermo Bellés, Bravo Portillo's top man and member of the Special Services Brigade, ran his own private 'commando' unit recruited from among his informers in the renegade Ferrer's own union branch, and from ultra-right-wing Catholic monarchist organisations as well as a network of lowlife ruffians. It was Bellés who had organised the Barret murder, and was responsible for identifying and targeting disaffected and vulnerable union members in the manufacturer's ordnance factory, which operated round the clock producing howitzer shells, grenades, and detonators for the French military. Over the years at least four unsuccessful attempts had been made to blow up Barret's factory, and who knows how many moves to disrupt production through strikes, ca' cannies and sabotage.

Belles's associates included two psychopath brothers, Valero and Espina Vandellós, who should have been smothered at birth, or at least committed to an insane asylum. Both were involved in earlier unsuccessful attempts to blow up Barret's munitions plant. Bellés paid Ferrer 15,000 pesetas for the murders, the money came, through Bravo Portillo, from the German secret services. Ferrer was a truly despicable character who claimed to be a revolutionary, but who never really understood the Idea—or if he did, had long since lost belief in it. Over the years I have met many people like him—articulate people who can talk with apparent ease and confidence and enthusiasm about socialism and the Idea, but always obliquely, using glib, abstract terms and an obscurantist language designed to conceal the fact that they have neither ideals nor morals. Cynical, shallow, ignorant, unprincipled fraudsters and opportunists, they deceive themselves and everyone they come into contact with; devious characters who betray their fellow man without compunction, be it for money, malice, power, or personal advancement. Their moral strength and courage is in inverse proportion to their rhetoric. Empty souls devoid of human empathy, their only concern is to fill their pockets and please powerful men whose ultimate ends are far beyond their victim's imagination.

THE PATRONAL AND THE CNT

The Patronal—which funded the pistolero campaign, being desirous of the end, though it shrank from the means—was the umbrella association that united Barcelona's largest employers. Its function was similar to that of the British chambers of commerce, except that it stalked darker territory. Formed in 1910 to protect employers' interests in the face of increasingly militant trade unionism, the Patronal had sufficient political clout to have the CNT outlawed shortly after its first national congress in 1911. But the CNT's enforced clandestinity didn't seriously damage the union, and it reemerged in 1915, larger and more dynamic than ever—and with considerably more influence throughout industrial and agrarian Spain.

ANDALUSIA IS BURNING

In the south, in May 1918, the previously independent Andalusian Regional Confederation of Landless Labourers, the Federación Regional Andalusia, had affiliated to the CNT. With unskilled day labourers working from sunrise to sunset in part slave, part feudal debt peonage hell for below subsistence-level wages, rebellion was never far from the surface. For centuries, the power of Andalusia's landlords, the terratenientes, had depended on the unlimited reserves of labour they could exploit at will. Whenever union organisers appeared, migrant workers from other areas would be shipped in as blackleg labour to coerce local workers into rejecting the union. In spite of the terrible conditions on the latifundios, the enormous estates where they were at the mercy of ruthless and often absentee semifeudal landowners, the peasants and day labourers of southern Spain were known for their tradition of sporadic insurrections that were ruthlessly and vindictively repressed by the Guardia Civil. This in turn fuelled further working-class anger and resentment and was a decisive factor in radicalising people.

But the news of the October 1917 Russian Revolution changed all that, especially in rural Andalusia where stories of land redistribution, spread by educated 'conscious workers' who could read and write, provided the revelatory example needed to ignite the hopes of the region's peasants and day labourers and inspire a mass insurrectionary movement.

The first wave of strikes began in Córdoba—a city of 'advanced ideas'— in March 1918. Public buildings were put to the torch, the big estates occupied and their fences torn down. Literally overnight hundreds of workers' centres sprang up across the south as groups of enthusiastic anarchist educators and speakers travelled from village to village across the plain of Guadalquivir and the surrounding mountains spreading the news of what everyone believed to be the arrival of the Russian Revolution in the Iberian peninsula. Agricultural workers and day labourers flocked in their thousands to join the CNT.

ANARCHISTS AND REVOLUTION

'Revolution', or rather what anarchists mean by the word revolution, isn't about transferring power or bringing down a bad government. The role of the anarchist is to educate by word and by deed, to make centralised, elitist governments unnecessary, to prevent new ruling groups taking over from the old ones and to spread the idea and practice of communal self-management. After all this—along with the burning desire for wrong-righting— is the whole point of the libertarian social revolution. Indeed, what happens after the Revolution determines whether or not the process can really be described as a social revolution at all. Clearing the ground for social change by sweeping away the old order after centralised power collapses is only the first step in this process.

The problem is that revolutions rarely go the way their initiators intend; factions emerge and manoeuvre to replace the state apparatus with new administrative bodies which, because of their drive for power, inevitably become reactionary and quickly begin to roll back the revolutionary process. A revolution can only truly be said to have begun when peoples' values change and power is distributed horizontally—not vertically—with the whole of society being brought into the decision-making process. And the only way people's values change is through education: reeducating adults and educating the young—with an emphasis on mutual aid, mutual respect, cooperation, and personal responsibility. The ruling classes have to be deprived of their power and wealth, and the land, the means of production, and all productive wealth put at the disposal of everyone. Those who are not workers now will become workers, as opposed to being rentiers and parasites who live off the labour of others. The anarchist's job is to defend the revolution by ensuring that no individuals or parties find the means or have the opportunity to form a new government themselves, thereby restoring privilege, rank, and the power to dominate among new or old party bosses or leaders.

There is only one way this can be achieved. When the revolution begins, it has to be pushed as far as it will go. As long as some people have the power to violate the freedom of others, the revolution remains unfinished. Even so, the pressures of fear, envy, spite, hedonism, corruption, and reaction are ever-present and ineradicable, so the revolution can never be said to be 'finished'. The struggle is forever; that is the true nature and, perhaps, even the necessary tragedy that blights the human condition. In the meantime, the violence that oppresses has to be opposed by whatever means of resistance are appropriate or available to each individual or community.

For anarchists, the essential precondition of revolution—of all actions that pursue the dream of the just society—is the safeguarding of the delicate moral thread between ends and means so that it remains unbroken. The dilemma is a familiar one: power that corrupts righteousness, the perverting tension between high ideals and the desire to use force and cunning to attain them. Power and authority are inescapable features of all social organisations, including anarchist ones; they are 'givens' that will persist no matter what the prevailing order of society. The problem is ensuring that they are perceived as legitimate, rational, competent, and subject to constant scrutiny and criticism. They must also be temporary.

The dangers thrown up during the revolutionary process don't come only from those who fear losing their wealth and influence. Dark personal forces emerge from the degenerative and corrupting process of the Revolution itself, especially from revolutionaries whose motives are shallow, whose mentality and sympathies are essentially elitist, and who would seek to direct the Revolution towards ends that are the opposite of egalitarian and libertarian. Revolutionary movements are, after all, made up of human beings, not only those selflessly heroic individuals with the capacity to persuade, inspire, and thrill; revolutions also sweep up in their wake many more ordinary people who, unexpectedly, find themselves pushed beyond what they can humanly bear. Since the time of Spartacus revolutionary movements have acted like magnets to obsessed, insignificant, weak, and deceitful men and women possessed by personal demons whose moral strength and courage is in inverse proportion to their vociferousness, and who will go to any lengths to acquire and retain concentrated social power and dominating authority. The only way to guard against this process was expressed most elegantly by Michael Bakunin:

> Not the writers, nor the philosophers, nor their books are sufficient to build a living, powerful, socialist movement. Such a movement can only be made a reality by the awakened revolutionary consciousness, the collective will, and the organisation of the working masses them- selves. Without this, the best books in the world are nothing but the- ories spun in empty space, impotent dreams.

The only alternative, I am now convinced, is to ignore and avoid the state as much as is possible, abandoning the search for the unobtainable and chi- merical 'City of the Sun'. If enough people did that and looked to building alternative nonhierarchical social relationships and structures, the state itself would eventually become superfluous, along with the obsessive and ultimately counterproductive drive to make the world 'perfect'. All we need focus on is making it better, and more just.

LIBERTARIAN COMMUNISM

The concept of libertarian communism was a fairly vague policy statement at the time, similar to the then recently adopted Clause Four of the British Labour Party, in which the Party claimed to seek to secure for the work- ers 'the full fruits of their industry, equitable distribution and the common ownership of the means of production, distribution, and exchange'. The dif- ference between the Labour Party and the CNT was that the latter meant what it said and actively pursued its goal—and came close to achieving it just seventeen years later in the Spanish Revolution between July 1936 and May 1937.

For the leadership of the British Labour Party, Clause Four was an imag- inative piece of carrot-dangling intended to keep the socialist rank and file in line and on message. Such a clear affirmation of socialism was always an embarrassment, but it had to be retained as it was the only socialist creden- tial the party had. Their socialism had nothing to do with ideals and princi- ples; for them it was purely about office and power, and adopting policies that would allow them to retain that power.

For the anarcho-syndicalists of the CNT, however, libertarian commu- nism wasn't something that could be achieved through legislation or the nationalisation of industry or of the land. It had to be taken by the people themselves, and at the earliest opportunity. After the Sants conference,

Archs, Figueras, and most other anarchist militants had much clearer ideas as to how libertarian communism could be achieved, and that meant acquiring weapons and setting up strategic arms caches around the country.

GERMANY'S PROPAGANDA MACHINE

The botched general strike and uprising of August 1917 proved a serious setback to the Entente's diplomatic relations with Spain. Germany's propaganda machine was quick to capitalise on the strike, taking advantage of it to spread, through the publications it controlled, the lie that British and French agents had been the 'hidden hands' behind what they claimed was an attempted Republican coup.

In a move to emphasise Britain's support for Alfonso XIII's pro-Entente position, the British ambassador, Hardinge, bent over backwards to distance His Majesty's Government (HMG) from contacts with anyone remotely radical, leftist or Republican. He even promised Prime Minister Eduardo Dato and his foreign minister, the Marqués de Lema, the services of HMG to investigate the allegations. Ironically, the men tasked with the investigation were our own 'friends in the north', Bruce and Marshall of the British Secret Service Bureau, who were now ingratiating themselves with the CNT and the anarchists.

Hardinge's protests that HMG had no involvement in the events of August hit a diplomatic brick wall; the British ambassador was unable to overcome the king's now rampant paranoia. A powerful pro-Central Powers lobby dominated the Spanish court, and Alfonso XIII and his queen, Victoria Eugenia of Battenberg, Queen Victoria's granddaughter, were, at that point, almost the only ones supporting the Entente. The king was also having lots of problems with the army unions, the 'defence juntas' of middle-ranking army officers, and with the ultra-Catholic anti-French lobby whispering constantly in his ear. He was now convinced that the whole thing had been an Anglo-French Masonic plot to destabilise the country, topple the monarchy, undermine the Roman Catholic Church, and embroil the country in war.

All this ignored the fact that Britain and France were Spain's main foreign investors and already controlled much of the country's economic resources, particularly its mines and heavy industries. The Paris-based Société Minère et Métallurgique de Peñarroya, for example, owned a fair number of mining monopolies and the industries and commercial businesses associated with the mines, with the Peñarroya lead mines being the jewels in the Société Minère's crown. The company president was French, as were many of its directors. The rest were well-connected European financial figures such as

Pierre Mirabaud, a former manager of the Bank of France; Baron Robert de Rothschild; Charles Cohen; Baron Antony de Rothschild's brother-in-law, Humbert de Wendel; director of the Banque de l'Union Parisienne and the International Suez Canal Company, Count Errico San Martino di Valperga; and two of the richest men in Spain—the Conde de Romanones and the Marqués de Villamejor. So although all the lead produced at Peñarroya was reserved exclusively for export to Germany, Minère et Métallurgique remained a French-registered and -controlled company.

Spain was also the world's largest producer of mercury, a metal indispensable for warfare, and most of its output came from Rothschild's mines at Almadén in Ciudad Real Province. The Rothschilds also controlled the country's most important railway lines, including the Madrid–Zaragoza line.

Britain and France were the main markets for the heavy industries of the Basque country and Catalonia. British investment was extensive in the iron mines around Bilbao, even the mines ostensibly owned by Spaniards. Orconera, an iron-mining district, was almost completely controlled by British companies. The same was true in most other iron-producing regions such as Desirto. Bilbao's dock facilities and the Transcantabrian Railway that carried the ore to the coast were also British-owned, as were the boats that completed the transport link between Britain and the Basque iron fields. Spain's iron played a big part in British armament plans. The Rio Tinto Company was another important London-based concern. Along with well important sulphur and iron mines, Rio Tinto also owned Spain's richest copper mines in Huelva Province, which produced most of Spain's average output of 540,000 tons a year.

Nor did King Alfonso's pro-German advisers point out to him that the Entente's political leaders would rather cut off their arms and legs than foment revolution—with all the political, economic and social disruption, and unforeseen consequences such events inevitably brought in their train. Regime change maybe; revolution no. Since the fall of the Tsar earlier that year, the domestic and international impact of the Russian Revolution had convinced the British and French governments that it would not be at all wise or productive to follow the example of the German High Command in providing financial and logistical support for revolutionaries such as Lenin and the Bolsheviks.

LESSON IN GEOPOLITICS

There was never any question that Bruce and Marshall wouldn't accept Archs's proposal that the British Secret Service Bureau should collaborate with the CNT Defence Commission. Time was not on their side; they were up against a formidable and long-established enemy in Spain. Since 1904, German agents had been aggressively pursuing their imperial interests in Morocco from Madrid, Barcelona, and Alicante—after being diplomatically sidelined by the British and French with the signing of the Anglo-French Convention. In return for a free hand in Morocco, France pledged to respect Spanish interests in the region. It was, effectively, the start of the Entente Cordiale.

The German secret service had been running its extensive destabilisation, infiltration, and sabotage campaign in Spain since the beginning of the war. The Germans had three main strategic objectives: controlling public opinion, damaging Entente interests and bringing down any anti-German administration. And, with at least eighty thousand German nationals living in Spain at the time, they had a substantial pool of potential agents to draw upon.

As for Britain and its allies, although the UK and Canada had extensive investments in Spain, the British Secret Service Bureau, the French Deuxième Bureau and the French Service de Renseignements (SR) had few reliable informants or agents in place. For this reason alone, Arch's walk-in offer was a godsend. Bruce and Marshall were desperate for timely, accurate, and verifiable information on German and Austro-Hungarian subversive plans, activities, and networks. Between the CNI and the wider anarchist movement there were probably around eighty to ninety thousand anarcho-syndicalist militants and affiliates spread across Spain, with antennae in every pueblo, town, and province, as well as in every industry, army barracks, ship, and naval base. Their extensive international networks and experience in clandestine actions were added bonuses.

For the most part, the militant syndicalists who formed the ideological core of the CNT were anarchists who wouldn't for a moment have considered themselves British agents. Ours, after all, was a struggle for justice and social revolution against an enemy intoxicated with ideological hate and hell-bent on the permanent subjugation of organised labour. Our degree of commitment to the Idea can really be understood only in the context of the revolutionary euphoria that was then lifting the spirits of oppressed people everywhere.

One enduring lesson I learned at that time about British foreign policy with regard to Spain was that it was entirely predicated on Gibraltar. As far as Britain was concerned Gibraltar's border began at the Pyrenees, and Spain, therefore, would always be a potentially hostile neighbour.

Bruce and Marshall's brief was to eliminate or neutralise the Central Powers' espionage and sabotage networks which were then wreaking so much havoc with Entente supply lines, particularly at sea. The CNT shared those objectives, albeit for different reasons, irrespective of what each of us thought about the rights and wrongs of the war. The Germans, for their part, depended on the connivance and resources of the powerful anti-cenetista cabal of right-wing employers, bishops, priests, nationalists, and monarchists controlling the police, the army, and the judiciary. The British wanted an end to Germany's highly effective submarine campaign and the consequent disruptions to the Entente's supply lines; we wanted an end to the repression.

It didn't work out that way. Although we were confident as to what we were fighting against, we didn't give too much thought to what the people with whom we were collaborating were fighting for.

FOURSQUARE BEHIND THE CENTRAL POWERS

Apart from the prime minister, the Conde de Romanones, the king and his Scottish born queen (who wasn't born in Glasgow by the way), the Spanish ruling class, almost without exception—the court, the oligarchs, the landed aristocrats, manic Carlists from the backwoods of Navarre, Maura supporters, the officer caste, the gentry, and the clergy—all stood foursquare behind the Central Powers. Although Alfonso XIII had married Victoria Eugenia in 1906, the queen still retained a sense of obligation to her country of birth, Britain. As for the king, one of his favourite sayings was 'Only the rabble and I support the Entente'—the 'rabble' being the workers. But after the Russian Revolution of March 1917, his sympathies shifted and he became increasingly pro-German.

Court support for Germany and Austro-Hungarian was mainly due to the influence of the Queen Mother, the Austrian Archduchess Maria Cristina. She was adamant that a Central Powers victory for Germany, Austria-Hungary, Turkey, and Bulgaria was the only guarantee of survival for the 'old order', a euphemism for her family and in-laws.

Spain's *gent d'ordre* also stood solidly behind imperial Germany and the Austro-Hungarian Empire. Unshakeable in their conviction that they were the West's last defence against Russian barbarism and bloody revolution, they believed a German victory would mean the return of Gibraltar and the annexation of French Morocco and, possibly, Portugal. That at least was the view of General Echagüe, Spain's minister for war.

However, after Italy entered the war in 1916, Spain was surrounded by Entente states making it unfeasible for it to openly support the Central Powers—hence the obsession with the appearance of strict neutrality, a policy that the Germans were determined to ensure at any price. It wasn't that Spain's elites were particularly Germanophile, rather that they were Francophobes, and the wax-faced Roman Catholic hierarchs were the most rabidly Francophobic of the lot. *El Debate*, the main Catholic newspaper, even hailed the Kaiser as 'God's Sword'—in spite of the fact that Wilhelm was a Protestant. The Vatican considered him an honorary prince of the Church who would restore the temporal power of the Papacy and the Habsburgs and chastise both Protestant Britain and immoral and faithless Republican France with temporal and divine vengeance. As far as the Roman Catholic Church was concerned, all the evils of the modern world could be traced back to the escape to Scotland of the Knights Templar, the fall of Jerusalem, the Protestant Reformation and the Grand Orient-inspired French Revolution. The view of the Roman Curia, the institutional hierarchy of the Church, was that the world had been seduced into a materialist mindset by the pivotal events of 1789, which conflated human happiness with materialism, rationalism, and egalitarianism, raised working-class expectations for a better life in this world and undermined the foundations of the unquestioning belief on which the Papacy was built, that the that the better life would come in the next world—'pie in the sky', as defined succinctly by the then recently murdered Wobbly organiser Joe Hill.

Since the beginning of the war, four years earlier, the Catholic Church had been the most unyielding in its political and ideological support for the German-Austro-Hungarian cause. Not even the invasion of plucky 'little' Catholic Belgium could weaken its stand. There were even some priests and bishops who argued that it was God's punishment on the Belgians for permitting a monument to be raised to the memory of the godless Francisco Ferrer i Guardia in Brussels.

The Anglican Bishop of Southwark, touring Spain in 1915, reported that the only senior clerics friendly towards the Entente were the Bishops of Madrid and Ciudad Real. The rest of the Spanish clergy, particularly the sinister Archbishop Soldevilla, were solidly pro-German and reserved their particular hatred for the French. Right up until the final hours of the war, Cardinal Pacelli—later Pius XII—was desperately pulling out all the diplomatic stops in an attempt to broker a deal that would prevent the collapse of the Hapsburg Empire, the last great Roman Catholic power of Europe.

ANARCHISTS AND THE WAR

Most cenetistas and anarchists opposed the war—but that didn't make us pacifists. We were internationalist and antimilitarist inasmuch as we believed in international working-class solidarity. As Glaswegian revolutionary John MacLean—an educator, like Ferrer—famously said: 'The only war worth waging is the class war!' But class war wasn't some theoretical abstraction; it meant something in those days.

I believed—emotionally and intellectually—that the war was an internal power struggle between competing capitalist interests, and that workers shouldn't have had to sacrifice their lives or take the lives of other fellow workers in what was essentially a folly of capitalism and statism. But after a few months in Spain, in my heart of hearts, I felt increasing hostility and resentment towards Germany, so I obviously wasn't as immune to the cultural influences of my environment as I liked to think I was. A lot of this was due to the loss of my friends and shipmates on the *Covenant*, but the issues weren't as straightforward as I originally understood them to be. Paradoxically, even though I rejected the state's right to wage war on my behalf, I now saw the war in more complex terms and increasingly found myself taking the anti-German side.

From bitter experience of political realities we know only too well that when the disenfranchised seize power they don't always act from the noblest of ideals; they can be as outrageous in their actions as the gangsters they replace. Revolutions, unfortunately, often go much further—and in different directions—than their militants ever intended. That is the corrupting nature of power, and it is precisely for that reason we are anarchists. For us it has never been simply a war between classes, the war is between freedom and servitude. There is no other enemy. Many anarchist activists and thinkers such as Kropotkin, Malatesta, and Faure, as well as Spanish, French, and Italian anarcho-syndicalists supported the Entente against German-Austro-Hungarian imperialism and militarism. To them the Entente represented the forces of progress; the Germans, on the other hand, particularly the ultra-conservative Prussians and Junker class, were the arrogant, sabre-rattling enemies of social progress who bore the main responsibility for the war.

Bakunin, long dead, was another anarchist who hated what Germany represented, especially after its role in the Franco-Prussian War of 1870-71. Bakunin's opinion of German socialists was that they were so uniquely authoritarian and craven in their deference to the institutions of state that they were beyond all redemption. He was of the opinion that Germany's military, political, and business classes were constantly contriving war in order to dominate Europe and believed that such a war would set back the cause of freedom immeasurably.

A theory at the time held that a popular war against the Prussians would develop into a revolutionary war, which actually wasn't far from the truth when you consider what was happening contemporaneously in Russia and elsewhere. Others argued along the lines that 'my enemy's enemy is my friend'. Max Nettlau, a German anarchist, believed, on the other hand, that it was Russia that was the main obstacle to socialism and for this reason he supported the Central Powers. It certainly took all sorts.

WAR AND THE NATIONAL PSYCHE

When war broke out in 1914, Europe's Social Democratic parties and most trade unions formed ranks enthusiastically behind their respective national governments. Randolph Bourne, a contemporary American libertarian commentator with remarkable insight into the cathartic and unifying effect of war on the national psyche, observed:

> The moment war is declared, the citizen throws off his contempt and indifference to government, identifies himself with its purposes, revives all his military memories and symbols, and the State once more walks, an august presence through the imaginations of men. Patriotism becomes the dominant feeling, and produces immediately that intense and hopeless confusion between the relations which the individual bears and should bear towards the society of which he is part.

In August 1914, the German labour movement was the largest and most powerful section within the Second (socialist) International. Even so, in spite of massive opposition to the war, Germany's socialist and trade union leaders arbitrarily overruled their rank and file's opinions on the grounds that it was 'progressive' and 'just' for advanced powers to declare war against less developed ones. And so, on 30 July 1914, a delegation of Social Democratic Party leaders met with the Prussian Minister of State to assure him of the German socialist movement's unquestioning loyalty to the regime. Four days later, they announced in parliament that 'the SPD stands by the Fatherland in its hour of danger,' and that the German unions had agreed to an industrial truce—a *Burgfrieden*—for the duration.

As trade unions were increasingly incorporated into the state structure, workers' demands and protests also grew proportionately, particularly in opposition to being conscripted into the mines. The reservoir of goodwill the German state had built up with organised labour in 1914 was becoming exhausted. By 1918 it had evaporated, the socialist and trade union leaders who negotiated the original *Burgfrieden* were discredited. The contagious example of the Russian Revolution overturning the old established order had also given legitimacy, credibility, and urgency to the argument for revolution.

In Austria-Hungary, the Social Democratic Party, the country's main Marxist party, nailed its colours to the mast by committing itself to keeping the Habsburgs in power. When war was declared, the Austrian socialist leaders justified their support for the regime as an 'unavoidable defence against Russian expansionism'. Without a single exception, every Social Democratic and Marxist member of parliament voted to support the war—and to outlaw all strikes and acts of rank and file 'insubordination'.

The only people with any integrity who objected to the war—and did something about it—were the Czechs, many of whom threw down their weapons when ordered to march against Russia. The anarchist writer Jaroslav Hašek's *The Good Soldier Schwejk* was probably more diary than fiction.

In Spain, CNT secretary general Francisco Roldán declared that if the government entered the war, the union would declare a revolutionary general strike. Segui and Pestaña denounced this off-the-cuff statement, but what no one knew or suspected at the time was that Roldán and a number of other prominent 'neutralist' cenetistas were already in the pockets of the German special services.

THE CENTRAL POWERS' ESPIONAGE OPERATIONS IN SPAIN

Since the first crisis over the international status of Morocco in 1905, Germany and Austria-Hungary had been particularly sensitive to Spain's strategic and logistical importance as a supplier of raw materials, manufactured goods and food, and had, since then, been running an extensive espionage network in the peninsula and North Africa for the previous fourteen years.

The activities of Central Powers' spies in Spain first came to light in October 1914, when one of their agents was discovered transmitting information from a Carmelite convent in Bilbao to German battleships in the Bay of Biscay, underlining the close links between the German secret services and the Roman Catholic Church. Jocelyn Grant, then British military attaché in Madrid, reported to the director of the British Secret Service Bureau in London on the close links between the German Embassy in Madrid and the Spanish clergy, the military, and the grandees. Grant also kept London briefed on the extent of German funding of Spain's right-wing newspapers. I later discovered from Henry Angliss and William Peel, two of the British special service officers with the Cairo Gang who had worked in Russia with Robert Bruce Lockhart and Sidney Reilly during the revolution, that one of their Leninist

Bolshevik agents, an Okhrana officer, was in fact *Pravda*'s editor-in-chief. Roman Malinovsky, the man who headed up the Leninist Bolshevik organisation inside Russia until 1914, was another British secret service 'asset'. It was certainly an eye opener for me. I remember thinking that perhaps they were trying to recruit me as an agent, as opposed to the temporary quid pro quo arrangement we thought we had with them at the time.

Spain's parliament, the Cortes, had been in the pocket of Germany's special services throughout the Kaiser's War, and since 1915 the Germans had spent in the region of half a million pesetas manipulating Spain's right-wing press—*ABC, El Correo Español, La Correspondencia Militar, El Debate, El Universo, La Acción, La Tribuna,* and *La Nación*—all of which presented the Central Powers' cause as synonymous with that of international 'law and order'.

On the other side, Spanish newspapers receiving financial subvention from the Entente powers included *La Epoca, El Diario Universal, El Liberal, El Heraldo de Madrid, La Correspondencia de España, El Imparcial,* and, of course, the paper of the man who started it all: Luis de Araquistain's *España*.

Through some sophisticated press manipulation by the Germans, the Kaiser was presented as the friend of the Spanish monarchy and the defender of the established order, while the Entente Cordiale leaders were portrayed as revolutionary, Republican, and Masonic in inspiration.

By 1918 Germany's special services controlled over five hundred local and national newspapers in Spain. They were helped in this by the high cost of newsprint which made the less scrupulous publishers—of whom there were many—more amenable to accepting financial support in return for running pro-German stories, such as presenting Germany's invasion of Belgium as a 'consequence' of the war, not its cause.

Spanish newspaper readers were fascinated by what was happening on Europe's battlefields and in its chancelleries. Most papers focused on nothing but the war, hence the heavy German investment in the liberal press and their interest in the widely read pro-neutral anarcho-syndicalist publications.

All this was difficult to prove as it was done behind closed doors, with the publishers and editors receiving what were reputedly substantial sums of cash in hand, some of which went to their paper, the rest into their pockets. The quid pro quo, however, was an editorial line firmly opposing any departure from strict neutrality.

Media criticism of the Central Powers—even a passing reference to 'innocent lives' lost in a submarine attack or reports of atrocities in Central-Powers-controlled territory—was considered tantamount to warmongering and a call to intervention. Spain's craven and corrupt national press even justified the torpedoing of Spanish vessels and the deaths of Spanish sailors, blaming 'greedy' vessel owners as the authors of their own misfortune, accusing them of smuggling contraband, war profiteering and siding with the aggressors. Germany, they claimed, was merely fighting to survive, an end that justified its means.

In 1916, before Germany's submarine campaign began in earnest, some pro-Central-Powers papers were regularly publishing lists of the Spanish companies producing and selling matériel to the Entente countries—identifying the ships that regularly carried cargoes to Allied ports.

THE IMPEX FILE

Madrid and Barcelona were the main operational centres of Central-Powers espionage, sabotage and political subversion in Spain; these two bases controlled most of the agents operating in the peninsula—Bilbao, Valencia, Malaga, Huelva, the Balearics, and the Canary Islands—as well as in Portugal and North and North-West Africa. Both centres also ran networks in Bordeaux, Le Havre, Cherbourg, Brest, Marseilles, and Toulon. The Madrid-based military attaché, von Kalle, was responsible for all of Germany's clandestine land operations in the Western hemisphere, from Hudson Bay to Cape Horn, while Captain von Krohn, the naval attaché, ran all Atlantic and Mediterranean maritime operations.

Cover for much of German-Austro-Hungarian covert operations was provided by the Barcelona-based German import-export firm Impex, which had offices in every major Spanish and Portuguese port. A subsidiary of a Madrid registered business, Impex imported a wide range of manufactured goods from Germany—machine tools, mining equipment, automobiles, dyes, and pharmaceuticals—and reexported strategic raw materials back to Germany and Austria-Hungary.

Trading under the name Ceuta Impex, a Spanish freight forwarding company that had been established as a front for the German and Austro-Hungarian secret services since 1914, Impex shared a front door, a hallway, adjoining offices, and an interior staircase with Ceuta Impex. Nor was it a coincidence that the same building housed the administrative offices of the Hamburg-based Atlas, Oldenburg-Portugiesische Dampfschiffs-Rhederei (OPDR) and Woermann shipping lines, which operated twice-weekly scheduled services to Morocco and the west coast of Africa.

Impex's warehouses were managed by gangmaster Luciano González, a fat slug of a thug who provided the lowlife muscle for the organisation's clandestine operations. According to the Defence Commission of the CNT Maritime Workers' Union, González's cutthroats, a gang of stevedores, were responsible for sabotaging ships, wharves, and warehouses, planting incendiary and explosive devices in the holds of boats with cargoes destined for Entente ports. These outrages were consistently laid at the door of the anarchists and the CNT.

Central and South America were key targets in the Central Powers' global war strategy. In Mexico they worked hard to destabilise and overthrow the corrupt pro-American Venustiano Carranza and his anointed successor, Ignacio Bonillas. Carranza's corruption didn't bother them; what did matter was that he and Bonillas, his Washington ambassador, remained pro-American. The Germans wanted Carranza replaced by someone favourable to the Central Powers and plotted a coup with General Pablo González of the Mexican army. González, a ruthless half-Yaqui *mestizo*, was a psychopath who hated *peones*, *rancheros*, and Zapatistas. In fact, there weren't many people he did like, or who liked him. The German plan was to goad the Mexican army into attacking the Yankees, thereby sucking America into a US-Mexican war. They were also causing trouble in the Azores, trying to get the islands to secede from Portugal.

Germany and Austria-Hungary's special services also targeted munitions factories and harbour facilities along the US seaboard—and in the Azores, where they successfully sabotaged the United States's only four K-Class submarines based there, along with their tender vessel, the *USS Bushnell*. German agents also successfully bombed ships heading for Allied European ports, blew up oil wells in Tampico, sabotaged mining operations in Chile, and poisoned Argentinean livestock destined for export to Europe.

Germany's secret services also used as cover a tuna and sardine canning company with fisheries in Galicia, the Basque country, the Canaries, and the Azores, while the Barcelona Centre operated a canning station on the small Balearic island of Cabrera, south of Mallorca, and other canneries as far down the coast as Valencia. The German and Austro-Hungarian navies used these out-of-the-way plants as forward supply bases for provisioning their Atlantic and Mediterranean submarine fleets. German submarines were also being provisioned along the Valencian coast by boats belonging to Juan March, a key player in organised crime in Spain. At the same time, German agents in Morocco's Spanish zone—Bartels, Koppel, and Richels—were providing funds, weapons, ammunition, and explosives to the Moroccan tribes that had risen in revolt against the French, while Germany's vice consulates in Tetuan, Larache, and Melilla were bases for clandestine operations and intrigues across the Maghreb. From those bases, local German agents provided Rif chieftains Abdel Malik and Raisuni with money and weapons which allowed them to continue their operations against the French. Koppel had to be expelled from Spain's North African protectorate after police unwittingly intercepted a million pesetas intended for Raisuni and half a million for Abdel Malik, a situation that was highly embarrassing for the Spanish government.

THE ETAPPENDIENST
Another, independent German naval intelligence service operating in Spain at the time was the Etappendienst, headed by U-boat commander Wilhelm Canaris, who operated from one of the many German merchant ships interned in the port of Cartagena. The German navy used these vessels as fuel, food, and matériel dumps for provisioning their Mediterranean U-boat fleet. Etappendienst agents had minimum contact with the German embassy in Madrid for radio communications with Berlin they had their own high-powered wireless telegraphy radio stations with Telefunken engineers and technicians operating from Spanish trawlers. Canaris had agents working in shipping and forwarding agencies, fishing companies and with the ports and harbours' authorities and regularly tried to recruit CNT members to provide information on ships' cargoes and arrival and departure times. There was even a postcard circulating of a surfaced German submarine in Cartagena harbour being openly refuelled and provisioned.

MARTHE RICHARD
Much of our information on Germany's special services came from a French compañera by the name of Marthe Richard—or Marthe Regnier to use her maiden name—von Krohn's mistress. For a spymaster, von Krohn was extraordinarily indiscreet where Marthe was concerned.

Marthe's story was unusual. As a child, she ran away from her home in Lorraine to Paris where she was soon caught and returned to her parents, who placed her in a convent. She promptly escaped again and returned to Paris where she fell in with a French anarchist, Alexandre Marius Jacob, and his partner, Rose Roux, who looked after the rebel twelve-year-old girl as their own. This time she wasn't caught, or perhaps even looked for. Unfortunately, Jacob, Rose and most of the members of his anarchist group were betrayed and arrested in 1905 for a string of spectacular burglaries of the rich and well-to-do across the length and breadth of France. They were sentenced to life imprisonment on Devil's Island, leaving the sixteen-year-old Marthe to fend for herself. She turned to prostitution to survive for a time, until by chance she met, fell in love with, and married an extremely rich patron who was able to indulge her every whim.

One of these whims was learning to fly and, now a wealthy woman, she took lessons, becoming one of the first women in France to obtain a pilot's certificate. Unfortunately, her husband was killed on active service shortly after the outbreak of the Kaiser's War. Ever the adventuress, she was recruited into the French secret service, the Service de Renseignements (SR), by spymaster George Ladoux and posted to Spain where she mixed in the highest circles of Madrid society. Even so, she always remained close to her libertarian roots and regularly passed on information she thought might be useful to her CNT and anarchist contacts in Spain.

During her time on the Madrid diplomatic cocktail circuit, Marthe became romantically involved with Baron Hans von Krohn, the head of German naval intelligence in Madrid. Von Krohn, always with one eye on the main chance and the other on beautiful women, quickly recruited her into his spy network, via the horizontal road to espionage. Before taking her on, however, the von Krohns—husband and wife—invited her to dinner to test her claim not to understand German, which she did, perfectly. Over dinner, the von Krohns and other selected German guests talked among themselves, blatantly and rudely, in German, about all French women being whores, implying also that the dessert was poisoned, then discussing how they would get rid of their guest's body. Marthe didn't bat an eyelid and continued eating as though she were totally oblivious to the macabre conversation going on around her.

Although she and von Krohn became lovers, the arrogant German aristo seriously underestimated her, taking her for a fool, which she most certainly was not. It wasn't long before this astute woman had wheedled important information out of the kraut spymaster about German operations in Spain, France, and Morocco—and the routes used by the Germans to infiltrate spies and saboteurs into France through the Pyrenees. Von Krohn even sent her to Argentina with a box of weevils, which she was supposed to introduce into Allied grain and food supplies. Another of von Krohn's schemes was poisoning Entente livestock—horses, mules, and cattle. Worse was planned. Marthe discovered that he had commissioned a mad Cameroonian professor by the name of Kleine to gelatinise cholera and typhus cultures that were to be dumped in rivers along the Portuguese border, the intention being to provoke panic and a diplomatic incident that would oblige Portugal to close its border with Spain and compromise its relationship with the Entente. The plot never came to anything. The French had Kleine under close surveillance and the only thing dumped in the Tagus was his body.

Marthe's master plan was to drug von Krohn, steal the contents of his safe, kidnap him with the help of an anarchist action group, and smuggle him across the border, but when it came to it, her French handlers refused her the drugs she needed to dope him, and would not return her passport so she could return to France. Sensing a double-cross in some nasty internecine Franco-German secret service game, Marthe took matters into her own hands and ended the affair with von Krohn, somewhat impetuously and publicly, during afternoon tea in the salon of the Madrid Ritz. She also told him, equally rashly, that not only had she been working for the French all along, but also that she was an anarchist and that she despised him and the regime and class he represented.

Had Marthe broken this bombshell in private there's little doubt von Krohn would have killed her there and then with his bare hands, but in such a public place he was powerless to do anything other than stare at her with incomprehension and a dropped jaw that must have looked like a urinal. To exacerbate matters, Marthe then telephoned the German ambassador, Prince von Ratibor, to tell him she had been von Krohn's lover—which he probably knew anyway—and that she was a French agent to whom von Krohn had been paying large sums of money out of secret service funds. She also told him that she had had free access to von Krohn's safe and regularly photographed its top-secret documents.

I imagine her intention in telling Prince von Ratibor all this was to put the proverbial cat among the equally proverbial pigeons and cause the maximum disruption, confusion, and embarrassment to Germany's special services, but she seriously underestimated von Ratibor's anger and von Krohn's malice. She soon realised they had put out a contract on her and that her life was in danger; it was time to leave the country. The first she knew of the contract on her was when von Krohn's *pistoleros* tried to kill her when she was out rowing on the Parque del Retiro boating lake in the centre of Madrid. When the shooting started she was hit in the shoulder, but escaped by jumping overboard and hiding below the upturned boat. It could have been much worse. The CNT arranged to have her smuggled across the border and into France.

Marthe was a unique source of information. Ethically she felt she had no choice, but the duplicity proved too much for her. It's surprising she put up with von Krohn for so long. He was a truly nasty piece of work, and probably deranged. A leading light in the Thule Society, he was involved in all sorts of arcane satanist practices. I'm unaware of his subsequent fate, but I suspect he was either sent home or severely reprimanded. Ratibor was not a forgiving man, and was not amused by his subordinate's lack of judgment.

German agents in Spain had much to answer for: the deaths of so many of our merchant navy compañeros sunk in the Mediterranean and the Atlantic. For years von Krohn's and Canaris's spy networks kept their submarine commanders informed as to cargoes, destinations, routes, itineraries, and convoy assembly points of all ships leaving Spanish, Portuguese, and French Mediterranean and Atlantic ports. The dangers were not confined to the sea; boats and lives were at risk in ports as well. Between 1916 and 1918, more than forty members of the CNT's Maritime Workers' Union were either killed or seriously injured by sabotage in the docks. Also, although Germany's secret war in Spain focused mainly on shipping, their agents and proxies murdered, bombed, and raised fires in factories and warehouses throughout the peninsula, including Portugal—and tried to incriminate cenetistas and anarchists as the perpetrators.

THE GERMANS AND *SOLIDARIDAD OBRERA*

The Madrid newspaper *El Sol*, had published a facsimile of a letter—leaked to them by French intelligence agents—from Dr Eberhard von Stohrer, the second secretary of the German Embassy at 4 Paseo de la Castellana in Madrid, to the then editor of *Solidaridad Obrera*, Pascual. The letter itemised German contributions towards the print costs of anarchist antiwar leaflets, payments that had been personally authorised by the German ambassador von Ratibor. To compound the problem, Pascual allegedly told *El Sol* that he had had regular meetings with two German Embassy attachés, von Stohrer and Grimm, who paid him to provoke disturbances, organise strikes—with the intention of disrupting Spain's export trade with France and Britain and to publish hostile editorials on the pro-Entente government of the Conde de Romanones.

Solidaridad Obrera's position had always been that if Spain entered the war it would be the workers who would suffer most, paying for it with their lives. *Soli* editorials also attacked the country's pro-Entente factions for being complicit in the orgy of exports that was tearing the country apart. As far as Pestaña was able to ascertain, most of the German money went into *Soli*'s press fund—as opposed to going into anyone's pockets—and had been doing so since mid-1915. The only other main 'left-wing' newspaper supporting the government's supposedly strict neutrality policy was the Republican *España Nueva*, which was also bankrolled by the German secret service. The company fronting the Central Powers' press campaign was the Madrid-based Sociedad Civil de Estudios Económicos, a German-owned firm operating from an office at 20 Calle Campoamor. Its chairman in Spain was a Spaniard, a former Austrian Embassy employee and a front man liaising between the German services and Spanish publishers, editors, and journalists. The brain behind the operation was his partner, a German secret service agent by the name of Gustavo Motschmann.

In 1918 *Solidaridad Obrera*'s editor was José Borobio. He was about forty-five years of age, but his broken nose and lumpy, scarred eyebrows made him look much older, and if he wasn't an actual German agent, he was certainly a German asset. Borobio's editorials argued that intervention served only the interests of the shipowners and manufacturers. The clergy and the oligarchs, he said, were plotting to bring Spain into the war against the class interests of the people, for whom it would mean more poverty and misery. This was true, but it raised the question as to what life would be like if Germany won the war. The more I read and discussed the issue with people who were much better informed than myself, the more I became convinced that the Austro-Hungarian government had been manipulated by the Germans into using Archduke Ferdinand's assassination in Sarajevo as an excuse to provoke Russian mobilisation—knowing full well it would lead to a war which they hoped would launch Germany as a world power.

My 'plague on all their houses' attitude had long gone, mainly as a result of long debates with myself on the question of greater and lesser evils. It had been very confusing. Macphail's death had changed me and taken me beyond the boundaries of my personal moral landscape, across my own 'line in the sand'.

Borobio had to be careful not to offend the CNT's then partner, the socialist UGT, with whom the CNT had signed a pact of unity, which was why the Catalan CNT—the Confederación Regional del Trabajo (CRT)—sent him to Madrid to discuss with the Socialist Party the risks they were running for the labour alliance by abandoning internationalism and pressing for intervention. The final decision, however, lay with the CNT's National Committee, which was largely pro-German, and suspicious of the UGT because of its treachery during the previous August's general strike.

The British and French were as up to their necks in this covert propaganda campaign as the Germans, but the latter were more efficient. The Entente didn't launch their propaganda effort until 1916, and that only happened under pressure from pro-Entente Spaniards like the socialist journalist Luis de Araquistain, who persuaded the Political Intelligence Division of Lord Beaverbrook's Ministry of Information Department MI7 (b) of the British Directorate of Military Intelligence to subsidise a media offensive to counter that of the Central Powers.

Germany was also quick to exploit the historic rivalry between Portugal and Spain. Portugal had been a republic since 1910 and its relations with Spain—which had been behind a number of unsuccessful plots to restore the Spanish monarchy to the Portuguese throne—were far from friendly. Spain's then prime minister, the Conde de Romanones, believed the war would allow Spain to absorb Portugal and extend its Moroccan territories. Until relentless German provocations forced Portugal into the war in 1916, Portuguese neutrality served the geopolitical interests of the Entente.

THE STRANGE CASE OF JEAN KISS

At the end of May 1918 Ángel Pestaña presented his evidence on the compromised relationship between *Solidaridad Obrera*'s editorial team and the German secret service to the Catalan Regional Committee of the CNT. The news didn't just rock the boat; it blew it out of the water. Until then everyone had been pleased with how well *Solidaridad Obrera* had been doing since Borobio and his editorial team took over the paper in May 1915: it appeared regularly and on time, and within budget, but no one had bothered to audit the accounts or ask where the money was coming from to pay the inflated costs of wartime newsprint.

I met Borobio a couple of times. He was a strange character. Most evenings, after putting *Soli* to bed, he would go straight to the music halls where he performed most nights under the stage name of 'Jean Kiss'—hypnotist and conjurer. I saw his show a few times in the Victoria theatre in the Paral·lel and he was an impressive conjurer and legerdemain artist. A few years later, in his film *The Thirty-Nine Steps*, Alfred Hitchcock based the character of the 'Memory Man' on Borobio—the performer who gets shot on stage at the London Palladium by the wicked German spymaster, Professor Jordan, when he automatically recites the answer to Richard Hannay's question from the audience: 'What are the Thirty-Nine Steps? Come on! Answer up! What are the Thirty-Nine Steps?'

'The Thirty-Nine Steps is an organisation of spies, collecting information on behalf of the foreign office of . . .' Then, bang, Professor Jordan shoots him dead.

Borobio wasn't shot, but when the German funding scandal broke he found himself ostracised by most of his old friends and union comrades;

the stage became his only source of income. But he wasn't the sort of man to bear a grudge. He took to travelling around Europe, putting on shows in schools, community centres, and music halls wherever he could hang his shingle. The last I heard of him was in the late 1920s when he performed in the Café New York in Budapest. His travelling act apparently so impressed a young thirteen-year-old Austro-Hungarian lad by the name of Matuska that he claimed at his trial—years later in Budapest in 1934—that he had fallen under the hypnotic power of Borobio/Kiss, who, he claimed, had hypnotised him into blowing up four rail bridges and two viaducts. 'Matuska the dynamiter' was, in fact, a severely disturbed young man—barking mad's the more appropriate description—who had been trained in sabotage techniques by the Austrian army; it was those army experiences, apparently, that tipped him over the edge.

Personally, I don't believe Borobio saw the moral contradiction in taking German money to keep *Soli* afloat; it didn't register with him that it might clash with his principles. Accepting German money wasn't a moral problem to him; his attitude was 'more fools them' for paying us to do what we believe in—preventing Spain being sucked into the plutocrats' war.

Borobio wasn't the only one; there were quite a few others who were more than willing to cooperate with the Germans once they had convinced themselves that they shared similar goals. The same could be said about those of us associated with Archs and the Defence Commission who were working with the British secret service. Glasshouses and stones spring to mind here.

Negré, on the other hand, *Soli*'s publisher, was a hot-blooded Valenciano who hated Sugar Boy and Pestaña intensely. He insisted to the end that the story of German funding was a misunderstanding. *Soli* had had problems with its print bills ever since it launched as a daily, until once, after a particularly heated dispute over an invoice, Negré, gave the print contract to another printshop, which led to an argument with Salvador Quemades, the graphic arts union secretary and a close friend of Salvador Segui. There was definitely some serious shit-stirring going on. It had been Quemades who first raised the question of *Soli* being funded by the Germans to support the Central Powers.

Soli's editorial line was unquestionably antiwar; its slogan was 'No war but the class war!' And, although it invoked plagues on both houses, there was a definite anti-French bias in its editorials, which probably led to the first rumours about *Soli* being financed by German gold—rumours that were spread and embellished by French secret service agents, some of whom were passing themselves off as anarchist deserters and conscientious objectors. The outcome of the investigation was that *Soli*'s entire editorial board was asked to resign, leaving Negré convinced that Pestaña, Segui, and Quemades had stitched him up. To make matters worse, Pestaña was appointed acting editor and immediately began recruiting a new editorial team. Whether or not Borobio and Negré had taken German money in return for maintaining *Soli*'s neutralist line in regard to the war was a moot point. The important thing was credibility: people believed it. There was no way any of them could have continued working on the paper without it losing all credibility.

The question of *Soli*'s German sponsorship never quite went away. Shortly after the story broke, a freelance journalist, an Andalusian by the name of Francisco Jordan—an occasional contributor to *Soli* who also wrote for the weekly La Rebeldía—approached Segui to suggest a meeting with two of the Republican demagogue Alexander Lerroux's tame journalists, Pierre and Leyn Rochyere, who told him it would be 'worth his while'. Intrigued, Segui met the two journalists who brazenly offered him a deal to make pro-German propaganda in his newspaper column.

'All right,' agreed Sugar Boy, 'but it will cost you 200,000 pesetas.'

Segui's price and the speed with which he agreed to their proposition took the Rochyeres by surprise. All they had on them, however, were 8,000 pesetas, which they promptly handed over, promising the balance within the week. 'Thanks, boys,' said Segui, rising to leave, 'for your welcome donation to the CNT's Prisoner's Fund!' Next day that amount was duly credited to the coffers of the CNT's *pro-presos* committee.

Soli's editorial position remained firmly antiwar, but under Pestaña's editorship it was now also markedly anti-German.

ON TREACHERY

Some comrades were easier prey than others for German agents, the Special Services Brigade, and provocateurs. The problem was that the vast majority of members, even the most apparently cynical, were very unworldly; like decent people the world over, they tended to accept people at face value and were generally unsophisticated in the devious and manipulative ways of bad people. But there were other, less class-conscious members whose reasons for joining the union had nothing to do with mutual protection and solidarity, but purely economic reasons of acquisitiveness and self-interest. They were more easily corrupted—expecting, as they did, far more from the big city than it could possibly provide.

Illiterate and credulous unskilled immigrants from Andalusia and Extremadura arrived in the city without jobs, money, family, or friends, believing their economic problems would be solved as if by magic. When things didn't improve or work out as they hoped, they found themselves homeless, hungry, disillusioned, and frustrated, blaming everyone except themselves for their situation. It was from the ranks of these malcontents that the police recruited many of their informers and gunmen foot soldiers. Traitors, informers, and confidentes—those amoral individuals whom states suborn or infiltrate into popular movements and organisations to undermine them from within—can be found in every walk of life, the weakest being the most vulnerable.

We uncovered a number of cases where Honnermann had been paying off CNT branch officials to foment industrial action in key factories and workshops involved in manufacturing strategic goods for the Entente. No matter what precautions were adopted, it was impossible to prevent the infiltration of spies and provocateurs; spies can and will penetrate to any position; there is no final defence against it.

Even the most idealistic of us can, at times, find ourselves psychologically vulnerable or compromised for all sorts of reasons: depression, fear of prison, disgrace or violence, protecting loved ones, being blackmailed for secret 'vices', having an affair, being homosexual, or whatever. We found evidence to suggest that a few apparently irreproachable compañeros were in fact on Honnermann's payroll, men such as Francisco Roldán, the former CNT national secretary; Villena, president of the Barcelona fabric and textile union; Gil, secretary of the Regional Committee of Catalonia; Irenofilo Diarot, a highly intelligent and personable compañero who worked with me on *Soli* and spoke French, English, and German; and Casildo Oses Bilbilis, a good journalist who covered all the CNT meetings and conferences for *Solidaridad Obrera*. I am not entirely convinced that Bilbilis worked for the police, at least not directly, but he was certainly on Alexander Lerroux's payroll.

Hardly a day went by after that without *Solidaridad Obrera* publishing more embarrassing information about German terrorist activity in the peninsula. Bruce and Marshall, with whom I liaised regularly that summer, fed us with as much of this material as we fed them with what we knew. In fact, Eduardo Dato's government was so compromised by the seemingly endless scandals, revelations, and leaks that the prime minister had to rush an Espionage Bill through the Cortes in an attempt to contain press speculation and prevent further embarrassing revelations. The speed with which they pushed through this legislation was clearly a sop to the German

ambassador, Prince Max von Ratibor who, ever since Pestaña's initial revelations in March, had been subjected to constant hostile press attention.
The law was a crude attempt to muzzle what little free press remained in
Spain, *Soli* in particular, and to avoid an embarrassing international diplomatic situation developing with the public unravelling of the German terrorist and espionage networks.

The public outcry was massive. The government lamely justified its
actions on the grounds that it was the only way to prevent the country's
'neutrality' being undermined by the negative unintended consequences of
'well-intentioned' press campaigns.

The penalties for providing agents of a foreign power with information compromising Spain's neutrality ranged from imprisonment to a fine
of between 500 and 20,000 pesetas. For publishing or circulating prohib-
ited information 'contrary to the respect due to the neutrality or security
of Spain' or spreading news 'of a nature to alarm Spaniards', the penalty
was imprisonment or a fine of up to 100,000 pesetas. Insulting, satirising
or exposing a foreign head of state, or a military or diplomatic representative to hatred or contempt—by word of mouth or in print or in illustration—
incurred a penalty of between 500 and 100,000 pesetas. The spies themselves faced a maximum fine of 20,000 pesetas, while the journalists and
publishers exposing them could receive fines up to 100,000 pesetas!

SPAIN AND THE RUSSIAN REVOLUTION

Surprisingly, there was much more enthusiasm among the anarchists for
the Russian Revolution than there was within the CNT, at least as far as *Soli*
was concerned. In December 1917, the newly formed Catalan Federation of
Anarchist Groups declared its support for the Revolution, and even adopted
the Bolshevik slogan of 'the dictatorship of the proletariat', although to give
them their due nobody seemed to know what the slogan meant or how it
squared with anarchist principles. People who should have known better
talked about the Bolsheviks as though they were some new tribe freshly
emerged from the rainforest to swell the ranks of the international anarchist movement—completely ignoring the controlling role of the Communist
Party. Editorials in the anarchist paper *Tierra y Libertad!* were equally naïve
as to the nature of the Bolshevik regime.

Even National Committee member, Manuel Buenacasa, one of the CNT's
most sensible and prolific writers on international and theoretical affairs,
was, for a short time, an enthusiastic Bolshevik supporter. As late as 1918
he was writing favourably about Lenin and Trotsky and their involvement at

Zimmerwald and Kiennthal, stressing how the Bolsheviks shared the CNT's desire to transform an imperialist war into a social revolution. He did, however, distinguish clearly between Bolshevism and revolutionary syndicalism:

> Bolshevism is state socialism, and represents a lesser ideology than syndicalism, which gives workers' control of all administrative functions. Even so—as did *Soli* and the CNT's National Committee—there is no question of not supporting the Russian Revolution, symbolising as it does the social war against capitalism. It will bring about a victory for Spanish workers by triggering social revolution throughout the peninsula; it is the first phase of a revolutionary process that will have a domino effect on all other countries, including Spain.

By the end of the summer of 1918, even though the Russian Revolution itself was still being championed by influential elements within the CNT, its apologists could no longer pretend that Bolshevism had anything to do with revolutionary syndicalism, or that it shared any of the Confederation's aims or principles. Apart from the Communist or Marxist syndicalists, supporters of the October Revolution began to differentiate between support for the social revolution in Russia and support for Bolshevism as an ideology.

THE RUSSIAN REVOLUTION AND BOLSHEVIK LENINISM

Sixty years on, it is difficult to imagine how different things were in 1918. It was, truly, another world. Social discontent across war-ravaged Europe had unleashed violent instability unlike anything anyone had seen since the days of the Paris Commune. Soldiers and sailors were mutinying, labour militancy was reaching critical mass, and large antiwar demonstrations and food riots were daily occurrences; landless agricultural workers had occupied the big estates in Andalusia, Italy, and Ireland, workers' councils had spread across industrial Germany, and in Russia Bolshevik success was demonstrating to Europe's elites the extent to which their power had been eroded. It seemed that the social cataclysm of 1789 in Revolutionary France was about to be replayed, this time across the whole of Western Europe.

Few people, however, including most anarchists, were aware of the duplicitous game being played by the Bolsheviks. To all intents and purposes the Russian Revolution of 1917 certainly conformed to most people's idea of revolutionary spontaneity, appearing to the world as a socialist dream come true, bestowing cult status on Bolshevism and the Bolsheviks. But in the euphoria of the moment their role was never properly analysed. There weren't many who understood the extent to which the revolution had been a consequence of the hunger and war weariness of a people forced into a conflict that no one other than the German High Command understood or cared about.

The outbreak of the revolution itself had taken everyone—Bolsheviks included—completely by surprise, although the Okhrana, the Tsar's secret police had been predicting it for months. The Russian Revolution began as food riots in the capital, Petrograd, and had little if anything to do with military defeat or discontent at the front. The demonstrations of February 1917 were primarily protests against the insufferable domestic social conditions that existed in the country. The reality was that the Russian army was probably a better and more efficient fighting force in 1917 than it had been at the outbreak of war. The conscription of the peasants and day-labourers, coupled with the railway network's inability to keep the armies supplied, led to food shortages in the towns, rampant inflation, and the enormous and ever widening gulf between rich and poor. Older soldiers from the Petrograd garrison who didn't want to be sent to the front joined the hungry food protestors, and after just three days of demonstrations, the Tsar's authority simply evaporated, especially after the Cossacks, sent to put down the demonstrations on 25 February, began fraternising with the protestors.

The extraordinary thing was that no one at the time really understood the significance of what was happening. The government ordered the dissolution of the Duma, the parliament, but its members ignored the order and continued their deliberations. It was at that point that the demonstrations, with their slogans calling for an end to Tsarism and to the war, took on a distinctly revolutionary flavour.

The decisive date was 27 February, when the Volynsky Regiment mutinied and joined the demonstrators in attacking the police. At ten in the morning, the crowd took over the Petrograd Arsenal, seizing forty thousand rifles, thirty thousand revolvers and ammunition. By 11 a m., the District Court and a nearby jail had been assaulted, its prisoners released and the buildings set on fire. Even when the crowds stormed the local police stations, the headquarters of the Petrograd Okhrana, Central Police headquarters and destroyed the telegraph office, it still wasn't clear that the Romanov Empire had collapsed. By noon that day around twenty-five thousand troops had mutinied, a fraction of the forces available to the government, a little more that 5 percent of the troops and police in Petrograd—but it was enough. Suddenly, to everyone's surprise, the Tsar abdicated and power passed into the streets. The problem, however, was that Tsarism hadn't been overthrown; it had imploded, leaving behind a government, the Duma, which patched together a provisional government of Liberals and a few Social Democrats under Alexander Kerensky, the self-appointed spokesman of this ad-hoc bourgeois government.

Kerensky's objective was to roll back what had become a full-scale revolution, but this proved impossible in the face of the emergence of a rival authority, the trades' councils—the soviets consisting of delegates from the factories, the armed services and some agricultural workers. Initially, the soviets didn't see themselves as governing bodies; their role, as they saw it, was that of radical pressure groups, to push the Provisional Government as far as it could go; but this 'dual power' situation couldn't last, with both groups operating in a political vacuum, and neither with sufficient strength to use what power they had.

LENIN IN SWITZERLAND

Lenin was in Switzerland when the February Revolution broke out, taking him and everyone else by surprise—everyone, that is, except the Russian secret police. The German High Command moved quickly to take advantage of the situation on the eastern front, and in April provided Lenin with funds and a safe conduct, and packed him off to Russia in a sealed train with Lettish bodyguards to oust Alexander Kerensky's provisional government. Kerensky was then being acclaimed as a hero by the Entente powers because of his commitment to continuing the war. Germany needed Russia out of the war to allow them to concentrate their forces on the Western Front.

The antiwar movement in Russia, meanwhile, continued to gather momentum throughout June 1917, with the anarchists playing a large part in the protests. In Petrograd they squatted the stately Durnovo Villa, converting it into a cultural centre and children's nursery. Durnovo was also the headquarters of the Petrograd Bakers' Union and the important Commissariat of the Workers' Militia.

It was when the Petrograd anarchists seized the offices and printing presses of a well-connected right-wing newspaper that their problems began, and they were quickly removed by force. But when the Minister of Justice tried to evict them from the Durnovo Villa it immediately provoked a wave of strikes in Petrograd's factories and brought out soldiers from the First Machine-Gun Regiment—and fifty anarchist sailors from Kronstadt, the island base of the Baltic Fleet, near Petrograd.

THE 'JULY DAYS'

Meanwhile, pressure to overthrow the Provisional Government continued to build. On 3 July, the First Machine-Gun Regiment again came out onto the

5 December 1917: Trotsky (second from right) at Brest-Litovsk to carve up Ukraine and sign armistice.

3 September 1918: Fanya Kaplan, Left Social Revolutionary, is executed for attempting to assassinate Lenin.

The Last Picture Show: the 'Captains and Kings' prepare to depart (funeral of Edward VIII).

German battlecruiser *Deutschland*.

Revolution sweeps Germany as Kaiser flees: radical soldiers and sailors man the guns.

Mutinying German soldiers in Kiel being addressed by Gustav Noske.

Marshal Foch accepts the German surrender on behalf of the Entente Cordiale.

The clock of revolution ticks towards midnight, 1919.

streets, calling for the disbanding of the Provisional Government. They also sent delegates to the nearby Kronstadt naval base to enlist support from the sailors who had earlier attempted to set up the independent republic of Kronstadt. This move was strongly resisted by local Bolshevik leader Fyodor Raskolnikov who saw it as a direct threat to party control.

Despite Bolshevik 'caution', unrest continued to grow. This was the start of what came to be known as the 'July Days' when a cohesive socialist movement began to emerge in the towns and cities, and in the countryside there was a wave of land seizures and widespread acts of jacquerie by landless peasants against the hated landowners.

Kerensky's government cracked down on the Kronstadt sailors, the First Machine-Gun Regiment, the Bolsheviks, and the anarchists, arresting and imprisoning their leaders and spokesmen. Lenin, Grigory Zinoviev, and other prominent Bolsheviks went on the run, disappearing to Vyborg in Finland where Lenin took time out to write his book *The State and Revolution*, which, duplicitously, appeared to turn the accepted Marxist view of the State on its head. Its publication caused widespread dismay among many of his own party who accused him of being an anarchist—which he most certainly was not! Lenin's brief flirtation with libertarian ideas was an opportunistic ploy— and greatly exaggerated.

On the night of 23–24 October, with rumours of a Bolshevik plot to seize power spreading, Kerensky sent cadets from the military academies to close two Bolshevik newspapers. These were promptly reopened the next day by troops loyal to the Military Revolutionary Committee of the Petrograd Soviet, the MRC, the closest thing at the time to a police force in the capital.

The following day, taking advantage of Kerensky's departure for the front to mobilise support for the Provisional Government, the Bolsheviks sent in Red Guards to seize the deserted General Staff building. At the same time they issued an ultimatum to the ministers in the Winter Palace to surrender by 9:20 p.m.; twenty minutes after the ultimatum expired, one of the big guns on the cruiser *Aurora*, anchored in the harbour close by, fired off one blank shot, scaring off the Palace's few remaining guards. As for the heroic storming of the Winter Palace—it never happened. The reality was much more mundane. At two o'clock in the morning of 26 October, the Bolshevik leader Antonov-Ovseyenko led a small detachment of Red Guards into the palace, squeezing in through a window in the servants' quarters, where, in the name of the people, they arrested the ministers of the Provisional Government. That was the sum total of the Bolshevik Revolution!

Shortly thereafter, Lenin and Trotsky appeared on the platform at the second meeting of the All Russian Congress of Soviets to announce that power now lay in the hands of the Soviets—and then proceeded to read out the names of the members of the new Soviet government—none of whom had ever been nominated or voted for by any Soviet, and most of whom were unknown to the assembled delegates. And that, in a nutshell, was how the Bolshevik propaganda machine fabricated the myth of the October Revolution and turned it into legend—forever corrupting and altering the course of the socialist movement, and establishing the pernicious example of Lenin and his ideological cronies as the paragons of socialist virtue.

The October Revolution was never a revolution of the masses, as had genuinely been the case of the earlier revolution in February. It was, in fact, a coup d'état comparable with Auguste Blanqui's 1848 attempt to seize control of France's revolutionary government. Nor did the Bolsheviks initiate it, even though they had talked about seizing power. Ironically, it was Alexander Kerensky who triggered the Bolshevik coup by moving against them prematurely, fully expecting them to collapse. Under Trotsky's leadership they resisted and, much to Kerensky's surprise, it was his own government that collapsed.

The Russian anarchists and other radical socialist groups did what they could to resist the Bolshevik seizure of power, but they weren't sufficiently organised, numerically strong or ruthless enough, and were among the first to fall victim to the Cheka's 'red terror'.

THE MYTH OF THE RUSSIAN REVOLUTION

Beyond Russia's borders the apparent success of the October Revolution of 1917 inspired giddy, contagious hope in a large part of the world's suppressed citizenry; but at the time it was the example of the February Revolution that inspired the Spanish labour movement to call the general strike. Bolshevism was the fashionable 'ism' of the moment, and to capitalise on this near-unconditional and uncritical support from international working-class organisations, Lenin and Trotsky convened a conference to be held in Moscow early in 1918. It was to be the first meeting of the Communist International, the Comintern, and the sinister institution that was soon to pervert and distort the ideas of socialism out of all recognisable shape.

Meanwhile, Lenin's new book *The State and Revolution*, recently translated into Spanish, was having its intended effect, reconciling, with ideological smoke and mirrors, a surprising number of anarchists to Bolshevism by creating the illusion that the Bolsheviks had abandoned the idea of the so-called dictatorship of the proletariat and democratic centralism, and were now endorsing revolutionary syndicalism, and advocating workers' control, press freedom, and the abolition of the state. In other words, Lenin was writing and talking like an anarchist.

Joaquín Maurín, a pro-Bolshevik Marxist who had manoeuvred himself into the position of secretary of the Lérida provincial federation of the CNT and editor of its newspaper—*Lucha Social*—mainly because most anarchists were in prison—waxed lyrical about Lenin's book, acclaiming it as 'the doctrinal bridge linking Bolshevism with syndicalism and anarchism'.

For non-Russian anarchists it was easy to believe in the Russian Revolution. Nobody outside Russia knew what was really happening there. What was clear was the fact that the hated Romanov regime had been replaced by factory committees and workers' and soldiers' soviets, and the slogan 'All Power to the Soviets' appeared to embody anarcho-syndicalist ideas on workers' control, local autonomy, and antistatism. It captured the imagination of everyone at the time, so we chose to ignore or gloss over the negative stories that were trickling out of Russia. Stories such as the arrest and torture of Maria Spiridonova, the respected Left Social Revolutionary. She was a Jenny Geddes figure who had denounced Lenin, accusing him and the Bolsheviks of betraying the industrial and agricultural workers by substituting state capitalism for the socialisation of industry, and institutionalising terror.

Also, nowhere in *The State and Revolution* did Lenin mention political centralisation, an omission that should have immediately aroused anarcho-syndicalist suspicions. But the book had its intended effect, and within six months membership of the new Bolshevik Communist Party leapt from 24,000 to 240,000, most of whom were would-be bureaucrats who saw joining as a career move, and an easy route to wealth, power, and influence.

It was all an illusion. Lenin had long since moved away from the idea of revolution as the 'midwife of history' to the concept of the 'Party as the midwife of revolution'. It wasn't long before the Bolsheviks reverted to type. 'Communism in Russia had to be defended at any cost against the nightmare threat of the "White" terror'—and they were the boys to do it. Now they held power, they were going to hang on to it, and those who questioned Party dictats or who didn't 'wholeheartedly support' the 'forces of order and discipline within the army' were demonised as 'traitors' who had to be 'ruthlessly destroyed'. To the Bolsheviks, people were never individual human beings with their hopes and dreams, flaws and ideals—they were mere integers in the realm of their political calculations.

PROLETARIAN COMPULSION AND NEW COMMUNISM

From the outset, Lenin set himself the objective of establishing state capitalism as the Party's top priority. Clinging uncompromisingly to Marxist theory as an established truth, his argument was that state communism would ultimately transform itself into a humane method of production that would benefit the people. But, like Marx, none of the Bolshevik leaders understood or had the slightest regard for the concept of freedom—nor did they appreciate the basic political truth that state power inevitably develops institutionalised interests of its own, at the expense of any honestly held or professed revolutionary ideals.

Nikolai Bukharin, Lenin's close friend and protégé, defined the Bolshevik position thus:

> From a broader point of view, that is the point of view of a historical scale of greater scope, proletarian compulsion in all its forms, from executions to compulsory labour, constitutes, as paradoxical as this may sound, a method of the formation of a new Communist humanity from the human material of the capitalist epoch.

'Precisely', noted Lenin in the margin.

LENIN AND FANYA KAPLAN

As the economy collapsed around them and their unpopularity grew daily, due to the draconian restrictions of 'War Communism', the Bolshevik leaders saw their hold on power slipping away. My view is they passed their tipping-point when they murdered the Tsar and his family in that Ekaterinburg cellar on 16 July 1918. The killing of the Romanovs was a bad decision—morally, ethically, and politically. The Bolshevik leaders panicked, fearing that the sixty thousand strong Czechoslovak Legion occupying nearby Kazan—who had seized eight train carriages of gold bullion from the imperial reserve—might try to free the royal family and use them as a rallying point to march on Moscow.

Earlier that July, political and social discontent had led to an unsuccessful revolt by Left Social Revolutionaries in which three hundred of them were killed. A few weeks later, Fanya Kaplan, another Left Social Revolutionary, almost succeeded in assassinating Lenin. Her action provided Lenin and Cheka head Felix Dzherzinsky with an excuse to unleash what they officially described as the 'Red Terror', a 'merciless mass repression directed against all the enemies of the revolution,' i.e. those who opposed the Bolsheviks—a terror that has continued now for more than fifty years.

Interrogated by the Cheka, Fanya made the following short statement:

> My name is Fanya Kaplan. Today I shot at Lenin. I did this on my own, and I will not say from whom I obtained my revolver. I will give no details, but I made up my mind to kill Lenin long ago as a traitor to the Revolution. I was exiled to Aktau for my involvement in an assassination attempt against a Tsarist official in Kiev as a result of which I spent eleven years at hard labour, and was only freed after the Revolution. I favoured the Constituent Assembly, of which I am still a supporter.

A state executioner shot Fanya Kaplan in the back of the head on 3 September 1918.

LENIN SELLS OUT UKRAINE

Even before the outbreak of war in August 1914, Germany's master plan had been to subvert the imperial structures of the countries of the Entente Cordiale, a plan that required Germany to secure its empire in the west, displace France and Britain as the dominant colonial and maritime powers, push Russia back as far as possible from Germany's border, and break her influence over her non-Russian European buffer states. That was why the German high command gave Lenin free transit to the Finland Station in a sealed train with a bodyguard of Lettish mercenaries—and the money he needed to fund and arm the Red Army.

Germany's military and political leaders may have been blockheads, but they understood that Bolshevik ambitions were, ultimately, a threat to their own class interests. At one point in 1918, General Ludendorff, who dominated German policymaking throughout the war, was prepared to send troops to finish off the Bolsheviks, but was overruled by the Kaiser and other German political leaders who had their own agendas.

When the Bolsheviks sued for peace with Germany at Brest Litovsk, it cost them massive territorial and economic concessions in Ukraine—which meant that by mid-1918 Lenin was back asking Germany for more military assistance to prosecute the Civil War in Russia. The collapse of the Russian front and Lenin's deal with the Germans at Brest Litovsk seriously damaged the credibility of the left everywhere and transformed anti-German sentiment into anti-Bolshevism and anti-radicalism.

In the United States, the editorial line of the populist Hearst press was that the Bolsheviks were German agents whose objective was to free up the Kaiser's troops to fight more effectively against the Entente on the Western Front. In Britain, the so-called 'Diehards' in Lloyd George's Cabinet, the

War Office, and even in some leftist circles, claimed Brest Litovsk was nail-in-the-coffin proof that all the antiwar, pacifist, and revolutionary socialist organisations were covert agencies of Germany's hidden hand, dedicated to exploiting industrial unrest as part of its military strategy.

One reason why the British Cabinet was so convinced of the conspiratorial links between German intrigues and pacifism, revolutionary rhetoric and internationalism, was because section MI7 (b) of the British Secret Service Bureau had been up to exactly the same subversive tricks in Germany and Austria, sowing dissent and fomenting revolution within the labour movements there. They achieved this by orchestrating an aggressive propaganda campaign that ranged from dropping revolutionary propaganda leaflets from aeroplanes to funding German antiwar and radical groups such as the Briefeinhall and Nemesis networks. They did exactly the same in Italy, funding—among other publications—Benito Mussolini's prowar paper *Il Popolo d'Italia*, in an attempt to combat pacifism and antimilitarism through newspaper editorials and street brawls.

NESTOR MAKHNO

Lenin's sell-out of Ukraine backfired on the Bolsheviks when large numbers of agricultural workers in the region began resisting the German occupation, the 'White' interventionists and Trotsky's Red Army, which was attempting to impose Bolshevik control over the area. As a result, many workers and peasants rallied to the anarchist guerrilla army raised by Nestor Makhno and his anarchist comrades. Because the anarchist movement in Russia and Ukraine was so small, news of Makhno's military and revolutionary successes took everyone by surprise, including the anarchists. East of the Dneiper, Makhno's anarchist militia controlled a large territory through the anarchist led regional Soviet of Workers, Peasants, and Insurgents. Makhno himself was elected chairman of the Gulayai-Polye Committee for the Defence of the Revolution, the body responsible for redistributing land, cattle, and agricultural equipment to peasant families, and for collectivising workshops in those parts of Ukraine it controlled.

Makhno began his campaign in January 1918 with small guerrilla units targeting German patrols; by September these small units had grown into an insurrectionary army that defeated an entire German army division. Makhnovschina partisans also took Ekaterinoslav. This was the dramatic occasion when Makhno and his men marched through the town to the jail, released the prisoners, blew up the prisons, and then shot the judge who had sent him to prison eleven years earlier.

The Makhnovschina organised themselves on three basic principles: voluntary enlistment, self-discipline, and the electoral principle—in which all units and ranks elected all officers and commanders. Soldiers' committees that were subsequently approved by all units drew up disciplinary rules. These rules were rigorously observed on the basis of individual responsibility and awareness of the possible consequences of poor discipline, not only on fellow soldiers but also on the wider movement in general.

Eight years later, when I met Makhno in Paris, he told me that around that time—June 1918—he was in a Moscow meeting with Lenin and Yakov Sverdlov, the secretary of the Bolshevik Central Committee. He'd gone to discuss strategy and tactics in Ukraine with fellow anarchists and, while he was there, he decided, on impulse, to visit the Kremlin and speak with Lenin.

It was a patronising interview in which neither Lenin nor Sverdlov had the slightest idea who Makhno was, what he was doing, or his politics; all they knew was that he came from what they called the 'tortured south of Russia'—a euphemism for Ukraine, the Russian equivalent of 'Red Clydeside'. The Bolshevik leaders were completely ignorant as to what the anarchist-led peasants of Gulayai-Polye were doing to resist both the Austro-German occupation troops and the soldiers of the Central Rada, Ukraine's national government. As far as the Bolsheviks were concerned, all southern peasants were either kulaks or supported the Central Rada. When it finally dawned on Lenin that his visitor was an anarchist, he became agitated and jumped up from his chair, pacing up and down, gesticulating spasmodically like a man with motor neurone disease:

> Yes, yes. You anarchists are big on ideas for the future, but in the here-and-now, you don't have your feet on the ground. It is deplorable. Can't you understand that your vacuous fanaticism means that you have no real links to the future . . . Have anarchists ever acknowledged their lack of realism in the 'here-and-now' of life? No!—it never occurs to them.

Lenin sniffed reflectively, spat awkwardly, and missed the spittoon by his desk. Makhno, restraining himself admirably, replied, politely, but with obvious irritation and muted sarcasm:

> Forgive me, comrade Lenin, I am only a poor and semiliterate peasant, and I will not be drawn into your peculiarly distorted understanding of what and how anarchists think and behave. You are completely

Russia's Provisional Government led by
Alexander Kerensky (centre), June 1917.

Lenin (with wife Nadezhda
Krupskaya): paragon of
socialist virtue?

Madrid, May Day, 1918: pro-Russian
demonstration.

Petrograd, 30 December 1917: Anarchist
Congress delegates.

Kronstadt, 1917: revolutionary sailors in main
square.

Petrograd, 1917: parade of workers' militia.

First meeting of the Petrograd Soviet.

Makhnovia 1917–18: Makhnovist sphere of
influence.

1918: Nestor Makhno, aged 30.

wrong, however, when you say 'anarchists have no grasp or ties with the here-and-now'.

We anarchists of Ukraine—or 'Southern Russia' as you Bolshevik Communists so dismissively describe Ukraine—have already furnished more than enough proof that we stand foursquare in the 'here-and-now'. And, for your information, the entire struggle of the revolutionary Ukrainian countryside against the Central Rada has been inspired and led by anarchist communists and Social Revolutionaries. To be honest, we fight against the Rada for different reasons. Your Bolsheviks don't, for the most part, exist in our part of the country, and where there are any, your influence is miniscule. Most peasant communes and associations in Ukraine are led or inspired by anarchist communists, and I have to add that all the resistance to the counterrevolution in general—and the Austro-Hungarian and German invading armies—has been led, exclusively, under the ideological and organisational banner of Ukraine's anarchist communists. You may not like to credit us with that, but those are the facts and you cannot dispute them. I imagine you are aware of the numbers and fighting capacity of Ukraine's revolutionary irregulars? You referred, after all, to the courage with which they have been heroically defending our common revolutionary gains, and more than half of them fight under anarchist colours. Mokroussov, Nikiforova, Chernyak, Garin, Lunev, and many other partisan commanders—I couldn't begin to list them all—are all anarchist communists, not to mention my own group—or all the other partisan groups and volunteers we have set up to defend the revolution, and of which the Red Guard command must surely be aware.

All of which underlines, rather forcefully comrade Lenin, the extent to which you are mistaken in your view that we anarchist communists don't have our 'feet on the ground', that our attitude in the 'here-and-now' is to be deplored—although it is true we are fond of thinking about the 'future' a lot. What I am telling you is the truth, and it contradicts the verdict you have just passed on us. Everyone—you included—can see the proof that we stand foursquare in the 'here-and-now'. But we also keep our eyes open for whatever brings us closer to the future—something we do think about, and very seriously at that.

Sverdlov at least had the grace to blush at this reproach and looked at the floor. Lenin, however, shook his head dubiously and carried on pacing the floor, waving his arms around like a demented semaphorist: 'Well, maybe I am mistaken,' mumbled Lenin, grumpily, snorting in his nose and spitting noisily—but successfully this time—into the spittoon by his desk. 'Who doesn't make mistakes, especially in the situation in which we find ourselves at the moment?' Sensing Makhno's growing irritation, Lenin stopped pacing, pulled at his braces, and sat down. He tried to steer the conversation diplomatically back on to less contentious topics, but by this time the wee man from Gulayai-Polye was really wound up at the Bolshevik's arrogance. Makhno left shortly after.

'I would have liked to have been a fly on the wall of that office after I left,' said Makhno to me when we met in 1926. 'I'd have shat in his caviar.'

APOCALYPSE NOW!
The conjunction of the Russian Revolution with the end of the Kaiser's War opened up the prospect of an exhilarating new phase in humankind's struggle for a just society. It was a time of tremendous euphoria and great social ferment, an open window in history when anything seemed possible. It was the most exciting time since the Paris Commune of 1870–71—and we were part of it. The Austro-Hungarian and the Ottoman empires had collapsed by this time and revolutions were breaking out across Germany, Bavaria, and Hungary, while in Russia foreign and anti-Bolshevik armies were marching on Moscow. The clocks could not be put back; the revolution was sweeping westwards, terrifying Europe's ruling elites—especially the Spanish grandees and bourgeois capitalists whose power and privileges for so long had depended on electoral falsification, patronage, and brute force. It seemed just a matter of time until the old system collapsed.

Ironically, it was at precisely this time that Adolph Hitler was being politicised in Vienna, albeit for different reasons. His radicalisation was rooted in his sense of shame that his beloved Fatherland had been forced to surrender to the Entente on such humiliating terms. Spain's ignorant, malevolent, reactionary, and greedy aristocrats, oligarchs, and gent d'ordre were equally convinced of the imminence of the apocalypse, especially after the Fatima prophecies.

For many, it was 'the end of days' prophesied in the Bible. Hell had emptied, and Satan and all his little helpers were stalking the world seeking out the righteous to devour. The recently translated anti-Semitic Tsarist police forgeries, *The Protocols of the Wise Men of Zion*—which was being read and taken seriously by the gullible everywhere as a serious *vade-mecum* on how society functions behind closed doors—stated unequivocally that the Antichrist was at hand: 'He is near, he is hard by the door.'

All this seemed to make perfect sense to the ultras, integrists, fundamentalists, and ignorant dyslexics who needed supernatural causality in their lives, and who couldn't tell the Antichrist from the anarchist. This was no random concatenation of unfortunately timed events; dark forces were behind this seemingly inexorable rise of social unrest, strikes, revolution, and the collapse of Spain's foreign markets and economy. The astronomical growth of the anarcho-syndicalist CNT was itself a clear sign that God was unhappy! The world inhabited by Spain's well-heeled capitalists and rentier bourgeoisie, its hierarchs and landed gentry had been transformed into a living and frightening Gustav Doré engraving in which the howling demons of liberalism were laying siege to God's fortress.

MEANWHILE, EAST OF SUEZ

In the East, German, Austro-Hungarian and Ottoman strategies focused on undermining the British and Russian empires by encouraging Muslim revolts in the Middle East, Central Asia, and British India. In Mexico they infiltrated and tried to suborn the revolutionary movement, and provoke the army into attacking the United States with the intention of tying down the Americans at home. It was this plot to bring Mexico into the war—uncovered with the interception and decryption of the so-called 'Zimmerman Telegram' by British Naval Intelligence under Admiral 'Blinker' Hall—that finally brought the United States into the war. The plot was greatly exaggerated by the incompetent, opportunistic, and vicious-minded Basil Thomson—then head of Scotland Yard Special Branch—who produced a dossier for the British Cabinet claiming to have unassailable 'intelligence' that a German army was plotting insurrection from some unspecified location in the US Midwest, that Germany was planning a surprise invasion of New York, and that the US Administration was riddled with pro-German sympathisers who were warning fellow conspirators of their imminent arrest.

In Spain—the Entente's largest neutral trading partner—German attention focused on disrupting the economy by sabotaging shipping and factories supplying the Entente with war matériel—as well as promoting a strategy of tension through sponsored terrorism and antilabour vigilantism. German tactics changed round about the time I arrived in Barcelona. With Russia effectively out of the war, the United States well and truly in and Austria-Hungary close to collapse, Germany's political and military leaders were beginning to realise that they hadn't the slightest hope of defeating the Entente. Their campaign of unrestricted submarine warfare wasn't working, food was in short supply, Entente bombing raids over the Fatherland were increasingly frequent and intense—and with the campaign of subversion by the British Secret Service Bureau's [MI7 (b)] feeding the ripening fruits of political instability, the German General Staff was highly conscious of the rising tide of working-class discontent. The only way to prevent dissent metamorphosing into revolution was an overwhelming military victory.

It was now or never. Germany needed to inflict a sudden, devastating blow of sufficient magnitude that would knock Britain and France completely out of the war, before US troops were fully in place. The Germans launched their massive 1918 offensive along the Western Front, from the Somme to Cambrai, in a last-ditch attempt to drive straight through the Entente's lines. Two more coordinated offensives, one at Hasbrouck and another in Aisne, did break through the British defences and brought the Central Powers' armies to within fifty-six miles of Paris, leaving the French ready to fall back to defend the capital, and the British looking nervously to secure their escape routes to the Channel ports.

THE 'BIG PUSH'

The Entente launched its first concerted military offensive against the Central Powers on 8 August 1918, when Field Marshal Foch began his massive counterattack, deploying French, British, and American ground forces. The Germans were quickly overwhelmed and fell back towards the Fatherland, drenching the ground behind them with mustard gas to slow up the pursuing Entente army. During their uncontrolled retreat, the morale of the German military plummeted, manifesting itself in mutinies and rebellions. For militarists such as Erich Ludendorff, Germany's brilliant strategist, this was the German army's 'Blackest Day'.

Meeting at Spa afterwards, the Kaiser's Crown Council agreed that victory was no longer possible and that they should negotiate an armistice, which provoked a heated argument between the crown prince and Ludendorff, who won the argument—so the war continued.

Two Entente victories followed in quick succession: one at Saint-Quentin on 31 August, and another in Flanders on 2 September, making the disagreements among the German high command irrelevant. With their armies retreating to the Rhine, the Germans ratcheted up their submarine campaign, hoping to gain some leverage when the time came to negotiate an 'honourable' peace. By 10 August, German submarines had destroyed around 20 percent of the Spanish merchant fleet and killed over a hundred seamen. The situation had deteriorated to such an extent that even ships bringing in goods intended exclusively for Spanish domestic consumption were now being torpedoed. Spain retaliated by threatening to seize the forty or so German ships that had been detained in Spanish ports since the beginning of the war. The Germans responded almost immediately. Within ten days, two more Spanish ships were sunk and Germany announced that it would declare war on Spain if any of its vessels were impounded. This was the last thing Britain and France wanted. If Spain joined the war it would mean territorial claims in North Africa and North-West Africa and other economic demands at the victors' table.

THE CAPTAINS AND THE KINGS DEPART

On 9 November 1918, Kaiser Wilhelm II chose discretion over valour by abdicating and fleeing to Holland in a twenty-carriage train—each carriage filled with huge quantities of luggage—leaving Germany free to sue for peace. Behind him he left a political wasteland with middle-class Social Democrats such as the trade union leader Friedrich Ebert and the so-called socialist Gustav Noske setting up ultra-right-wing vigilante units of former soldiers to counter the workers' councils movement that now controlled most of the cities and towns.

Much the same occurred in Austro-Hungary. The last Hapsburg emperor signed away his empire in a hastily pencil-scribbled abdication note, leaving all its disparate regions to declare their independence. In Bavaria, King Louis fled while the Duke of Brunswick and five other German kings, princes, and grand dukes abandoned their castles and large estates, and escaped into exile. In Italy, day-labourers took over the big estates, and industrial workers declared workers' control and seized the factories. In Ireland, there were widespread general strikes with land seizures and workers took over the running of towns and cities. This happened not only in large centres like Limerick, but also small towns like Dungarvan where, for a month, nothing could be bought, sold, or brought into town without union approval. Anyone found breaking the blockade had their carts overturned and their goods confiscated or destroyed. The strike committee even had its own rationing and distribution system. In Scotland and England, there were a number of cases of mass insubordination and disaffection among the returning troops, some of whom formed workers' and soldiers' councils.

END OF AN EPOCH

Prior to 1914, Catalonia's main industries had been textiles and construction, but low productivity, lack of investment in machinery and poor quality control meant neither the region nor the country was in a position to compete on the world market. Everything now depended on the impoverished domestic market. In 1914, for example, 98 percent of all spindles used in the Catalan cotton industry came from Britain; Spanish industry simply couldn't meet the country's need for machinery, steel, iron, ships, coal, and coke.

By the time war broke out, many of the raw materials, finished products, and even much of the foodstuffs Spain needed were being imported, and most industries—metals, chemicals, mining, electricity, and tram and railway systems—were dominated either by foreign capital or by the fabulously wealthy Jesuits who controlled a large part of the county's economy, including the only independent banks, railways, utility and shipping companies, orange plantations, many of the copper and lead mines of Peñarroya, the mercury mines at Almadén, pyrite and iron ore mines, and much of heavy industry.

Spain's 'neutrality' had been a financial godsend to the country's businessmen, but particularly so for the Society of Jesus. The money invested by the Jesuits during the war brought them considerable political power as well as fabulous profits. They controlled at least a third of Spain's working capital, around sixty million pounds sterling, they dominated the antique furniture business, supplied Madrid with fresh fish and controlled its theatres and cabarets. The moral problem facing this spectacularly wealthy Christian order was: whose interests were they to defend?

When it came to the crunch, it certainly wasn't the interests of the poor and the dispossessed!

German capital was another important influence in the country. Prior to—and throughout—the war, German agents had scoured Spain and Spanish Morocco for investment opportunities, meticulously buying up land, properties, and companies linked to strategic industries such as dyes, potash, and mines. This wasn't only because Germany needed these raw materials for its war effort; they were deeply worried about the possibility of postwar inflation and feared that their healthy cash balances in Spanish banks could be wiped out overnight, hence their hunger for real estate, property, and assets they could exploit after the war—whether they won or lost.

The war changed everything for Spain's capitalists and monied oligarchs such as the Conde de Güell whose powerful Transatlántico group of companies included banks, oil, shipping, tobacco, cement, and construction. Neutral Spain began selling goods not only to the European belligerents, but also on the world market from which, prewar, they had been excluded by the great powers: France, Holland, Germany, the United States, and the enormous British-dominated Central and South American market. Overnight new Spanish companies mushroomed to meet the world's needs for capital goods and equipment, all of them relying on a cheap, placid, and plentiful workforce. Initially, this boost to the export market led to a favourable trade balance, the first Spain had had since its loss, to the United States in 1898, of what remained of its empire in Cuba, Puerto Rico, Guam, and the Philippines. But the astronomical profits made by Spanish and Catalan businessmen, fertilised by the blood and misery of four years of war, were all frittered away on extravagant lifestyles: expensive foreign cars, jewels and furs for their wives, apartments for their mistresses, properties in Paris and Berlin—and German currency speculation. Little, if anything, was reinvested in their factories or the workers. And so, on 11 November 1918, no sooner had the ballroom clocks chimed the eleventh hour marking the end of hostilities than the engines of international commerce moved back into gear and the great industrial powers began clawing back their markets, leaving Spain with virtually nothing.

. . . FOR WHOM THE BELL TOLLS . . .

By the end of November 1918, Spain's commerce and industry had reverted to its pre-1914 status, with the collapse of most of the fly-by-night opportunist firms that were launched to provide export substitutes to the countries of the belligerent alliances. In spite of the enormous wealth they had acquired during the war, Spain's greedy and short-sighted entrepreneurs made no attempt to modernise their factories, improve efficiency, or find new markets or products. Nor had they initiated any civic projects or attempted to improve working conditions or address any of their workers' serious grievances. The resultant downturn immediately hit profit margins. Before the end of November at least 30 percent of Catalonia's factories had gone out of business. Unable to repay their loans, they dragged with them some of Spain's richest banks.

Like the rest of Spain's grandees, landowners, and businessmen, the Jesuit bankers had been so convinced of Habsburg and Hohenzollern victory that, even as late as the summer of 1918, the Society of Jesus continued to invest its substantial war profits in German industry, as well as purchasing property and land in Berlin and Wiesbaden. As for the big Catalan manufacturers, with bankruptcy and economic recession staring them in the face, the only recourse open to them was to lay off their workers and

cut back on production. Now, however, there was an angry bee in the oint-
ment: the CNT, a confederation of industrial unions committed to the idea
of a better and more just world—libertarian communism—to be achieved
through the revolutionary general strike. It was now the strongest union in
Spain. Antiparliamentarian and ideologically opposed to collaborating with
political parties, a substantial number of its militants were hostile even to
the idea of negotiating over pay and conditions with employers! Their attitude was uncompromising: 'get rid of the bosses altogether,' and agricultural and industrial workers should take over the land and the factories.

Employers had little choice. In the dramatically changed political-eco-
nomic context of the postwar period, the CNT was the main obstacle to the
introduction of so-called 'labour flexibility', which—for the bosses—meant
shifting the costs of the crisis onto the workers. The anarcho-syndicalists
had to be crushed, totally, and the working class subdued and returned to a
state of deference, by force if necessary. The Employers' Federation would
settle for nothing less. The war between the states might be over, but a new
phase of the class war had begun! Elsewhere in the industrial world, powerful liberal and reformist elements among the bourgeoisie had taken on
the aristocracy and the big landed interests and won, but not the cowardly
and self-satisfied Spanish middle classes.

PLANNING THE NEW WORLD ORDER

The cabal of armed and militant ultra-conservative fundamentalists calling
themselves the Hiéron du Val d'Or was a semioccult sect founded by Miró
i Trepat's friend and business partner, Baron Alexis de Sarachaga—a charlatan endorsed by Pope Leo XIII. Its members included bishops, cardinals,
a clique of venal historians and writers together with a clutch of conspira-
torially minded manufacturers, businessmen, politicians, civil servants, and
senior army, police, and intelligence officers. Their objective was Europe-
wide 'moral rearmament' and counter-revolution against the democratic
and socialist movements of the twentieth century. Their strategy was to
infiltrate and 'reform' freemasonry with the idea of 'fusing the religious pas-
sion of the people with the cold power of the State into one great counterrevolutionary force' that would hopefully shake society to its foundations
and somehow stave off chaos. Had their plan succeeded it would certainly
have profoundly transformed autocratic Spain and—by anticipating the later
phenomenon of Fascism—made it considerably more powerful.

Central to the arcane beliefs and esoteric rituals of the cult of the Hiéron
du Val d'Or was an obsession with Eucharistic symbolism, geometry, and

sacred architecture. It was all nonsense, of course, but the importance of this organisation lay in its political influence, its obsession with the imminent onset of 'proletarian barbarism' and the prevention of the catastrophic happenings prophesied by 'Our Lady of Fatima' in her brief appearance as a vision to three young children. It championed the cause of 'returning Europe to the original nobility of purpose and spiritual primacy of a Catholic Christianity modelled on the old Holy Roman Empire'.

The thrust of Hiéron du Val seminars and conferences wasn't simply to dissect and counter Masonic, Bolshevik, liberal, or anarchist 'subversion' and 'contain' the advance of Godless communism and 'Masonic free thought', but to actually confront the enemy by launching a four-hundred-year rollback. It was what they euphemistically called 'expanding Catholic values', 'mobilising true faith into action', and 'spreading the social reign of Christ'.

People like Miró and Milans del Bosch weren't interested in negotiating with the modern world; only 'extreme measures' could halt the onward march of liberal interventionism and the working-class militancy that was challenging the foundations of belief on which the Papacy and the Monarchy were built. What society needed, they believed, was a purging and patriotic 'White Terror'.

The kernel for this White Terror was already in place in a number of European countries. It functioned through secret, likeminded Catholic army officers' organisations such as 'Tradition, Family and Property' and the 'Compass Rose Society', which, in Spain at the time, was headed by ninety or so senior officers representing all the major army regiments and civilian security forces. Central to this Europe-wide web of integrist malcontents was the Hiéron's 'Clandestine Planning Committee', the organisational body responsible for supervising and coordinating resistance to the impending revolution—and for giving strategic direction to its campaigns of terror.

With the end of the war in sight, the warnings of 'Our Lady of Fatima'— herself a prism of signs and wonders—and the smell of revolution in the air, the prophecies of the Book of Revelation were coming true in front of their very eyes. And so, for three days in mid-September 1918, the Catalan chapter of the Hiéron began planning for the postwar world and the fortress of Montjuïc became the venue for a 'discreet' international conference on the theme of 'Bolshevism—An Instrument of World Expansion'. The catalyst for the conference was the phenomenal success of the Bolshevik seizure of power in Russia, and the mushrooming of the CNT following the Sants Congress, which had terrified the bankers and thrown Spain's urban and landed elites into a real panic.

Antonio Maura y Montaner, prime minister of Spain—March–November 1918 (above right with Alfonso XIII).

Eduardo Dato, Maura's Interior Minister, 1918.

José Maestre Laborde, the Conde de Salvatierra.

Pistolero patron: Juan Cardinal Soldevilla y Romero (29 October 1843–4 June 1923).

Barcelona's 'men of order' on the Ramblas,

The prelates.

Above: Spain's grandees; below: the bourgeoisie.

The rich by Helios Gómez.

Nominally organised under the aegis of the Fomento Nacional del Trabajo, the national employers' organisation, the event had in fact been sponsored by the Hiéron and the counterintelligence bureau of the Spanish secret service, with whose members it cultivated close relations. General Milans del Bosch and Guillermo Graell, the Fomento's secretary-general and Spain's most prominent ideologue of militant lay clericalism, chaired the sessions jointly.

Graell, a reactionary on principle and honest in the service of his class, was the author of a shelf of tracts, pamphlets, and books such as *The Religious Question* and *An Essay on the Necessity to Return to Religion*, which expressed the pre-Fascist, integrist, employers' desires for religious order by arguing for the closest possible ties between the Catholic Church, the workforce and the business community, while extolling the virtues of an idealised lost world, a never-never land in which peaceful, happy, and devout workers and peasants belonged to a trade guild, attended religious processions, confessed and expiated their sins while doffing their *boinas*—flat caps or 'bunnets'—to their betters.

The ideological stars of the Hiéron conference were an eclectic international group of extreme right-wing journalists, academics, and theologians. Some sought to define what they saw as the present threat to the social order, while others prescribed the means by which it could be overcome. Their enemies were everywhere and included everything and anything that promoted what they defined as heresy or moral laxity, or undermined faith, good order, and discipline. It was a broad canvas that covered science, reason, and even a belief in the goodness of man. In their rogue's gallery of the Great Beast's acolytes were such hate-filled blasphemers as Descartes, Bacon, Hobbes, Kant, Leibniz, Rousseau, Hegel, Adam Smith, Michael Bakunin, Pierre Joseph Proudhon—and, last but not least, Francisco Ferrer i Guardia.

The study of science and rationalist philosophy, for the Hiéron organisers, led inevitably to heresy via Protestantism and anarchy. Protestantism because it promoted the notion of individualism and resistance to princes on spiritual and temporal grounds; anarchy because it denied the authority of Rome.

One after another, the speakers stood up to denounce materialism, liberalism, and workers' mutual aid with equal vehemence. As for labour unions, Jesus had more to offer workers than did union organisers. Resignation, submission, and suffering were extolled as essential to the human condition, and the only ways to win 'God's love'. Heaven's entrance fee could be paid only through suffering in this life. According to their world view, people living in poverty were happier than the idle, bored, and joyless rich who had acquired their wealth through questionable means—and spent it in frivolous consumption:

> The Great War will be followed [said one of the keynote speakers at the Hiéron conference] by a social war that will jeopardise the great temporal and spiritual institutions of Europe. Even as we speak, Bolsheviks, anarchists and liberals are capitalising on the instability of the situation. By progressively poisoning the minds of the impatient and enthusiastic poor, radicalising and provoking the weaker members of society into refusing to accept their lot with their normal deference, submission and resignation they are pushing matters to the edge of the abyss.

A panel of police, military, and security speakers proposed various strategies to counter the subversive onslaught against family, nation, tradition, and property, but the one that was given the most enthusiastic reception came from a hitherto unknown and new face in town, the Baron de Koenig, who delivered a paper on how to 'break' the CNT and end the social unrest 'crippling' Barcelona.

This ideological snake oil salesman knew exactly what emotional and psychological buttons to press in his audience. His comprehensive and studiously calibrated plan for pacifying the working class ranged from infiltrating agents into the unions to act as informers and provocateurs, to physical and psychological intimidation. He even hinted at 'eliminating' troublesome trade unionists. The Baron's paper, delivered with unselfconscious irony, outlined a semicovert organisation of what he described as 'plausibly deniable' security auxiliaries and cells, who, in the event of a revolution, would give 'unhesitatingly ruthless, energetic, and unorthodox' battle to the enemy. These auxiliaries were to be recruited from ideologically selected and trusted Catholic, Royalist, and middle-class organisations, and led by an operational nucleus of reliable, disciplined, and highly motivated officers from the police, security, and armed services. The Baron continued:

> The threats facing Spain today are real, multiple, and potentially devastating. Unless we exert a strong and ruthless hand immediately, the Bolsheviks and anarcho-syndicalists will soon make totally unreasonable demands upon management and employers in the pursuit of their ultimate objective—social revolution.

The greatest danger comes from the CNT. Their leaders are desperate men driven by millenarian faith-based idealism in pursuit of unworkable and ungodly ends. They are a festering sore on the body politic, a cancer that gnaws into the vitals and saps the moral life of Spain. There is no alternative. We have to destroy them physically and psychologically. We are not dealing here with the accommodating union officials of the UGT. These are irrational men. They cannot be bought or brought into the system—nor will they concede without a fight.

To sum up. We require a special action service, a clandestine and unconventional body that operates parallel to the official security forces, similar to the Sometent; one capable of organising national resistance to an anarchist or Bolshevik revolution that would provide civilised Spain with a militant bulwark against the Godless hordes of anarchism, Bolshevism, atheism, subversion, terrorism and the new unionism of the CNT. Its role would be to straddle the grey area between the normal military and police operations carried out by men in uniform, and the clandestine political and psychological warfare operations conducted by civilian agents. Its job will be to safeguard the nation's institutions and maintain the status quo by confronting and neutralising—anywhere and at anytime—the gravest of Bolshevik and anarchist threats.

Even if there is no revolution or need for an underground resistance movement, we will still have an instrument of control that will be capable of conditioning the political life of the country and preventing any further advances towards liberalism; an instrument that will allow us to manipulate and control popular mass movements— and, when necessary, eliminate them. When a nation asks its security forces to take on enemies such as the CNT who use terror and intimidation to compel a normally apolitical and indifferent workforce to join its ranks and provoke a repression that will, in turn, outrage national and international public opinion, then the forces of law and order cannot avoid using extreme measures in retaliation.

The only way to prevent revolution is to confront the enemy—in this case the terror cells of the CNT and the Bolsheviks—with every means at our disposal. Facing the dangers we face, caution is a luxury we cannot afford. We must treat them as the enemies of humanity that they are—beyond the protection of the law. The courts and the judicial system may not be able to handle them, but we can—and we will!

But our intelligence capabilities must be adequate to the task. We need to create an extensive network of informers and agents who will monitor the radicals, dissidents, militants and sympathisers—actual and incipient—and report on all subversive talk, publications, activities and movements. With good intelligence we can manipulate, neutralise and, when necessary, physically eliminate the enemy.

Remember, friends, we are at war. The exceptional nature of the threat we face today justifies everything—and I mean absolutely everything, no matter how apparently brutal or immoral. The enemy is no longer at the gate, he is inside the city. 'Babylon the great is fallen and become the habitation of devils, and the hold of every foul spirit, and a cage of every unclean and hateful bird . . .'

We can no longer afford to think in terms of bourgeois morality; we must do what is practical and timely. If you have a gangrenous finger, what do you do? Do you allow the whole hand, and then the body, to become poisoned?—or do you amputate the finger? Our mission demands results, and will require extreme and exceptional measures, but remember—that which corrupts an entire country and its people has to be pulled up like weeds infesting a field of wheat Some will call us butchers, but get it into perspective, we are butchers surrounded by vampires!

The assembled plutocracy of Catalonia rose as one to give the Baron an enthusiastic standing ovation. With the applause still echoing around the auditorium, Miró i Trepat, his protégé and patron, stepped up to the lectern. 'Are we all agreed, then?' he asked. 'We refuse to negotiate with the enemies of Spain and God. The terms of surrender are nonnegotiable! We will employ only those workers who agree to work on our terms, and our terms alone, no one else's. Those who resist us will be neutralised—or eliminated!'

On the podium, the captain-general, the police commissioner and the Conde de Güell clapped and nodded approvingly while Soldevilla, the Archbishop of Zaragoza, raised his hand and made the sign of the cross, giving the proceedings the Church's seal of approval.

THE BARON DE KOENIG

After his presentation at the Hiéron du Val d'Or conference, the Baron went to ground under the direct protection and patronage of Miró i Trepat. A few days later, he moved out of his small rented office in a mansion at No 71 Carrer Vallirana in San Gervasión to more prestigious premises located at the Maison Meuble in the Carrer Santa Ana where he hung out the shingle of his new, discreet, 'private detective agency'—BK Services (BKS). It was, in fact, a terrorist private army.

Bruce and Marshall knew of the web-spinning Baron by reputation— from Paris, Brussels, Amsterdam, Caracas, and London. De Koenig was as much a Baron as I was. The real name of this latter-day Count Cagliostro was Friedrich Rudolf Ställmann, a forty-four-year-old fraudster, chicane, charlatan, professional gambler, racketeer, carpetbagger, and double, triple, or possibly quadruple secret agent from Potsdam, near Berlin. Known variously as Fritz Kölman, Alberto Colman, Federico or Fritz Stagni, Von Rosbdel, and Colonel Lemoine, he served many masters, the latest of whom was Miró i Trepat. He was also on the payroll of both the French and German secret services—and, although Bruce and Marshall denied it, probably the British Secret Service Bureau as well!

No one knew much about the Baron's background. As with Cagliostro, everything was hearsay. One story had him joining the French Foreign Legion at eighteen to avoid a prison sentence for robbery and murder, and while he was in French North Africa, Marseilles, and Corsica, striking up friendships with local gangsters where he acquired the deadly skills of the milieu, including how to use a knife and kill without compunction. Neither Archs nor Pestaña, old Algeria hands, knew anything about him however.

The next anyone heard of the Baron was after his father died, when he settled in Brussels and opened a cabaret club, which he ran for a year before selling and reinventing himself as a professional gambler, acquiring a reputation in the Brussels casinos as an adroit and dexterous card sharp. There followed a number of scandals after which he moved to Berlin where he was arrested on charges of fraud. Released on bail he fled to France and thence to Buenos Aires where he lived for a time under the cover of an Alsatian engineer by the name of Alberto Colmann. In Argentina, he married Mlle Lemoine, the daughter of a respected Parisian doctor, who adopted the identity of the Baroness Rene Scalda, and whom he introduced into polite Argentinean gambling circles through a Polish Jew by the name of Heinrich Mayer—whom he later defrauded of fourteen thousand pesos. Mayer committed suicide soon after.

The 'Baron' later turned up in Caracas, claiming to be an official representative of the Monte Carlo Casino, and set up a 'branch office' in the Venezuelan capital under the name of Federico Stagni—a venture that attracted the attention of the police who quickly closed him down. From

Above: the Gran Casino, San Sebastian, run by the 'Baron von Koenig' from 1915 to 1917.

The 'Baron von Koenig'—a quadruple secret agent from Potsdam arrived in Fuenterrabía in mid-1915 with two beautiful, elegant women the 'Baroness' René Scalda and his mistress, CJ (illustration by Helios Gómez).

Friedrich-Rudolf Stallman, a.k.a. 'Baron von Koenig', a forty-four-year-old confidence trickster who served many masters. In Spain he was the confidant of Cantabria's movers and shakers who appointed him director of Fuenterrabía and San Sebastian's exclusive Casino, a position which gave him unique access to political and military intelligence until mid-1917.

Fuenterrabía: Puerta de San Nicolás, where the 'Baron von Koenig' first arrived in Spain.

The 'Baron von Koenig', fraudster, blackmailer, spy, pistolero chief (early and only known photograph).

Contemporary cartoon satirising relations between Bravo Portillo and the 'Baron von Koenig'.

Venezuela he moved on to Egypt, Turkey, Persia, and then South Africa, where he was arrested and held for a time on suspicion of murdering a diamond trader in the Transvaal. Returning to Europe he made his mark as a professional crook and fraudster in London and was eventually arrested under the name Von Rosbdel and deported to Germany, where he was jailed in 1910, this time under the name Baron de Koenig. It was possibly around this time that he was recruited as an agent of the German special services, because not long afterwards he reappeared, a free man, involved with a gang of international swindlers and burglars operating along the wealthy Côte d'Azur in France. He was later sighted in Amsterdam and Belgium where an arrest warrant was issued against him on suspicion of having cut the throat of an undercover Belgian counterintelligence officer in Brussels in July 1914, immediately prior to the German invasion.

Bruce and Marshall told me he had offered his services to the British vice consul in Barcelona, though they denied employing him. But they would say that anyway!

By the time he surfaced at the Hiéron conference, the 'Baron' had been living in Spain for three years, having arrived at the Spanish town of Fuenterrabía, near San Sebastián, on the Bidasoa, the border river between France and Spain, in August 1915, after being expelled from France for various frauds. The likelihood is that he was allowed to escape from France because he was also working for the French Secret Service, the Deuxième Bureau, and had been, apparently, since 1902. He arrived in Fuenterrabía in typically ostentatious fashion, in a splendid red Mercedes cabriolet with a black roof and gold trim, complete with a liveried chauffeur decked out in the same colours. Accompanying him were two beautiful and elegant women: one was his wife, the 'Baroness Rene Scalda', and the other his mistress, CJ. Cars didn't come flashier in those days, nor did their occupants.

A charming, charismatic and ruggedly handsome man in his late forties, the Baron was tall, slim, clean-shaven, and tanned with a dress sense that showed a fussy correctness which came perilously close to being prissy. He saw himself, however, as 'spruce and elegant'. His well-groomed, thick, jet-black hair skimmed the collar of his brilliant-white starched, cuffed shirt and brushed the jacket collar of his bespoke English-cut suit, made from Mongolian cashmere. The suit complemented everything else about him: the monogrammed red silk handkerchief drooping out of the breast pocket, fine handmade Russian leather shoes, embroidered silk socks, elegant watch, and simple silver cufflinks. He had a few slightly nervous traits or mannerisms, such as fiddling with the twinkling square-cut yellow diamond ring which covered the whole joint of his little finger, or the knot of his colour-ful silk tie, or running his hand over his hair and tucking it behind his ears.

An accomplished confidence trickster, it didn't take 'the Baron' long to worm an entrée into the highest aristocratic, financial, commercial, and fash-ionable circles in town, winning everyone over with his sharp, lightly ironic wit, alert intelligence, apparent social status, cultivated self-deprecating man-ners—and generosity. His first port of call in Fuenterrabía had been to the Mayor's office where he introduced himself as a French citizen, and pomp-ously handed over 500 pesetas to be distributed among the town's needi-est families. For some time after, any needy townspeople looking for alms were usually generously accommodated if they turned up at the Baron's door. His largesse quickly bought him the 'respect and esteem' he needed along the length of the coast as far as Irún. He was helped by his enormous vanity and arrogance, and by the Christian names of the wide 'friendship' circle of powerful contacts he claimed to have in the chancelleries of Europe, names that he dropped carefully into every extravagant anecdote and conversation.

The 'Baron' soon became the idol of Guipúzcoa's middle and upper classes—and the most prized and sought-after dinner guest at the region's exclusive salons where he gave the impression of having a great deal of money at his disposal. All anyone knew about him, however, was based on the vaguest rumours and stories which either originated with him, his beautiful 'Baroness Rene Scalda', or his equally attractive mistress, CJ, all of whom lived together in what was—for the time—an unusually open ménage a trois in the aristocratic chalet they rented in town.

Within months of his arrival, 'the Baron' had established himself as the trusted confidante of the cream of Guipúzcoa's 'movers and shakers', and before you could say 'Jack Robinson' he had been appointed direc-tor of Fuenterrabía's and San Sebastián's exclusive Casino, a position that gave him free rein to fleece and blackmail the victims of his choice. It also gave him unique access to military and political intelligence, which he was selling on to both the French and German secret services, and who knows how many others.

'The Baron' managed both Casinos until mid-1917 when stories about his shady past as a fraudster and card sharp in Germany, Holland, France, and England finally began to catch up with him. Warned by the local police chief about his imminent arrest, the Baron quickly moved his operations first to Bilbao, and from there to Palma de Mallorca, Cartagena, Malaga, Seville, and Cadiz before finally ending up in Barcelona—the 'Paris of the South'—in September 1918. Like Milton's Satan, de Koenig was one of those amoral characters for whom times of disaster and trouble mean opportunities, and Barcelona, a hotbed of intrigue and conspiracy, offered plenty of those!

Using his tried-and-tested techniques of targeting and ingratiating himself with local powerbrokers and the city fathers, de Koenig set out to win the trust and confidence of Miró i Trepat, posing as an 'agent of influence' commissioned by the French government to provide confidential reports on social movements and labour conflicts in Spain, particularly in Catalonia. This was to some extent true as he was, in fact, reporting to Captain Février of the Deuxième Bureau office in Barcelona—and to the Germans. And it was through Miró i Trepat that 'the Baron' was introduced to Manuel Bravo Portillo to whom he spun the same yarn when he visited him in prison. It was a fantasy that won the trust and confidence of the surprisingly gullible and snobbish Bravo Portillo, whom the Baron visited regularly during his short stay in the Modelo prison.

JOAN MIRÓ I TREPAT

Joan Miró i Trepat, president of Pavimientos y Construcciones, one of the biggest building firms in the whole of Spain, was probably the wealthiest, most influential, and reactionary of all of Catalonia's employers. Tall and distinguished-looking with his wide-brimmed Panama and gold fob watch with a heavy chain that hung in an arc between the two pockets of his mustard-coloured waistcoat, Miró i Trepat's trademark accoutrements were a small gold Sacred Heart of Jesus pin on his jacket lapel, a silver handled walking stick in one hand, and a Romeo y Julieta cigar in the other.

Miró i Trepat was a man with a mission, an obsession to restore to Spain—and Europe—the spiritual and temporal hegemony of the Roman Catholic Church. In the light of Germany's defeat, the fragmentation of the Austro-Hungarian Empire, and the likelihood of apocalyptic terror and world revolution, this mission now seemed more urgent than ever. A hardline, paranoid integrist, Miró i Trepat clung, barnacle-like, to the Tridentine traditions of Holy Mother Church. His life and enormous fortune were dedicated to advancing the cause of Rome. In his Weltanschauung, the Roman Catholic Church—in its perfect sixteenth-century manifestation—was the only institution of spiritual and temporal power through which the unity and glory of Europe could be restored to what it had once been under Charlemagne's Reich, the Holy Roman Empire.

Miró i Trepat believed absolutely and unquestioningly in the divine inspiration and the literal truth of the Bible as the Word of God—the divinity of the Virgin-born Jesus, his vicarious atonement on the Cross for a fallen mankind, and his bodily resurrection. All the cataclysmic events and great upheavals that were now taking place were, he truly believed, prophesied in the Bible. They were the harbingers of the final stygian nightmare battle between Christ and the Antichrist in which the bodies of the baddies would 'burst open from head to toe at every word!' Facing the warrior Christ, 'their flesh will dissolve, their eyes melt, and their tongues disintegrate'.

Spain and Europe's volatile condition was not, he believed, fortuitous; it was the result of deliberate manipulation by evil, clandestine organisations controlled by the Grand Orient of France, hiding behind the veneer of liberal, democratic, and revolutionary movements whose sole objective was spreading their secular, humanist ideas and destroying Christianity. The Antichrist was near at hand. Spain had to repent; it had to plead with God to cleanse the moral stains infecting the nation and its godless inhabitants—and Miró i Trepat was the man to do it! Had it not been for the references to Spain, the sentiments he expressed could have come from any 'Wee Free' Church of Scotland Minister between Gretna and Stornoway.

This eccentric entrepreneur's significant moment of clarity had occurred the previous year on hearing that the Virgin Mary had appeared to three shepherd children near Fatima in Portugal, or rather had appeared to two of them: Lúcia de Jesus dos Santos and Jacinta Marto, the latter a bossy, sulky, and manipulative little crucifix kisser. The third, a young lad called Francisco, simply repeated whatever the two girls told him. 'Our Lady', as the shepherd children called her, had chosen them to pass on to the world three pieces of crucial information: two of which threatened hell on earth. The threat was explicit: Godless 'communist' Russia must return to the fold of Holy Mother Church and be consecrated to the 'Immaculate Heart of Mary'.

Since the Bolsheviks' seizure of power the previous October and their overthrow of the bourgeois Constituent Assembly, the Virgin Mary's warnings about Russia, as communicated through the youngsters, had become even more apocalyptic. 'If Russia doesn't convert,' she "told" the children, 'her errors will spread throughout the world, promoting wars and the persecution of the Church. The good will be martyred, the Holy Father will have much to suffer, and nations will be annihilated.' Adding a touch of drama to her warnings, 'Our Lady' even made the sun above Fatima 'dance in the sky' then 'precipitate itself from the sky to almost on top of the beholders'.

The third 'secret', to which only a handful of people were privy—one of whom was the well-connected Miró i Trepat—concerned a 'bishop clothed in white' falling to the ground, 'shot dead by a gunman'. This last piece of information put the fear of God into the church hierarchy, particularly the then Archbishop and soon to be Cardinal Juan Soldevilla y Romero of Zaragoza. He, along with Spain's devout aristocrats and upper and middle classes, began recruiting pious and not so pious thugs to protect them from the gunmen of the 'Antichrist', a word which, to the dyslexic and the ignorant, seemed very similar to the word anarchist!

In spite of having more in common with medieval society than that of Spain in 1918—at least in matters of religion, ethics, and philosophy—Miró i Trepat was, to all outward appearances, an urbane and practical politician and businessman well able to conceal his bipolar eccentricities, fantasies, fanaticism, and his behind-the-scenes role as the architect of terror. The man was a sociopathic zealot:

'My life has been dedicated to preventing hell predominating over an indifferent population, and to achieve this I am convinced we must create a confederal and theocratic Europe ruled by devout Habsburg-Bourbon elector princes—under the papacy—who will wield absolute temporal and spiritual power and defend the *Pax Católica* under the Kingship of Christ.'

The type of society envisaged by Miró i Trepat was that of a pre-Reformation absolutist medieval monarchy administered by vengeful theocrats ruling over a quiescent and deferential populace, the dream no doubt, give or take a couple of technical specifics, of all authoritarians and bureaucrats. Miró i Trepat's aim was to neutralise or eliminate prominent working-class leaders and humiliate, intimidate, and terrorise union rank-and-file-activists. Milans del Bosch, the captain-general of Catalonia and other members of the antimodernist Hiéron du Val d'Or shared Miró i Trepat's ideas.

Miró was an enthusiastic sponsor of 'closed seminars' and 'study groups' for Hiéron members, inviting speakers such as the Cistercian monk, Joerg Lanz von Liebenfels, the editor-publisher of the occultist, racist magazine *Ostara*, and the founder of 'The Order of the New Templars'. And until the recent death of the money-grubbing, purgatory and Mass trafficking French 'Sacred Heart of Jesus' priest Bérenger Saunière, Miró had also been his patron and sponsor of his baroque Church of Mary Magdalene in Rennes le Château, just over the border, near Carcassonne.

GENERAL JOAQUIN MILANS DEL BOSCH I CARRIO
Almost without exception, the whole of Spain's officer class supported the Central Powers, as did the police, Civil Guard, and the big landowners, the *latifundistas*. In Catalonia, German and Austro-Hungarian interests were protected by Joaquín Milans del Bosch i Carrio, the newly appointed captain-general of Catalonia.

1918: meeting of the Patronal, the Catalan employers' association.

Alejandro Lerroux: demagogue and provocateur.

Josep Bertrán i Musitu: Patronal boss, Sometent chief, and ideologue of 'pistolerismo'.

General Joaquín Milans del Bosch i Carrió (1854–1936), captain general of Catalonia from 1918 to 1920 and chief architect of 'pistolerismo'.

Milans del Bosch had only recently taken up this post on his return from Morocco, where the Spanish army had been fighting El Raisuni's Rif rebels in the ongoing Second Moroccan War, and where he had worked closely with the German special services who had been fomenting rebellion in neighbouring French Morocco. One of the rising stars among his young officers in Morocco, whose career he nurtured and whom he promoted to major, was Captain Francisco Franco de Bahamonde.

Milans, a sixty-four-year-old career army officer, came from a long line of army officers. With his shaven head, narrow, close-set eyes, square jaw, stern expression, and trim military moustache he had all the physical characteristics of a Junker fencing master. He behaved like one as well. Obsessed with discipline and form, Milans del Bosch was always immaculately dressed, in either a top hat and frock coat, or full ceremonial uniform, dripping with gold braid and campaign medals, and one of those hats with a chicken on top, just like Ramsay Mac, in court dress, on his way to the Palace, and just as silly.

The Barcelona posting suited him perfectly. It was a position with the vice regal plenipotentiary powers he had wielded so ruthlessly in the colonies. In spite of his affected piety, or perhaps because of it, he was notorious for harsh and pitiless measures; his concentration camps at Guantánamo Bay in Cuba and at Marinduque in the Philippines predated by a decade those used by the British against the Boers in South Africa. Hundreds of thousands of suspected rebels and sympathisers died of starvation and disease in his camps; he also had a predilection for the summary execution, without regard to legal process, of anyone he deemed to be a threat.

Milans del Bosch possessed a bunker mentality. His entire military career had been dedicated to the defence of the indefensible and fast receding Spanish empire. He had fought guerrilla insurgents in Cuba and the Philippines in the 1890s, and then the United States during the Spanish-American War of 1898, when the Americans decided to 'bring democracy' to the Cuban people and free them from their Spanish oppressors at the battle of Guantánamo Bay. The Spanish-American war ended forever Spain's pretensions of being a global colonial power, and for the rest of his life Milans was haunted by the thought that he had in some way been responsible for his country's loss of empire. But he assuaged his sense of guilt by blaming the Madrid politicians for their pusillanimity in supporting the army and navy in their time of need.

Milans's background as a colonial administrator made him the ideal candidate for the Barcelona posting: he had no qualms about violating human rights and ruthlessly suppressing dissent. Another point in his favour was his willingness to tolerate corruption and administrative malfeasance in the name of efficiency.

He was a respected figure among his fellow officers and NCOs, hence Madrid's decision to appoint him to this important post at a time of growing unrest within the army, with the rise of the *juntas militares de defensa*, military trade unions who threatened mutiny if their grievances were not resolved. Mindful of the fact that it was the defection of the Russian army that had precipitated the fall of the Tsar and triggered the Russian Revolution, Madrid quickly conceded to many of the infantry juntas' demands.

Another problem facing Milans in the office of captain-general was the emergence of a radical Catalan separatist movement. Although Catalan himself, Milans was first and foremost a Roman Catholic, an officer, a 'gentleman', and a 'man of honour'. His primary duty was to defend an undivided Catholic Spain and his own class interests—and prevent the country being dismembered by Republican separatists and revolutionaries. Of all of these concerns, however, his one unfaltering obsession was the CNT. In the monochrome world inhabited by Milans del Bosch there were no shades of grey, and he stubbornly refused to listen to anything that might possibly disturb his absolute conviction that the knotted tangle of Spain's social problems could be traced to a single source of evil, the anarchist-led CNT. Get rid of the CNT and the evil would be eradicated.

For Milans there was no such thing as the 'social question', only good discipline and public order. He shared his beliefs and values, which were rooted in his social conditioning and the teachings of the Catholic Church, with most of the diehard urban bourgeoisie of the Employers' Federation, the Patronal, who quickly adopted Milans as their 'man on a white horse'.

THAT WAS THEN...

From my present vantage-point in time—1976—it must be difficult for the present generation of militants to understand what life was like for activists at the end of the Great War. It seems an obvious thing to say, but it's difficult to share the cruelty and tragedy of the period. Things were so much harder in those days, and it wasn't just the poverty and lack of the minimum comforts of life, it was also the fact that we had to keep the faith on our own—or in small groups—during long periods of vicious repression and in the face of a public opinion controlled and manipulated by the Church and the press. On reflection, perhaps things haven't changed all that much. They've always been that way, I suppose, but in spite of the constant moral struggle and inflation-fuelled misery, the end of the war was also a time of focused anger and enormous optimism, of a hope and enthusiasm that we could recreate mankind afresh and transform the world. Workers were flocking to join the union, and *Solidaridad Obrera* was now a daily, its circulation almost doubling from seventeen thousand to thirty-two thousand copies. Another positive indicator of the growing level of popular radicalisation was the number of libertarian and rationalist cultural centres and schools that were opening, offering all sorts of educational facilities and lectures on every conceivable subject from astronomy to theosophy and zoology.

Day labourers on the march by Helios Gómez.

Above and below: Cafe de L'Europe, Rue des Couronnes, Belleville, Paris (October 1976)
© Farquhar McHarg (F.M., with scarf, is standing beside Laureano, seated).

Laureano Cerrada Santos (1902–1976).

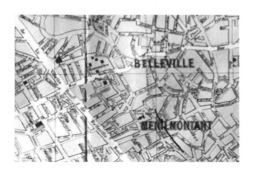

Murder scene.

Recommended Reading List

Anarchism and the City: Revolution and Counter-revolution in Barcelona, 1898–1937, Chris Ealham, Oakland: AK Press, 2010, ISBN: 9781849350129.

Anarchism, Revolution and Reaction: Catalan Labour and the Crisis of the Spanish State, 1898–1923, Angel Smith, Oxford: Berghahn, 2007, ISBN: 1845451767.

The CNT in the Spanish Revolution, vol. 1, José Peirats Vals (Edited by Chris Ealham), Oakland: PM Press, 2011, ISBN: 9781604862072.

Durruti in the Spanish Revolution, Abel Paz (Diego Camacho), Oakland and Edinburgh: AK Press, 2007, ISBN: 9781904859503.

El eco de los pasos, Juan García Oliver, Paris and Barcelona: Ruedo Ibérico, 1978, ISBN: 8485361067.

El Movimiento Obrero Español 1886–1926, Manuel Buenacasa, Madrid: Ediciones Jucar, 1977, ISBN: 8433455109.

El Sindicalismo Español antes de la Guerra Civil, los Hijos del Trabajo, Ricardo Sanz, Barcelona: Ediciones Petronio, SA, 1976, ISBN: 8472504875.

L'anarquisme i les lluites socials a Barcelona, 1918–1923: la repressió obrera i la violencia, Maria Amàlia Pradas Bacna, Barcelona: Publicacions de l'Abadia de Montserrat, ISBN: 848415484X.

Lo que aprendí en la vida, vol. 1, Ángel Pestaña, Madrid: ZYX, 1971.

Los años del pistolerismo: ensayo para una guerra civil, León-Ignacio, Barcelona: Planeta, 1981, ISBN: 8432036005.

Mujeres de temple, Sara Berenguer, València: L'Exiam, Colección Roja y Negra, 2008, ISBN: 9788496014770.

Red Barcelona: Social Protest and Labour Mobilization in the Twentieth Century, Angel Smith (ed), London: Routledge, 2002, ISBN: 0415279054.

Terrorismo en Barcelona (memorias inéditas), Ángel Pestaña, Barcelona: Planeta, 1979, ISBN: 8432006157.

ABOUT PM PRESS

PM Press was founded at the end of 2007 by a small collection of folks with decades of publishing, media, and organizing experience. PM Press co-conspirators have published and distributed hundreds of books, pamphlets, CDs, and DVDs. Members of PM have founded enduring book fairs, spearheaded victorious tenant organizing campaigns, and worked closely with bookstores, academic conferences, and even rock bands to deliver political and challenging ideas to all walks of life. We're old enough to know what we're doing and young enough to know what's at stake.

We seek to create radical and stimulating fiction and non-fiction books, pamphlets, t-shirts, visual and audio materials to entertain, educate and inspire you. We aim to distribute these through every available channel with every available technology — whether that means you are seeing anarchist classics at our bookfair stalls; reading our latest vegan cookbook at the café; downloading geeky fiction e-books; or digging new music and timely videos from our website.

PM Press is always on the lookout for talented and skilled volunteers, artists, activists and writers to work with. If you have a great idea for a project or can contribute in some way, please get in touch.

PM Press
PO Box 23912
Oakland, CA 94623
www.pmpress.org

FRIENDS OF PM PRESS

These are indisputably momentous times — the financial system is melting down globally and the Empire is stumbling. Now more than ever there is a vital need for radical ideas.

In the three years since its founding — and on a mere shoestring — PM Press has risen to the formidable challenge of publishing and distributing knowledge and entertainment for the struggles ahead. With over 100 releases to date, we have published an impressive and stimulating array of literature, art, music, politics, and culture. Using every available medium, we've succeeded in connecting those hungry for ideas and information to those putting them into practice.

Friends of PM allows you to directly help impact, amplify, and revitalize the discourse and actions of radical writers, filmmakers, and artists. It provides us with a stable foundation from which we can build upon our early successes and provides a much-needed subsidy for the materials that can't necessarily pay their own way. You can help make that happen — and receive every new title automatically delivered to your door once a month — by joining as a Friend of PM Press. And, we'll throw in a free T-shirt when you sign up.

Here are your options:

- **$25 a month** Get all books and pamphlets plus 50% discount on all webstore purchases

- **$25 a month** Get all CDs and DVDs plus 50% discount on all webstore purchases

- **$40 a month** Get all PM Press releases plus 50% discount on all webstore purchases

- **$100 a month Superstar** — Everything plus PM merchandise, free downloads, and 50% discount on all webstore purchases

For those who can't afford $25 or more a month, we're introducing Sustainer Rates at $15, $10 and $5. Sustainers get a free PM Press T-shirt and a 50% discount on all purchases from our website.

Your Visa or Mastercard will be billed once a month, until you tell us to stop. Or until our efforts succeed in bringing the revolution around. Or the financial meltdown of Capital makes plastic redundant. Whichever comes first.

The CNT in the Spanish Revolution Volume 1

José Peirats
with an introduction by Chris Ealham

ISBN: 978-1-60486-207-2
$28.00   432 pages

The CNT in the Spanish Revolution is the history of one of the most original and audacious, and arguably also the most far-reaching, of all the twentieth-century revolutions. It is the history of the giddy years of political change and hope in 1930s Spain, when the so-called 'Generation of '36', Peirats' own generation, rose up against the oppressive structures of Spanish society. It is also a history of a revolution that failed, crushed in the jaws of its enemies on both the reformist left and the reactionary right. José Peirats' account is effectively the official CNT history of the war, passionate, partisan but, above all, intelligent. Its huge sweeping canvas covers all areas of the anarchist experience—the spontaneous militias, the revolutionary collectives, the moral dilemmas occasioned by the clash of revolutionary ideals and the stark reality of the war effort against Franco and his German Nazi and Italian Fascist allies.

This new edition is carefully indexed in a way that converts the work into a usable tool for historians and makes it much easier for the general reader to dip in with greater purpose and pleasure.

"José Peirats' The CNT in the Spanish Revolution *is a landmark in the historiography of the Spanish Civil War . . . Originally published in Toulouse in the early 1950s, it was a rarity anxiously searched for by historians and others who gleefully pillaged its wealth of documentation. Even its republication in Paris in 1971 by the exiled Spanish publishing house, Ruedo Ibérico, though welcome, still left the book in the territory of specialists. For that reason alone, the present project to publish the entire work in English is to be applauded."*
— Professor Paul Preston, London School of Economics

" . . . this is a wonderful work and an essential resource for anyone interested in the history of the CNT and the Spanish revolution. Indeed, reading Peirats' work you see how much other historians (and other anarchists) have lifted from it in their books. It is great to finally have the work available in English."
— www.struggle.ws

"For those whose field of study is modern Spain, this is indeed an obligatory purchase. Given that this edition has been indexed and footnoted it may prove more useful to scholars than the original Spanish-language editions."
— Kate Sharpley Library

The Floodgates of Anarchy

Stuart Christie and Albert Meltzer

ISBN: 978-1-60486-105-1
$15.95   144 pages

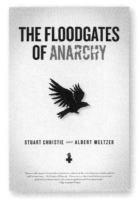

The floodgates holding back anarchy are constantly under strain. The liberal would ease the pressure by diverting some of the water; the conservative would shore up the dykes, the totalitarian would construct a stronger dam.

But is anarchy a destructive force? The absence of government may alarm the authoritarian, but is a liberated people really its own worst enemy—or is the true enemy of mankind, as the anarchists claim, the means by which he is governed? Without government the world could manage to end exploitation and war. Anarchy should not be confused with weak, divided or manifold government. As Christie and Meltzer point out, only with the total abolition of government can society develop in freedom.

"Anyone who wants to know what anarchism is about in the contemporary world would do well to start here. The Floodgates of Anarchy *forces us to take a hard look at moral and political problems which other more sophisticated doctrines evade."*
— *The Sunday Times*

"A lucid exposition of revolutionary anarchist theory."
— *Peace News*

"Coming from a position of uncompromising class struggle and a tradition that includes many of our exemplary anarchist militants, The Floodgates of Anarchy *has a power and directness sadly missing from some contemporary anarchist writing. It is exciting to see it back in print, ready for a new generation to read."*
— Barry Pateman, Associate Editor, The Emma Goldman Papers, University of California at Berkeley

Portugal: The Impossible Revolution?

Phil Mailer
with an afterword by Maurice Brinton

ISBN: 978-1-60486-336-9
$24.95   300 pages

After the military coup in Portugal on April 25, 1974,
the overthrow of almost fifty years of Fascist rule, and
the end of three colonial wars, there followed eighteen
months of intense, democratic social transformation
which challenged every aspect of Portuguese society. What started as a military
coup turned into a profound attempt at social change from the bottom up and
became headlines on a daily basis in the world media. This was due to the intensity
of the struggle as well as the fact that in 1974–75 the moribund, right-wing
Francoist regime was still in power in neighboring Spain and there was huge
uncertainty as to how these struggles might affect Spain and Europe at large.

This is the story of what happened in Portugal between April 25, 1974, and
November 25, 1975, as seen and felt by a deeply committed participant. It
depicts the hopes, the tremendous enthusiasm, the boundless energy, the total
commitment, the released power, even the revolutionary innocence of thousands
of ordinary people taking a hand in the remolding of their lives. And it does so
against the background of an economic and social reality which placed limits on
what could be done.

*"An evocative, bitterly partisan diary of the Portuguese revolution, written from a
radical-utopian perspective. The enemy is any type of organization or presumption of
leadership. The book affords a good view of the mood of the time, of the multiplicity of
leftist factions, and of the social problems that bedeviled the revolution."*
—Fritz Stern, *Foreign Affairs*

*"Mailer portrays history with the enthusiasm of a cheerleader, the 'home team' in
this case being libertarian communism. Official documents, position papers and
the pronouncements of the protagonists of this drama are mostly relegated to the
appendices. The text itself recounts the activities of a host of worker, tenant, soldier
and student committees as well as the author's personal experiences."*
—Ian Wallace, *Library Journal*

*"A thorough delight as it moves from first person accounts of street demonstrations
through intricate analyses of political movements. Mailer has handled masterfully the
enormous cast of politicians, officers of the military peasant and workers councils, and
a myriad of splinter parties, movements and caucuses."*
—*Choice*

The Angry Brigade: A History of Britain's First Urban Guerilla Group

Gordon Carr
with prefaces by John Barker
and Stuart Christie

ISBN: 978-1-60486-049-8
$24.95   280 pages

"You can't reform profit capitalism and inhumanity.
Just kick it till it breaks." — *Angry Brigade, communiqué.*

Between 1970 and 1972, the Angry Brigade used guns and bombs in a series
of symbolic attacks against property. A series of communiqués accompanied
the actions, explaining the choice of targets and the Angry Brigade philosophy:
autonomous organization and attacks on property alongside other forms of
militant working class action. Targets included the embassies of repressive
regimes, police stations and army barracks, boutiques and factories, government
departments and the homes of Cabinet ministers, the Attorney General and the
Commissioner of the Metropolitan Police. These attacks on the homes of senior
political figures increased the pressure for results and brought an avalanche of
police raids. From the start the police were faced with the difficulty of getting to
grips with a section of society they found totally alien. And were they facing an
organization—or an idea?

This book covers the roots of the Angry Brigade in the revolutionary ferment of the
1960s, and follows their campaign and the police investigation to its culmination
in the "Stoke Newington 8" conspiracy trial at the Old Bailey—the longest criminal
trial in British legal history. Written after extensive research—among both the
libertarian opposition and the police—it remains the essential study of Britain's
first urban guerilla group. This expanded edition contains a comprehensive
chronology of the "Angry Decade," extra illustrations and a police view of the
Angry Brigade. Introductions by Stuart Christie and John Barker (two of the "Stoke
Newington 8" defendants) discuss the Angry Brigade in the political and social
context of its times—and its longer-term significance.

"*Even after all this time, Carr's book remains the best introduction to the culture and
movement that gave birth to The Angry Brigade. Until all the participants' documents
and voices are gathered in one place, this will remain* the gripping, readable
and reliable account of those days. It is essential reading and PM Press are to be
congratulated for making it available to us."
— Barry Pateman, Associate Editor, The Emma Goldman Papers, University of
California at Berkeley

Revolution and Other Writings: A Political Reader

Gustav Landauer
edited and translated by Gabriel Kuhn

ISBN: 978-1-60486-054-2
$26.95   360 pages

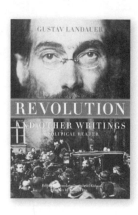

"Landauer is the most important agitator of the radical and revolutionary movement in the entire country." This is how Gustav Landauer is described in a German police file from 1893. Twenty-six years later, Landauer would die at the hands of reactionary soldiers who overthrew the Bavarian Council Republic, a three-week attempt to realize libertarian socialism amidst the turmoil of post-World War I Germany. It was the last chapter in the life of an activist, writer, and mystic who Paul Avrich calls "the most influential German anarchist intellectual of the twentieth century."

This is the first comprehensive collection of Landauer writings in English. It includes one of his major works, *Revolution*, thirty additional essays and articles, and a selection of correspondence. The texts cover Landauer's entire political biography, from his early anarchism of the 1890s to his philosophical reflections at the turn of the century, the subsequent establishment of the Socialist Bund, his tireless agitation against the war, and the final days among the revolutionaries in Munich. Additional chapters collect Landauer's articles on radical politics in the US and Mexico, and illustrate the scope of his writing with texts on corporate capital, language, education, and Judaism. The book includes an extensive introduction, commentary, and bibliographical information, compiled by the editor and translator Gabriel Kuhn as well as a preface by Richard Day.

"*If there were any justice in this world—at least as far as historical memory goes—then Gustav Landauer would be remembered, right along with Bakunin and Kropotkin, as one of anarchism's most brilliant and original theorists. Instead, history has abetted the crime of his murderers, burying his work in silence. With this anthology, Gabriel Kuhn has single-handedly redressed one of the cruelest gaps in Anglo-American anarchist literature: the absence of almost any English translations of Landauer.*"
—Jesse Cohn, author of *Anarchism and the Crisis of Representation: Hermeneutics, Aesthetics, Politics*

"*Gustav Landauer was, without doubt, one of the brightest intellectual lights within the revolutionary circles of fin de siècle Europe. In this remarkable anthology, Gabriel Kuhn brings together an extensive and splendidly chosen collection of Landauer's most important writings, presenting them for the first time in English translation. With Landauer's ideas coming of age today perhaps more than ever before, Kuhn's work is a valuable and timely piece of scholarship, and one which should be required reading for anyone with an interest in radical social change.*"
—James Horrox, author of *A Living Revolution: Anarchism in the Kibbutz Movement*

Liberating Society from the State and Other Writings: A Political Reader

Erich Mühsam
edited by Gabriel Kuhn

ISBN: 978-1-60486-055-9
$26.95   320 pages

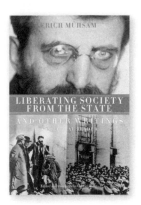

Erich Mühsam (1878–1934), poet, bohemian, revolutionary, is one of Germany's most renowned and influential anarchists. Born into a middle-class Jewish family, he challenged the conventions of bourgeois society at the turn of the century, engaged in heated debates on the rights of women and homosexuals, and traveled Europe in search of radical communes and artist colonies. He was a primary instigator of the ill-fated Bavarian Council Republic in 1919, and held the libertarian banner high during a Weimar Republic that came under increasing threat by right-wing forces. In 1933, four weeks after Hitler's ascension to power, Mühsam was arrested in his Berlin home. He spent the last sixteen months of his life in detention and died in the Oranienburg Concentration Camp in July 1934. Mühsam wrote poetry, plays, essays, articles, and diaries. His work unites a burning desire for individual liberation with anarcho-communist convictions, and bohemian strains with syndicalist tendencies. The body of his writings is immense, yet hardly any English translations exist. This collection presents not only *Liberating Society from the State. What is Communist Anarchism?*, Mühsam's main political pamphlet and one of the key texts in the history of German anarchism, but also some of his best-known poems, unbending defenses of political prisoners, passionate calls for solidarity with the lumpenproletariat, recollections of the utopian community of Monte Verità, debates on the rights of homosexuals and women, excerpts from his journals, and essays contemplating German politics and anarchist theory as much as Jewish identity and the role of intellectuals in the class struggle. An appendix documents the fate of Zenzl Mühsam, who, after her husband's death, escaped to the Soviet Union where she spent twenty years in Gulag camps.

"It has been remarked before how the history of the German libertarian and anarchist movement has yet to be written, and so the project to begin translation of some of the key works of Mühsam—one of the great names of German anarchism, yet virtually unknown in the English-speaking world—is most welcome. The struggles of the German working class in the early 20th century are perhaps some of the most bitter and misunderstood in European history, and it is time they were paid more attention. This book is the right place to start."
— Richard Parry, author of *The Bonnot Gang*

"We need new ideas. How about studying the ideal for which Erich Mühsam lived, worked, and died?"
— Augustin Souchy, author of *Beware Anarchist: A Life for Freedom*

Black Flags and Windmills: Hope, Anarchy and the Common Ground Collective

scott crow
with a foreword by Kathleen Cleaver

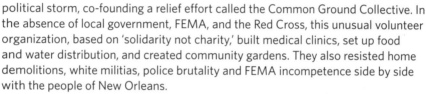

ISBN: 978-1-60486-077-1
$20.00   256 pages

When both levees and governments failed in New Orleans in the Fall of 2005, scott crow headed into the political storm, co-founding a relief effort called the Common Ground Collective. In the absence of local government, FEMA, and the Red Cross, this unusual volunteer organization, based on 'solidarity not charity,' built medical clinics, set up food and water distribution, and created community gardens. They also resisted home demolitions, white militias, police brutality and FEMA incompetence side by side with the people of New Orleans.

crow's vivid memoir maps the intertwining of his radical experience and ideas with Katrina's reality, and community efforts to translate ideals into action. It is a story of resisting indifference, rebuilding hope amidst collapse, and struggling against the grain. *Black Flags and Windmills* invites and challenges all of us to learn from our histories, and dream of better worlds. And gives us some of the tools to do so.

"(scott crow is a) . . . prominent anarchist community organizer behind a host of organizations including Radical Encuentro Camp, and Treasure City Thrift . . . "
— Austin Chronicle

" . . . a living legend amongst anarchist circles . . . "
— *This American Life*

" . . . depending on your sense of humor or your sense of irony . . . (crow and common ground) . . . are the good anarchists."
—CNN

" . . . crow is a puppetmaster . . . "
— Federal Bureau of Investigation

Moments of Excess: Movements, Protest and Everyday Life

The Free Association

ISBN: 978-1-60486-113-6
$14.95   144 pages

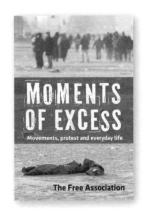

The first decade of the twenty-first century was marked by a series of global summits which seemed to assume ever-greater importance—from the WTO ministerial meeting in Seattle at the end of 1999, through the G8 summits at Genoa, Evian and Gleneagles, up to the United Nations Climate Change Conference (COP15) at Copenhagen in 2009. But these global summits did not pass uncontested. Alongside and against them, there unfolded a different version of globalization. *Moments of Excess* is a collection of texts which offer an insider analysis of this cycle of counter-summit mobilisations. It weaves lucid descriptions of the intensity of collective action into a more sober reflection on the developing problematics of the 'movement of movements'. The collection examines essential questions concerning the character of anti-capitalist movements, and the very meaning of movement; the relationship between intensive collective experiences—'moments of excess'—and 'everyday life'; and the tensions between open, all-inclusive, 'constitutive' practices, on the one hand, and the necessity of closure, limits and antagonism, on the other. *Moments of Excess* includes a new introduction explaining the origin of the texts and their relation to event-based politics, and a postscript which explores new possibilities for anti-capitalist movements in the midst of crisis.

"More than a book, Moments of Excess *is a tool for 'worlding' . . . it speaks to questions that are crucial in creating a better world, all the while asking and opening more questions . . . Reading this book, I felt like a part of a conversation, a conversation that I didn't want to end."*
— Marina Sitrin, editor of *Horizontalism: Voices of Popular Power in Argentina* and (with Clif Ross) *Insurgent Democracies: Latin America's New Powers*

"Reading this collection you are reminded that there is so much life at the front-line, and that there is no alternative to capitalism without living this life to the full. The message is clear: enjoy the struggle, participate in it with your creative energies, be flexible and self-critical of your approach, throw away static ideologies, and reach out to the other."
— Massimo De Angelis, author of *The Beginning of History: Value Struggles and Global Capital* and editor of *The Commoner*

"Wonderful. Fabulous. The Free Association's work have been writing some of the most stimulating reflections on the constantly shifting movement against capitalism— always fresh, always engaging, always pushing us beyond where we were . . . exciting stuff."
— John Holloway, author of *Change the World Without Taking Power* and *Crack Capitalism*

Demanding the Impossible:
A History of Anarchism

Peter Marshall

ISBN: 978-1-60486-064-1
$28.95   840 pages

Navigating the broad 'river of anarchy', from Taoism
to Situationism, from Ranters to Punk rockers, from
individualists to communists, from anarcho-syndicalists
to anarcha-feminists, *Demanding the Impossible* is an
authoritative and lively study of a widely misunderstood
subject. It explores the key anarchist concepts of society and the state, freedom
and equality, authority and power and investigates the successes and failure of
the anarchist movements throughout the world. While remaining sympathetic
to anarchism, it presents a balanced and critical account. It covers not only the
classic anarchist thinkers, such as Godwin, Proudhon, Bakunin, Kropotkin, Reclus
and Emma Goldman, but also other libertarian figures, such as Nietzsche, Camus,
Gandhi, Foucault and Chomsky. No other book on anarchism covers so much so
incisively.

In this updated edition, a new epilogue examines the most recent developments,
including 'post-anarchism' and 'anarcho-primitivism' as well as the anarchist
contribution to the peace, green and 'Global Justice' movements.

Demanding the Impossible is essential reading for anyone wishing to understand
what anarchists stand for and what they have achieved. It will also appeal to those
who want to discover how anarchism offers an inspiring and original body of ideas
and practices which is more relevant than ever in the twenty-first century.

"Demanding the Impossible *is the book I always recommend when asked—as I often
am—for something on the history and ideas of anarchism.*"
— Noam Chomsky

"*Attractively written and fully referenced... bound to be the standard history.*"
— Colin Ward, *Times Educational Supplement*

"*Large, labyrinthine, tentative: for me these are all adjectives of praise when applied to
works of history, and* Demanding the Impossible *meets all of them.*"
— George Woodcock, *Independent*